Women and Careers

The unifying theme of *Women and Careers* is women's educational and employment success, with the objective of profiling supportive public policy in global contexts from Atlantic Canada to Western Europe, Australia and China. The book takes up the career processes of women from marginalized groups who have been under-represented historically: women who are the first generation to graduate from university in both Atlantic Canada (New Brunswick) and China, and rural women from the eastern-most Canadian province (Newfoundland and Labrador). It examines the situation of marginalized Protestant women in Belfast, Northern Ireland, who benefit from a European Union programme that supports their political and social involvement in an economically underdeveloped region, previously unimagined in a country once wrought by sectarian violence. A policy analysis of an Atlantic Canadian region after the dominant forestry industry leaves takes up policy options and women's possible agency, should economic support return for small business networks and social enterprise, e.g., credit unions, retail food and social housing cooperatives. Proactive employment equity programmes in Finland's Applied Science Institute and Switzerland's Forestry Institute provide cutting-edge examples of diversity and inclusion policies in education and academia. A comparative study of Canada and Australia of two leading public service employers illustrates incremental outcomes for women managers and professionals but raises the ultimate question of the pace and necessary political will required to remove barriers to gender equality in countries with major gender inequities.

Women and Careers examines a series of institutional contexts transnationally and the impact of policies, programmes and economic restructuring on career outcomes. It displays the latest research on the topic and will be of interest to students at an advanced level, academics, reflective practitioners and diversity managers. It addresses the topics with regard to women's education and employment, and will interest researchers, academics and policymakers in the fields of women's employment and career studies, diversity programs, organization studies, development policy, gender studies and globalization.

Marilee Reimer is a Professor of Sociology at St. Thomas University in Canada. She is the Editor of an earlier collection of articles entitled *Inside Corporate U: Women in Academia Speak Out*, Sumach Press (2004), Toronto, Canada.

Routledge Studies in Gender and Organizations

Series Editor: Elisabeth K. Kelan

Although still a fairly young field, the study of gender and organizations is increasingly popular and relevant. There are few areas of academic research that are as vibrant and dynamic as the study of gender and organizations. While much earlier research has focused on documenting the imbalances of women and men in organizations, more recently, research on gender and organizations has departed from counting men and women. Instead research in this area sees gender as a process: something that is done rather than something that people are. This perspective is important and meaningful as it takes researchers away from essentialist notions of gender and opens the possibility of analysing the process of how individuals become women and men. This is called 'gendering', 'practising gender', 'doing gender' or 'performing gender' and draws on rich philosophical traditions.

Whilst Routledge Studies in Gender and Organizations has a broad remit, it will be thematically and theoretically committed to exploring gender and organizations from a constructivist perspective. Rather than focusing on specific areas of organizations, the series is to be kept deliberately broad to showcase the most innovative research in this field. It is anticipated that the books in this series will make a theoretical contribution to the field of gender and organization based on rigorous empirical explorations.

1 **Gender and the Professions**
International and Contemporary Perspectives
Edited by Kaye Broadbent, Glenda Strachan, and Geraldine Healy

2 **Postfeminism and Organization**
Edited by Patricia Lewis, Yvonne Benschop, and Ruth Simpson

3 **Women and Careers**
Transnational Studies in Public Policy and Employment Equity
Edited by Marilee Reimer

Women and Careers

Transnational Studies in Public Policy and Employment Equity

Edited by
Marilee Reimer

Routledge
Taylor & Francis Group
LONDON AND NEW YORK

First published 2019 by Routledge

2 Park Square, Milton Park, Abingdon, Oxon, OX14 4RN
605 Third Avenue, New York, NY 10017

Routledge is an imprint of the Taylor & Francis Group, an informa business

First issued in paperback 2020

Library of Congress Cataloging-in-Publication Data
Names: Reimer, Marilee, editor.
Title: Women and careers: transnational studies in public policy and employment equity / edited by Marilee Reimer.
Description: New York, NY: Routledge, 2019. | Series: Routledge studies in gender and organizations | Includes index.
Identifiers: LCCN 2018035404 | ISBN 9781138633735 (hardback) | ISBN 9781315207162 (ebook)
Subjects: LCSH: Women—Employment. | Women—Vocational guidance. | Sex discrimination in employment. | Diversity in the workplace.
Classification: LCC HD6053 .W6273 2019 | DDC 331.4—dc23
LC record available at https://lccn.loc.gov/2018035404

ISBN: 978-1-138-63373-5 (hbk)
ISBN: 978-0-367-73285-1 (pbk)

Typeset in Sabon
by codeMantra

Contents

List of Contributors vii

Introduction: Social and Policy Directions and Women's Careers 1
MARILEE REIMER

PART 1
Transnational Studies of Careers, Programmes and Policies: Introduction to Part 1 5
MARILEE REIMER

1 Atlantic Canadian Women University Graduates: Creative Career Strategies for First Generation Women 9
MARILEE REIMER

2 Gendered Choices in Post-Secondary Education—Math and Science or Liberal Arts? A Study of Women Students from Rural Newfoundland 29
MONIQUE BOURGEOIS

3 Postgraduate Transitions in Transforming China: Exploring Lived Experiences of First Generation Female Students in Two Chinese Universities 47
YIXI LU

4 Towards the Good Society: Expanding Women's Capabilities through Community Education and European Social Policy in Northern Ireland 67
SUSAN HODGETT

5 Considering Gender and Economic Development Policy: Gender Relations, Engagement and Institutional Practice 89
A. MARGUERITE CASSIN

PART 2
Equity in Education and Government: Making the change in work-life equity—does it really happen? An Introduction to Part 2 107
LIISA TIMONEN AND MARILEE REIMER

6 Reflections on Equity in the Finnish Working Life: A Case Study on Master's Students as Diversity and Inclusion Promoters 110
LIISA TIMONEN AND ERJA TURUNEN

7 Diversity and Inclusion in Institutional Development in Science and Engineering in Switzerland: A Bird's-Eye View 132
URSULA GUT

8 Are We There Yet? Advancing Women at Work in Canada and Australia: Similar Goals, Different Policies 140
EDDY S. NG AND ERICA FRENCH

Conclusion 162
MARILEE REIMER

Index 167

List of Contributors

Monique Bourgeois is a researcher working in higher education in the US. She earned a master's degree in sociology from Memorial University in Newfoundland and Labrador, and grew up in a small town on Newfoundland's west coast.

A. Marguerite Cassin is Associate Professor of public policy and public-sector management at the School of Public Administration at Dalhousie University, Halifax, Nova Scotia, Canada. She has been active in theorizing and teaching the practice of the institution of the Canadian public service, introducing gender equality and inclusion as part of merit and public service management, and introducing institutional ethnography as an approach for exploring economic development policy analysis. Dr Cassin has advised public services internationally and presented expert testimony on topics of gender equality and race relations and equality in legal and administrative adjudication.

Erica French is an Associate Professor of Management at Queensland University of Technology Business School, Brisbane, Queensland, Australia. Her research focusses on equal employment opportunity and equity management, including gender and age discrimination, and women in management and project management. She is an author of *Managing Diversity in Australia: Theory and Practice* with Professor Glenda Strachan and Professor John Burgess, and is an Associate Editor of *Equality, Diversity and Inclusion, an International Journal.*

Ursula Gut is an Institutional Developer and Diversity Coordinator at the Swiss Federal Research Institute for Forest, Snow and Landscape (WSL), Birmensdorf, Switzerland.

Susan Hodgett is Professor of Area Studies at the University of East Anglia, Norwich, England. She has published widely on Area Studies, narratives and the Capability Approach. She is currently Chair of the Area Studies sub panel in the UK Research Excellence Framework. She was Principal Investigator of the Arts and Humanities Research Council's *Blurring Genres Network* (https://www.ulster.

ac.uk/faculties/arts-humanities-and-social-sciences/schools/applied-social-policy-sciences/research/blurring-genres) and is currently writing on Politics, Narratives and the Visual Arts with Professor Rod Rhodes of Southampton University.

Dr Yixi Lu is an Associate Professor at the Institute of Development at the Southwestern University of Finance and Economics, Chengdu, Sichuan, China. She received her PhD in Sociology from the University of Saskatchewan in Canada. Her areas of interest include international migration, gender and health, sociology of education and the Chinese diaspora.

Eddy Ng is a Professor of Organizational Behaviour and the F.C. Manning Chair in Economics and Business at Dalhousie University, Halifax, Nova Scotia, Canada. His research focusses on diversity and inclusion, including public policy on fair treatment (e.g., employment equity and affirmative action) in the workplace, managing diversity for organizational competitiveness and managing an intergenerational workforce. He is the Editor-in-Chief of *Equality, Diversity and Inclusion, an International Journal*, and an Associate Editor for *Personnel Review*.

Marilee Reimer is a Professor in the Sociology Department and is Women's Studies Gender Studies Coordinator at St. Thomas University, Fredericton, New Brunswick, Canada. Her past work focussed on pay equity for public-sector office workers as well as on equity policies for women in universities. She is a dual citizen of the US and Canada.

Dr Liisa Timonen, PhD (Education), MSc (Social Sciences), is Head of International Affairs at Karelia University of Applied Sciences, Joensuu, Finland. She has extensive expertise in strategic internationalization of education and partnership development. She specializes in diversity and inclusion management, competence-based teaching and learning and global services.

Erja Turunen, LicEcon (Management and Organisations), is a Principal Lecturer and Team Supervisor for master's education at Metropolia Business School of Metropolia University of Applied Sciences, Helsinki, Finland. Her academic interests lie in educational development of organizations from the competence, learning and diversity perspectives. Internationalization of professional higher education is a special goal she has worked for throughout her career.

Introduction

Social and Policy Directions and Women's Careers

Marilee Reimer

This book comes at a time when women are questioning—and allies are joining in—to ask what conditions need to be addressed to change women's inequality globally. One of the vocal movements, the #MeToo Movement, has for over a decade raised critical questions about the sexual harassment and violence women experience in workplaces, and has only recently taken off after a decade of efforts (Ohlheiser, 2017).

Of central importance are the socially structured forms of inequality in terms of access to education and training, workplace equality and pay, career advancement and political marginalization.

The core of this collection's authors participated in the 8th Equality, Diversity and Inclusion (EDI) Conference of 2015, entitled 'Dealing with Diverse Identities', in Tel Aviv, Israel, that addressed policies supportive of women's equality. We approach the area by introducing discussions of women's differential access to education, jobs and careers in a range of countries and contexts. Women's access to higher education, jobs and careers is assessed in both Eastern Canada and China by examining 'first generation' women university students who are the first in their families to graduate from university.

Transnational Studies of Careers, Programmes and Policies

With the rise of globalization we see a push for more privatization of state services such as higher education. We can see one example of a contrary policy direction in which women's informal education in a Northern Ireland community development project gives previously marginalized women a chance to interact with other women's organizations and to have input into a community project and more extended social and political contexts. This is one of many European Union (EU)-funded projects directed at community economic development of some of the least economically successful regions in the EU. We have also seen economically marginal rural and first generation women in the Canadian provinces of Newfoundland and Labrador and New Brunswick defining a university career path that fits with their cultural, occupational and practical circumstances. In China, a study of first generation women shows the specific conditions under which a university degree can be an asset and an alternative, for many, to a future of housekeeping in one's village.

First generation women's access to higher education and EU-sponsored projects are areas where women have some means of overcoming the inequality that they face. In Canada, funding for both early childhood education and higher education has been a priority in response to creating a skilled labour force (OECD, 2015).

The pressure to remove state funding for publicly funded state schools has been increased recently in the USA by the Donald Trump administration as public and elite universities are seen as having a liberal bias (Martin, 2018) or as tending towards 'leftist brainwashing factories'. The funding cuts include states such as Arizona and Louisiana, where funding per college student has been cut by almost half. This administration is creating new taxes on college endowments of well-heeled schools and new caps on state and local deductions, expected to have the same impact as educational cutbacks.

This approach to reducing the state funding of higher education is contrary to not only the efforts of EU countries to support community economic development but also the human rights goal of greater diversity amongst its workforce. In Part 2, we see a second example in Timonen and Turunen's chapter, which outlines a Finnish project at a university of applied sciences. There we see a master's program where human resources practitioners develop employee-friendly projects that address the diversity concerns of their workplace colleagues, for example, for younger, senior and women employees. Likewise, as Gut notes, diversity goals are a part of a project in the Swiss Federal Institutes that addresses women scientists' possible career involving qualitatively high end research. The Swiss, Finnish and Northern Ireland examples are more in line with the Canadian province of Quebec's approach to education, where maximizing access to higher education for first generation students is seen as a priority in a reorganized higher education system.

Similarly, an emphasis on community economic development is taken in the Atlantic Canada Opportunities Agency projects discussed in northern New Brunswick by Cassin. She considers the impact of community economic development policies on women in rural Northern New Brunswick and considers the future participation of women in jobs, community organizations and local governance.

While the ongoing changes identified by the reorganization of local businesses are recognized as globalization, the attempts to use the principles of advancing the capabilities of the community members complement some of the EU's programmes and the United Nations Development Program, which emphasized how community development enlarges people's choices.

Equity in Education and Government

On 15 October 2017, American actress Alyssa Milano posted a tweet urging women to speak up and out about their experiences with sexual assault or harassment (Mahdavi, 2018). By the end of the first day, there were similar movements in multiple languages, including Arabic, Farsi, French, Hindi and Spanish. Today women in 85 different countries are using it to demand change.

It's not just a Hollywood issue … and that's the reason the movement is working so hard to support women in other industries, such as female farm workers, women in medicine, women in academia, women in hotel service and domestic workers (Siddiqui, 2018).

Canada, along with Norway and Sweden, is one of three countries in the world addressing issues of misconduct and harassment as a collective industry, according to David Sparrow, President of the Alliance of Canadian Cinema, Television and Radio Artists (Omar, 2018).

The Canadian government has instituted an anti-harassment bill that will better crack down on employees who do not take workplace harassment seriously enough, extending protections to political staffers working on Parliament Hill for the first time. It will amend the Canada Labour Code to make harassment and violence, including sexual harassment, activities that employers are required to prevent and act on under occupational health and safety provisions, and will require employers to investigate and report on any incidents brought to their attention (Connelly, 2018). Also included in the legislation will be parliamentary and political staff.

Lest you leap to the conclusion that this puts Canada ahead of the pack, Bill C-65 followed a government survey in February and March of 2017 of 1,350 mainly female federal staff asking their experiences with harassment and violence in the workplace. They found the following:

60% experienced harassment at work
30% experienced sexual harassment
21% experienced violence
3% experienced sexual violence in the workplace
75% reported the most recent experience
41% nothing was done to address the abuse.

In 'Part 2—Equity in Education and Government', we conclude by examining Ng and French's comparison of employment equity policy measures in two countries with advanced equity policies, Canada and Australia. To the question 'Are we there yet?', we have to consider the very elaborate equity regimes that exist in these countries, yet the degree to which they are enforceable is an open question. The lack of success of Australia and Canada's equity policies—pay equity and employment equity—is disappointing and questions policies lacking enforcement mechanisms. However, Ng and French are able to identify the 'positive action' approach taken in the Canadian province of Ontario as the most reliable strategy overall. Their analysis of the slow progress of women's entry and advancement within management and nontraditional work areas suggests minimal progress, given the large availability pools of skilled women in the labour force. This raises the need for an accountability movement in women's workplace matters as never before.

References

Connelly, A. (2018) *Bill C-5: Here's what the anti-harassment bill does and how it will affect you.* January 29, 2018, www.globalnews.com.

Mahdavi, P. (2018) *How #metoo became a global movement.* March 6, 2018, www.globalnews.com.

Martin, L. (2018) *As with most everything in the US, education has now become egregiously politicized.* January 3, 2018, www.globeandmail.com.

Ohlheiser, A. (2017) *The woman behind 'Me Too, knew the power of the phrase when she created it – 10 years ago. The Washington Post,* October 19, 2017.

Omar, N. (2018) *What Canada is doing to help protect women in the workplace.* March 25, 2018, www.globalnews.com.

Organization of Economic Cooperation and Development. (2015) *Policy outlook educational, Canada.* pp. 4–6. Siddiqui, S. (2018) *Sophia Bush on sexual assault: 'Women everywhere have been exposed to this'.* May 17, 2018, www.theguardian.com.

Part 1

Transnational Studies of Careers, Programmes and Policies

Introduction to Part 1

Marilee Reimer

This first section of this book includes five transnational studies of women students from relatively marginalized backgrounds—rural and mostly lower-income families, where parents do not themselves have post-secondary education. Three studies are set in Atlantic Canada (Reimer, Bourgeois, Cassin), one is set in China (Lu) and one is set in Northern Ireland (Hodgett).

Each study addresses critical questions around how women navigate post-secondary educational opportunities, the choices they make about areas of study and future career and life chances.

The research is timely. The broader context is one in which the value of post-secondary education, particularly in liberal arts, is in doubt. While the enrolment of women in post-secondary education has been increasing everywhere, tuition costs have risen and financial returns have fallen as more graduates compete in shrinking job markets. The prevailing neo-liberal view of post-secondary education, made explicit in the Newfoundland Government's White Paper, is instrumental: the point of education is to prepare students for the new knowledge economy, ideally focussed around STEM subjects—science, technology, engineering and mathematics. The route to gender equity in incomes is most readily achieved by promoting science education for women. The counter view, favoured by the theorists Pierre Bourdieu, Paulo Freire and Amartya Sen, is that an education in liberal arts is more valuable than one in STEM studies because the liberal arts promote a broader range of human capabilities—ones that add to quality of life, happiness and community building skills. The studies included in this section explore how their informants themselves assess the value of post-secondary education, the choices they made and the measures they consider most important. From their perspective—is an education in liberal arts 'worth the money'?

Marilee Reimer's research (Chapter 1: Atlantic Canadian Women University Graduates: Creative Career Strategies for First Generation Women) begins with the hypothesis that students might have internalized an instrumental view of liberal arts and that better-informed parents who themselves had post-secondary education would encourage their daughters to specialize early, in preparation for a postgraduate professional degree. Other students might find themselves triply disadvantaged, unfamiliar with how universities operate, fearful of debt, combining their studies with part-time jobs and more likely to graduate without necessary prerequisites for professional advancement. These findings were correct in some respects but also surprisingly wrong in that the non-specialist students felt happy with the work that they eventually found and were successful and appreciated by their employers.

Monique Bourgeois (Chapter 2: Gendered Choices in Post-Secondary Education—Math and Science or Liberal Arts? A Study of Women Students from Rural Newfoundland) similarly found that women students from rural Newfoundland communities commonly held vague and unfocussed ideas about future work opportunities yet felt optimistic and happy about their future life chances and valued the sense of intellectual freedom that liberal arts gave them to think beyond the narrow world views of other women in their rural home communities.

Female students in Lu's study (Chapter 3: Postgraduate Transitions in Transforming China: Exploring Lived Experiences of First Generation Female Students in Two Chinese Universities), located in Northwest China, expressed the highest level of concern about their career chances. Half of the 20 students in the study had graduated with no immediate job prospects. They were well aware that they faced multiple challenges as females in a culture that overtly favoured males; as graduates in a decade during which there had been a sevenfold increase in the number of students pursuing higher education; and as there had been a sudden steep rise in tuition fees that hit rural, poor and female students the hardest as well as a steep decline in the job market following the global economic recession of 2009. Yet none of the students expressed doubts about the value of their choices and the hardships they endured in pursuing higher education.

The two studies by Susan Hodgett and Marguerite Cassin, set in Northern Ireland and rural Atlantic Canada, respectively, are markedly different from the first three in that they focus not on university students but on women who occupy marginalized social status. Hodgett's (Chapter 4: Towards the Good Society: Expanding Women's Capabilities through Community-Education and European Social Policy in Northern Ireland) respondents are women who participated in community-based adult education projects sponsored by the European Union in communities that rank close to the bottom on measures of numeracy, literacy, poverty, ill health and mental trauma caused by years of sectarian conflict. It is this study, however, that develops the strongest measures of the value of education beyond simple economic indicators. These measures focus on the subjective well-being of participants, assessed through stories they tell about how they feel empowered to build their communities, create alliances with women across the sectarian divide, promote discussion, agree on targets and overcome opposition from administration to achieve positive changes in their communities and support each other in challenging domestic and sexualized violence. Hodgett's study leaves no doubt about the power of community-based adult education to enhance women's capabilities.

Cassin's study (Chapter 5: Considering Gender in View of Community and Economic Development Practices in Rural Atlantic Canada) investigates how agency is institutionalized, sequenced and enters people's lives. Economic development public policy and practice is examined for how it shapes changes in gender relations in rural industrial communities in crisis. Cassin illustrates the agency and structuring of public policy implementation as it sets new conditions for politics, community life, jobs, opportunities and gender relations when large industrial businesses close in rural communities. She uses her institutional ethnography of northern New Brunswick to show the changes, opportunities and responsibilities of women as the impact of job losses, social dislocation and political decline reshapes this region. She then speculates on the potential of social enterprise as a community economic development policy and as part of the future participation of women in jobs, community organizations and local governance. Existing literature generally characterizes economic decline in passive terms. The focus of discussion is how local people must and do adapt to changes not of their own making; it documents a decline in community confidence and capacity, and a shift in gender equality. Cassin's work, like Hodgett's, shifts focus from decline to considering individual and women's agency in revitalizing local economies. Women have the potential to assume roles in the context of rural industrial decline. Early indications suggest interest in creating social enterprises in their communities—enterprises that can effectively combine business and social goals. In the process, women are also actively restructuring gender relations. Cassin observes that economic development agencies might explore social enterprise for its potential in revitalizing community and fostering equality-oriented and inclusive institutions, and in view of such investigation consider economic policy implications.

It is this sense of subjective well-being, measured through the stories that women themselves tell, that best explains why respondents in these diverse studies answer the overarching question 'Is an education in liberal arts worth the money?' with such a resounding 'Yes'. Respondents in all these studies, in different ways, and in very different contexts, express their common agreement that they feel enriched and empowered in their careers and their lives, over and above financial returns on investment. The true value of education lies not simply in career preparation for professional or high-income jobs but in enhancing people's capabilities to shape positive choices to achieve the kinds of lives that they value.

1 Atlantic Canadian Women University Graduates

Creative Career Strategies for First Generation Women

Marilee Reimer

Introduction

This chapter[1] follows the career paths of women liberal arts university graduates. It focusses on career outcomes for first generation women students who are the first in their family to complete a university degree, hereafter referred to as first generation students. The study was conducted as an institutional ethnography as a part of a larger study on access to student support services for undergraduates who are first generation graduates in their family.

In the Canadian province of New Brunswick, 51 per cent of university graduates are the first generation to graduate in their families, representing the highest proportion provincially (MPHEC, 2009). This paper analyzes first generation and middle-class career outcomes, with a special focus on first generation women students in liberal arts majors. As an institutional ethnography, it is aimed at capturing the institutional practices and social relations that contribute to successful career outcomes. I conducted seven in-depth interviews with both first generation students and their mothers on the career process in the last year of university as well as subsequently in post-graduation—six with students in the liberal arts and one for comparison in the sciences. Three more interviews were done with middle-class mothers of at least second generation students, on their more typical career paths in the professions, including administration, accounting and one science-based career. While career outcomes are still in progress for some, these are assessed along with university choices, specialized degrees and work strategies during university and post-graduation.

I am using a restrictive definition of first generation students as high school graduates whose parents have little or no university studies and lack a university degree (Kamanzi et al., 2010). This group is well known in the literature for a range of disadvantages that are seen to affect access and retention in university programmes (Grayson, 1997; Pascarella et al., 2004; Terenzini et al., 19964; Turcotte, 2011; Tym et al., 2004). This applies to their access to university, family support, number of hours worked, parents' income and education, and general rates of success.

First generation students are more likely to have taken time off between finishing high school and starting university; they are more likely to drop out of university before completing all requirements for a degree, and once they graduate, they are significantly less likely to continue studies into postgraduate degrees. The possibility of professional success is very small for first generation students, according to National Educational Longitudinal Study of 2000, which found that ten years out, only 0.3 per cent of the aspirants for professional or doctorate degrees and 2.6 per cent of those for master's degrees had succeeded (McCarron & Inkeles, 2006). Yet for Canada, Kamanzi et al. (2010) found in the Youth in Transition Survey for 2005 that enrolment in graduate studies after graduation included 17 per cent of first generation students and 24 per cent of non-first generation students.

Canada has one of the highest levels of schooling in the advanced industrial world (MPHEC, 2009). However, the high proportion of first generation university graduates in New Brunswick, 51 per cent, reflects its character as an economically somewhat marginalized rural province, heavily dependent on resource extraction industries built around forestry, fishing, potato farming and ancillary support services. A decades-long decline in resource industries is pushing young people to consider other options for earning a living, including being the first in their families to consider attending university.

Furthermore, in English Canada more generally, the ability to translate schooling into a career path is unevenly distributed—by gender, social class, ethnicity, aboriginal status, etc. This research addresses the public and academic discourses on careers through an exploration of students' lived experiences at university. It explores the factors that determine their student success, or lack thereof, in achieving career goals in relation to an unfolding public discourse on access to university and the worth of university degrees.

Much of the sociological and economic literature points to the importance of parental education to labour market outcomes (Finnie et al., 2010). Our research makes a contribution by demonstrating the importance of university career supports in helping highly talented first generation graduates to achieve their career goals. The high proportion of graduates from this student population illustrates why career-related programming is necessary to launch a career. We move the focus away from 'parental education' as the major explanation of labour market discourse on career outcomes; alternatively we investigate how a first generation group forges unique career paths more conditioned by their employment and education histories.

Public Discourse

Ontario provincial Premier Mike Harris (elected in 1995) was known for criticizing liberal arts as having nothing to offer on the job market. *Globe and Mail* journalist Margaret Wente commonly writes about liberal arts graduates with such catchy headlines as 'Do You Want Fries with that Job?' (Wente, 2013). In this article, she cites extensively from a book that used US data to draw conclusions about the likelihood of liberal arts graduates landing a training relevant job or one that pays better than the fast-food chain McDonalds. Bill O'Reilly, formerly on the *O'Reilly Factor*, jeered at a liberal arts degree as not even qualifying as an investment in your future (The O'Reilly-Lehrer Hour, 2013).

Contradictory evidence that Canadian university graduates generally are doing better than their American counterparts tends not to get the same media attention. One report calculates that about 80 per cent of Canadian graduates land training relevant jobs, compared with 39 per cent of American graduates, and argues that this may help to explain why Canadian universities have been attracting increasing numbers of American students in recent years (Karambelas, 2013). In this argument, the author does not separate out the programmes of study that students select. The Canadian data do, however, support a more positive, although still instrumental, view of the value of university education in general. This view, which we will call the working-class view, is that university education is a good option because university graduates generally earn more than high school graduates. Hence, it might be worth doing if the jobs available after high school seem dead end or to be going nowhere in a region facing economic decline.

It is the students with higher amounts of student debt upon graduation that are likely to take media messages to heart. The statistics show that they are much less likely to complete the career process and opt for immediate jobs to address indebtedness (MPHEC, 2007). If we consider the entire career process and its invisibility to many without higher education in their families, the many steps students take in the career process come to mind: we would have to raise the issue of knowing the competitive character of achieving admission into graduate and professional programmes and one's dependence on faculty for references or on special programmes like honours degrees and upgrading, to qualify for scholarships.

The University Career Process

Three second generation, middle-class students (in the comparison group) share background assumptions and career processes most familiar to the families of professionals. Middle class parents were involved, as you would expect of a group of six parents with an average of 1.5 degrees each, including one Master's of Engineering and Education, two Bachelor's of Education, a Bachelor's of Science in Nursing and two Bachelor's of Business. These parents worked in various professions as, respectively, engineers, a psychiatric nurse, an officer of a professional association, an employee of a commercial enterprise and a housewife. They assumed that all of their children would and should attend university. This was a given in family discussions well before the children finished high school and formulated some intentions of future career aspirations and courses of study before starting university. They went to university straight from high school, with their eyes on the prize of getting a professional degree as fast as possible. They were confident in the knowledge that their parents could afford to support them financially, whether or not they supplemented their studies with part-time jobs and student loans. This pattern was markedly different from the lived experiences of the first generation students that are the main focus of this research.

First Generation Students: Forming the Intention to Attend University

Not surprisingly there were a couple of stories that highlighted the experience of students who were ambivalent about attending university, those who lacked self-confidence and a clearly thought-out direction. Two of the seven took time off to get a paid job after finishing high school, one of whom married young, had a child and worked for survival.

One student, who was quite unusual, having two International Baccalaureate credits when she began university, did not apply by midsummer and ran into one of the teachers who was familiar with her high marks. He asked if she had applied for the liberal arts university and pointed out, 'if you don't get your application in, I am going to kill you'. She said she was a bit afraid of him, so she got the application in and was accepted with a scholarship.

The second example of a first generation student who required a bit of motivating was a single mother who met regularly in a small group of other single parents who were familiar with her wish to attend university. One, a single father in his sixties and a family friend, casually mentioned one day, 'by the way, I registered you in a six credit English course today at the liberal art university'. That included paying her fees! Although these two examples surfaced, most of the students are very well versed in the necessity of further education—even when many are not sure how they will finance it.

Financing the Process

Two policies stand out as problematic in terms of how students were received as first generation students or as mature students: one, a single-parent student, emphasized that her post-secondary experience did not support her career path. As an 'A' student, she sought recognition for top grades but only received rock-bottom scholarships due to the necessity to moderate her full-time load to four courses per term and, therefore, a five-year undergraduate degree. Two mature women students did not receive recognition of their 'A' averages and were on a par with nonworking traditional students, taking five courses per term and finishing in five years. Second, when these students began their undergraduate programmes, the absence of a distinctive First Generation Orientation, Academic Mentorship or bursary programme may have affected their career readiness, their confidence and their available hours.

Since both mature first generation women students took the better part of a Master's in Education degree, it is important to mention that the lack of substantial scholarships and dean's list recognition as undergraduates has a cumulative effect when they became graduate students. The fact of their having received little academic recognition underlines the different conditions in which they went through and the lesser likelihood of receiving a scholarship at the graduate level. In any event, these students did not receive substantial scholarships as they were working at full-time or near full-time jobs to support themselves.

Supporting either oneself or a family means that, when first generation women land increasingly well-paying and interesting jobs, the attractiveness of more schooling is reduced. For one, during the last year of university, her parents' financial situation changed, and she assumed a greater portion of financial responsibility. Since documenting this for Canada Student Loans took time, the loan corporation contacted her, demanding that she repay them $2,000. In order to complete the degree, she was forced to get a very quick personal loan.

Many students have a limited tolerance for increasing student loan debt with no clear career goal. Mothers also weighed in on the experience:

> She had a big crisis here a little while ago, about what she was going to be when she grew up. And I said I don't really care what you do: I want you to do what makes you happy. And she said that if she finished school and didn't get a better paying job, she's got to start paying back her student loans, and that's where the worry came in,

for paying back the student loans ... that drives her bananas. She got that from me—hates worrying about money.

(Fieldnotes, January 15, 2010)

Four Years of Less Informed Choices

Many first generation students are not aware until their third or fourth year that postgraduate training is essential for professions beyond the 120 credit hours they need in liberal arts. Their parents have jobs that don't require any university education, although it is evident that having a degree is good for getting a good job these days.

First generation students are likely to come from lower-income families, with collectively fewer family members who entered what we think of as a career—a profession or occupation that confers the middle-class possibilities of occupational advancement and income level that contribute to property accumulation and social class position (Reimer & Mueller, 2006). The students' parents often have little to contribute in the way of knowledge of career preparation or surplus income for university but are acutely aware of the growing debt of their offspring.

When students are not aware of the competitive process to getting into professions, they are more likely to choose courses without regard to the prerequisites, the importance of honours or the need to compete for postgraduate degrees. They don't know about faculty references and the need to form closer relationships with faculty, in contrast to second generation students. In addition, many first generation students miss the preparation required to enter an honours programme, whether it is a given sequence of courses, a minimum grade point average or a project and professor who will supervise.

The immediate pressure on many students who graduate is to pay off student debt. While many writers have attributed a tendency to work to pay off such debt as a matter of having parents who are 'debt adverse' and job focussed, this does not give a balanced picture of why students focus on debt at a time when their career demands are the greatest. In New Brunswick, many of the first generation students we interviewed were unaware of the specifics of the competitive process for receiving graduate scholarships, an honours degree and career outcomes. Most have picked up the message from liberal arts university administrators that university graduates are more likely to be employed and receive superior lifetime earnings compared to high school graduates and that it is the liberal arts degree itself that provides this benefit. It is only when a common 'third year panic' sets in that many begin to realize that the job market is more specialized than they had thought. Since overall, 52 per cent of Canadian students have already decided to take further graduate or professional courses in their first year, the uninitiated first generation students have already encountered some committed students on a career path, with many of the former having accepted the assurances that the liberal arts degree itself will prepare them for training-related work (MPHEC, 2007).

One large difference we see between first generation and non-first generation students is in their persistence in graduating with a bachelor's degree. First generation students are about half as likely to attend and complete university: a 23 per cent rate of completion compared to 56 per cent for students in English Canada whose parents have a degree (Statistics Canada, 2012; Turcotte, 2011). We address the ongoing process these students confront, of conceptualizing a career when the student support services they access to address their difficulties often frame their situations in psychiatric terms (Reimer, 2012; Reimer & Ste-Marie, 2011; see also Tudiver, 1999). Most of the first generation students we interviewed are from New Brunswick or elsewhere in Atlantic Canada, some of the most rural regions in the country. Many of the women had little knowledge of career paths, and when this is perceived as a crisis, counsellors, health practitioners and university advisors often framed their problems as ones of depression, not recognizing the connection with the ongoing struggle for a first generation woman to obtain a degree or attend a graduate school.

The first generation status is especially common among Canadians from rural areas, where farming and fishing, and resource-based industries are being phased out, thus boosting the number of students who turn to a university degree as a ticket to the future (Reimer & Mueller, 2006). However, the career process remains invisible to many first generation students. When commentators critical of the liberal arts showcase the underemployed among these graduates, their futures are cast in very dire terms.

This raises the question as to why many students are being led to believe that the choice of a university education— particularly in liberal arts, humanities and social science—will destine them to wage and debt servitude for the rest of their working lives. The problem stems largely from media sources that have not moved away from the university discourse that presumes middle-class males are the traditional student body. In this case, first generation women students remain invisible and marginal to the main agenda of student services. The fact that the labour market is segmented by gender in many areas is taken for granted by public commentators who attribute the problem of low wages to individual choices, particularly those of women who work in low-pay sectors.

A second feature of public discourses is the focus on the immediate and relative economic gains after graduation—a focus that largely bypasses the actual process of learning the prerequisites for professional careers and the additional training and degrees that go into specialization. By trumpeting the relative disadvantages of those graduates who have not yet gone on to specialize, the long-term benefits of ever doing this appear to be nonexistent. By focussing on the immediate economic payoff of the first degree, the career process itself is not visible in terms of how students seek long-term career gains.

The University Career Process: Analysis

An underlying problem for first generation students is the lack of visibility—and their lack of participation—in career planning as undergraduates and in high school. Many of the very best students do not go on to graduate or professional school. Some of these 'A' students and go-getter graduates commonly find employment in government agencies doing research, in middle management or in the service industry.

This research was done in a period of economic retrenchment in the universities and provinces: funding was scarce for counselling and orientation programmes that address the career-related difficulties students have in a more corporatized university environment. Finding her voice and career path more likely occurred when her situation as a woman was taken seriously and the transitions she sought. Kamanzi et al.'s (2010) study of first generation students in French-speaking Quebec found that once in university first generation students are just as likely to graduate as non-first generation students but significantly less likely to continue on to graduate studies.

At the University of Quebec's eight campuses, no significant difference exists in the rates of graduation in the survey findings for these two groups. Kamanzi et al. (2010) explain this as the outcome of setting up the Quebec post-secondary educational system with the express objective of integrating and supporting marginalized groups. At the beginning of the Quiet Revolution in Quebec (the early 1960s), this referred largely to the relatively undereducated francophones (French speakers) in rural and urban areas. This was accomplished with the CEGEP (Collège d'enseignement général et professionnel, the general and vocational college) system that allowed students a transition from the eleventh year of high school to two years in a local CEGEP and then three years of relatively affordable university. The CEGEP in Quebec creates great savings for the first year of university, and the final three years in university are the lowest annual tuitions in the country at $2,774 versus $4,481 for the year 2012–2013 (Statistics Canada, 2012).

Other university co-op-type programmes also bridge the transition for first generation students, such as the University of Waterloo programme that has ties with government and corporate internships, which are incorporated into the school and summer terms. The three-year-old programme at the University of Regina also purports to have an extensive focus on careers, which includes a co-op programme offered to every student, with the benefits of career counselling, mandatory job preparation and networking workshops (CBC, 2013). While 97 per cent of graduates obtain employment, if they are unable to find a job related to their chosen career within six months, they are able to return to the university for free to improve their skills.

One might argue that by identifying participation and persistence in university, the problem of accessibility to educational opportunity has been addressed substantially. That is not true in New Brunswick, which has one of the highest proportions of first generation university students in the country. A much more telling piece of career information is whether a student continues down the path of preparing for a career, e.g., a graduate or professional degree programme that prepares one for a profession or occupation with specialized training.

Why does such a large difference exist between those who go into graduate-professional school the following year versus those who plan to do so at some future time in the following ten years? Some students consider or begin a graduate degree but find that the ongoing pressure to work affects their desire to complete a graduate degree.

Research Methodology

Addressing the Dominant Discourse on Jobs versus Lived Experience: Institutional Ethnography

In examining the public and academic discourses on careers for university students we explore the ongoing processes that first generation students confront in conceptualizing a career—processes that are largely invisible to the uninitiated. Grounded in institutional ethnography, this approach values the lived experience of marginalized groups (Smith, 1999, 2005). We study first generation students' insights into what it is like to fashion a career path with little formal guidance or career coaching in contrast to more experienced urban and middle-class students. The actual lived experiences of women are not usually a major focus in mainstream labour force analysis.

Smith has directed us into a detailed study of the life experiences of people as they are embedded in the wider relations of the ongoing institutional practices that shape and limit their life chances. These are practices that theorist Dorothy Smith refers to as the 'relations of ruling', the frequently subtle, seemingly unimportant and disregarded ways in which hierarchies of opportunities and wealth are reproduced. Institutional ethnography deliberately treats ordinary, everyday lives as problematic. It begins with the lived experiences of individuals, going about their mundane, everyday lives, and then tracks outward from these to unpack or discover the active practices of power that shape them.

Institutional ethnography involves an analysis of dominant discourses in the context of the work practices that create the relations of accessibility to career options. The prevailing explanation for the lower rates of university entrance and completion of undergraduate studies among first generation students focusses on the role of parents. Lower parental education correlates statistically with lower labour market outcomes for children, suggesting that these parents are somehow less capable of preparing or motivating their children for educational achievement. The research in this study takes a different approach. It focusses attention on the wider pattern of career-producing processes in which students and their families are embedded.

Career Outcomes and Family Contributions

The immediate outcomes highlight a divide where the middle-class students enter professional training and master's degrees, and then enter their careers, with three of the first generation students entering professions. However, four of the first generation graduates had to be more flexible in entering careers in the non-profit sector, the clerical-administration-management stream or hospital work. It is the four 'flexible' career patterns that are interesting to examine as the Bachelor of Art's students combined their work experience and interest to shape one of the valued career paths, allowing them to stay in Atlantic Canada and to enjoy what they considered interesting areas of work. Two of these graduates are currently in a management employment stream, and the third is training on the job from an administrative position in commercial real estate.

While my findings were not anticipated, they highlight the claim by the liberal arts universities that such a degree really does lead to coveted careers in areas related to the undergraduate training.

The Institutional Ethnography Interviews and the New Brunswick Profile

While an institutional ethnography does not attempt to be representative of a random sample, this group of ten families and students nonetheless was typical of the population in Atlantic Canada and New Brunswick. These first generation families were primarily English-speaking and French-speaking, with five 'anglophone' couples and two mixed francophone and anglophone, with one of the latter an aboriginal (American Indian); the middle-class/second generation families included two francophone couples and one mixed anglophone and English-speaking Asian. In a province with less than 5 per cent visible minorities and 45 per cent francophones, this group was close to the average ethnically in the only officially bilingual province in Canada and counted two parents out of twenty who were immigrants.

Second Generation Student Career Outcomes

In the middle-class group that were at least the 'second generation' to attend university, two of the graduates were drawn to firms in the richer job market for francophones in the province of Quebec: one had completed a master's degree in biology and obtained a job as a quality control manager with a medically oriented firm, and the other had completed a Bachelor's of Administration and obtained an administration position with a human resources firm. Both were still working for these firms ten years after they were hired. While the first two students received degrees from New Brunswick universities, the third was completing an accounting degree in a Montreal English university and taking courses to improve her French in the summer; she eventually got a full-time summer job requiring spoken French while finishing her degree. All three had been traditional students, going straight into university from high school.

First Generation Student Career Outcomes: Professional Group

The first generation student outcomes highlight some of the career possibilities that might be unexpected for such a group. Of the students who took Bachelor's of Social Work and one who took Optometry, all achieved what many would identify as expected professional success: two were employed immediately in their field—a social worker in a permanent, full-time casual position for a government-run hospital and the optometrist graduate in a private practice. A second social worker opted not to continue at the hospital, choosing a more varied if less secure position in a community centre with a range of community-based programming.

'Flexible' or Employment Conditioned Careers: Four Career Paths

The unexpected career paths of the remaining four students present outcomes that resulted from their unusual flexibility as well as the demand that they work during schooling and after graduation. They also demonstrate that, in the cross section of an ethnographic grouping, there are women advancing into management ranks and managers willing to promote talented employees who commit to progressive social change in non-governmental organizations, to company success through progressive management in corporate food distribution and to promoting commercial real estate goals and smooth functioning surgeries in the hospital sector.

One of these graduates is the Coordinator of a community social development group in a large non-profit organization. Two are being mentored to move into more specialized management work than the lower management and administrative positions at their companies. The fourth is doing hospital work that has proven to be challenging for her and has taught her to see in an applied setting a number of jobs in which she could utilize her psychology degree and several hospital-related career pathways requiring additional training.

The lived work experiences of the first two mature students and the second two 'traditional' students (straight from high school four years through) display a commonality: work conditioned career paths.

The First Student

The first mature student became a 'Program Delivery Officer' for a non-profit organization for several years prior to being interviewed for this study. She specifically benefited from doing a philosophy honours degree as knowing how to make an argument put her in a good position for writing grant proposals for the organization. Her salary wasn't bad for someone with a BA degree, although it was not as high as that of a starting teacher in New Brunswick: $49,774 for 2014–2015 (Statistics Canada, 2017). The student's ten courses in the Master's of Education programme were helpful in providing adult education in the direct service aspect of her job to people who experienced aggression or trauma (Fieldnotes, June 18, 2015). She described how her career path had developed from programme delivery to developing and overseeing programmes, and hoped to be in a leadership role in another organization with a similar mandate.

A year later, she was made the top administrative officer (Coordinator) of a community social development project within a large non-profit organization that administers multiple services. Her work as a Program Delivery Officer at two different non-profit organizations and her volunteer involvement in community development work (including background research on multiple service delivery for the affected communities over ten years) no doubt went a long way towards such a career accomplishment. The five years she took for a degree was typical of mature students who needed to work part-time; however, her sophistication with community social development and thus programme management set her apart as unusually talented and capable of assuming a leadership position within ten years after graduation.

The Second Student

The second graduate who started university as a mature student is also in an administrative position as a 'Management Specialist' in a food distribution company. She manages the flow of goods by the dealers, solving issues and exercising independent decision-making. Having worked in several high-profile positions—for example as the Administrative Assistant to the President of a job placement company and Project Officer/trouble shooter in a large shipping company—she was placed in a position working closely with dealers: she monitors their work and finds creative strategies to ensure compliance. In Operations, she carried out the everyday managing of dealers, helping them navigate the software, escalating compensation issues and ensuring that people who purchase the service are acknowledged in a timely fashion.

The graduate's senior manager supports her career progression in a number of ways: she is sponsored in taking in-house computer courses, was promoted a level within the management hierarchy and was deliberately assigned a manager with insights into 'soft' management skills (people skills), given that she sees a future in management work. She is particularly taken with the progressive management philosophy espoused by her mentor and hopes to achieve a career path managing dealers more directly and using humane management practices. Her manager is attempting to give her the skills to succeed in hands-on managing, which is a growth area for her.

She was very close to completion of a master's degree in education that she had undertaken and abandoned when hired in a more challenging job. However, she was singled out by the President of a job placement agency, who pushed her to advance beyond her then job as a bilingual Executive Assistant because she was 'too bright' for that position and helped her locate the job she has now. Starting as an anglophone, this graduate is now completely bilingual, an important skill in a bilingual province situated next to a large French-speaking one (Quebec) and while working for a nationally based company. Bilingualism is something this graduate achieved through schooling, both in New Brunswick and in Quebec, and with the help of her francophone grandparents' companionship while her father worked in Quebec.

In the last year and a half she gained skills in her former role as Project Coordinator through on-the-job training, working more on the corporate side, which involved independent decision-making and a lot of technical skills, such as Microsoft Office applications, as well as a lot of online learning courses, e.g., the Project Management Work Supply course. Her manager has taught her 'soft skills' in management, i.e., working with people in a way that allows you to achieve your work goals but also in a way that encourages them to submit their input and comply. A Project Coordinator would make less than a beginning teacher salary, but her new management position is close in salary to that of a teachers. In future, she hopes to manage people in a more direct way. She understands that such a position with a budget is what is considered a 'true manager', and with such excellent mentoring she hopes in future to manage at that level in this company.

The Third Student

The following two 'traditional' first generation students went directly to work after a four-year degree and graduation. One is an Administrative Assistant in a commercial real estate company in New Brunswick, a position that she obtained after graduation with a Sociology degree:

> I like the field — learning what the market in the area is, what companies want, how to get stores in ... from the landlord's point of view ... I get to know all the tenants issues and serve the company and the tenants. I'm looking forward to more study now that I know what I want to do: accounting. I like seeing the flows of money in and money out — this interests me. I never would've seen myself in this when I was in school ... working in commercial real estate. But I'm really, really happy.
>
> (Fieldnotes, May 14, 2015)

She is in a support position that requires her to help her whole department. She is learning what companies want from the landlord as well as the tenants' or commercial renters' point of view. After working for nine years, since junior high, in commercial establishments—such as the ones renting from this company—she finds that she is the only individual in her office with any retail employment experience. She has recently been trained in the Property Administrator's position from the accounting side in order to do the rent collections while the incumbent is sick. She is asked to work wherever she is needed, including the marketing department or on specialty leases, and is learning about the building management system. She took a French course on her own time, so she is able to communicate with any French-speaking commercial customers who come in as well as for possible work in connection with the Quebec office. She finds that there is always something new to learn, a source of great job satisfaction.

Similar to the student in the second example, she is in charge of a project, producing a handbook for General Managers, and of accounting work that might prepare her for a more advanced position in this company, particularly if she obtained an accounting degree. It is also helpful that her employer will fund half of her community college degree, once completed. She is very pleased with her salary—not quite a beginning teacher's level but impressive compared to many graduates in this part of the country.

The Fourth Student

The fourth graduate, who was a 'traditional' first generation student (by beginning and finishing university in four years) and is currently a Medical Instruments Re-processing Technician at a local hospital, is using her job as a 'foot-in-the-door' to indulge her curiosity about which hospital jobs would draw upon her courses in psychotherapy and which would draw on her general interest in science. Because she sees her job as 'exciting and very satisfying' for a first hospital job that takes her across departments and exposes her to a range of occupations, she has used this job to identify two possibilities: a similar job in Pathology and a Patient Aid/Counsellor in the Psychiatry ward. She is still entertaining an interest in how medicine affects the mind, and this underlying interest in psychology may ultimately guide her in choosing to specialize.

She had decided to try for more of a 'high-end' upgrade and thus trained in a 12-week informal hospital apprenticeship in surgery equipment provisions. This job involves researching on the hospital website all surgical tools and technology in pertinent surgeries (from orthopaedic to general to cardiac). The suppliers provide educationals on different updates and new practices, and each surgeon introduces individual stipulations they must learn. This is really challenging work that the graduate quite enjoys. Working around the clock increases her overall pay.

This graduate is also in the process of renewing her bilingual certificate as the hospital aims to have 20 per cent of employees bilingual in French and English. While French skipped a generation in her mother's family, as the schools didn't provide it prior to the mid-1970s, she took it at school and was tutored by her French-speaking grandmother. Bringing in this income will not erase her student loan in a hurry, but her job still compares well to the unionized hospital jobs of psychology graduates and even some social workers making $21 an hour. The graduate's position and the in-house jobs requiring a psychology degree or further technical training have provided a real-world, living example of a set of employment possibilities with concrete payoffs that did not appear accessible while she was doing undergraduate courses.

Conclusions

These women were not at all satisfied with simply finding a work-oriented major, as the graduates' paths suggest for the four 'A' students on their overall grade point averages. Although the value of the liberal arts degree may not have been obvious to them as they entered their successful careers, clearly all four of the 'flexible' career paths benefitted from liberal arts education and their receptiveness to training on the job as well as exceptional written, oral and critical thinking skills that primed them to be receptive to management skills and on-the-job forms of training.

While these students were unable to benefit from the 2016 New Brunswick government's Free Tuition Program (PETAL, 2016), they would do so, if going through university today. Nonetheless, two policies in particular stand out as problematic in terms of how students were received as first generation students: first, the manner in which single parents and, by extension, first generation students, are treated in policies of recognizing achievement for career purposes on the Dean's list and scholarships, and, second, when they went through, the absence of a distinctive First Generation Orientation, Academic Mentorship or bursary programme, as some universities across the country have implemented.

The Program Manager who became Coordinator is the most successful in landing a true management job in a non-government organization ten years after her undergraduate studies, and certainly the first three in management and administrative positions had cooperative support from managers and superiors who believed in their competence. The graduate working as a technician organizing materiel supplies and technical equipment for 'high-end' surgeries similarly knows how to train into some of the more novel work. Three of these 'flexible employees' also made maximum use of their ongoing French courses by studying to make their oral skills as broad as possible in the New Brunswick context of bilingualism as an everyday reality in government, social services and the corporate sector.

While the two mature students would not have been affected as they graduated already, the following policies could have affected them. While it may not appear to be a likely policy to see recognition for family responsibilities, in New Brunswick, the Liberal Party assumed government in 2014 and changed the policy for student loan 'forgiveness' over a certain level ($26,000) to enable students with 'family responsibilities' or 'temporary illness' to be treated exceptionally if they took longer than four years to graduate, a condition for receiving loan forgiveness (Post-Secondary Education, Training and Labour (PETAL), 2015). In a province where 51 per cent of university graduates are first generation, the new government apparently also felt that the student loan policy should be changed to remove the 'parental contribution' eligibility requirement that actually disqualifies many students, necessitating thirty-plus hour workweeks. In 2017 the New Brunswick government also gave free university tuition to residents whose family income is below $60,000 (PETAL, 2016).

The 'parental contribution' is still prevalent in many Canadian provinces and results in many students receiving little or no money from the federal-provincial student loan plan; many students thus work over 40 hours a week—even in the Sociology honours programme, where I have seen the vast majority of a class working these excessive hours. Nonetheless, all four of the graduates described in the last section were student loan recipients, and at least three of them were evaluated similarly under the current Canada Student Loans programme, requiring high levels of employment for some of them. The tendency to migrate west for higher-paying jobs is related to high student debt levels and places a damper on short-term plans to enter and complete master's or other graduate programmes for many students (MPHEC, 2007).

Thus, we see policy stipulations that are set by both university established scholarship and academic achievement recognition as well as provincial/federal government student loan and debt forgiveness policies that impact students mid-career and at a crucial time for their committing to further career training. One of the students with experience as a jobs counsellor identified the 'business model' of post-secondary institutions that orients to attracting the greatest number of full-time students and traditional students who enter and complete university directly from high school. In addition to changing policies to be more inclusive towards parents with family responsibilities or students without parental contributions, the most obvious approach would be to address the needs of mature students and those who had interrupted their career path with full-time employment, which is common for first generation students.

Inclusive policies would be of two sorts: (a) Orientation and Pre-University programmes that address the unique situation of first generation students who are more likely to have non-standard career paths (Stephens et al., 2014) and (b) recognition of prior learning schemes, e.g., prior work experience, military training and community college up to a maximum number of credits. One 'Difference-Educational Intervention' was even successful in reducing the social class achievement gap for first generation students by 63 per cent by the end of their first year and easing the transition to campus life, with numerous psychosocial outcomes (Stephens et al., 2014).

The Quebec approach described earlier was designed for a marginalized French-speaking student population that benefitted from an inexpensive two years in the CEGEP (twelfth grade and one year more), and then university tuition at half the national average for three years. Less comprehensive pre-university programmes have been offered for over ten years, and some of these include those at the University of Toronto, Carleton University, King's College at Western University and McMaster University. Lehman (2009) recommends such a preparation in order to allow 'working class students to understand their unique status in a social institution they entered as outsiders and a labour market that is characterized by traditional forms of social closure'.

The benefits offered in such programmes vary but include academic mentorship programmes (King's College, 2015), first generation bursary and work-study of 10–15 hours (St. Thomas University, 2015) as well as less extensive academic and structured supports, such as promoting inclusion through mature students' associations and socializing.

While academic and financial barriers to first generation students may benefit from 'remedial programming and an "environment that affirms students" strengths and encourages their educational pursuits', the policy changes raised by this institutional ethnography suggest that for those performing at a very high level, the standards have not been adjusted to include all students regardless of social class, family responsibility and likelihood of employment.

When we realize that approximately 17 per cent of students whose parents have a high school education or less go on to university compared to approximately 50 per cent of students with university educated parents, we see that a university-based career path is much less accessible for first generation students than it is for their middle-class counterparts. The barriers that exist to academic recognition and financial support for the high performing women in this study suggest that completing their career training at the post-secondary level becomes more stressful and demands an increasing number of years to complete compared to middle-class, second generation students following a more traditional career in the professions.

At the same time, the first generation students who were able to capitalize on a flexible career path that combined the benefits of a liberal arts education and previous job experience were able to carve unique career paths into community service work, administration, managerial and hospital career paths. With recent employed population losses in the New Brunswick workforce of about 2,000, carving out such a career path may be considered quite an accomplishment, yet it might still be considered a reasonable long-term trajectory, given the job losses due to retiring skilled labour projected by 2020 (NBJobs, 2017). In a market with an increasing skilled labour deficit, academic and financial supports for first generation women students can be seen to be more important than ever so that these students are able to capitalize on the liberal arts degree. Equally important is that the New Brunswick government publicizes the ways in which students with work experience have connected their ongoing work expertise with undergraduate degrees, such as the examples given by the 'flexible careers' in this chapter. And given the fact that women continue to comprise the majority (56 per cent) of current university undergraduates (OECD, 2015), it might also be a good time for employers to utilize employment equity programmes in order to tap into the talented women employees entering the Canadian work force.

Acknowledgements

I am very grateful for the opportunity to do the original fieldwork that is referenced and for the ability to work with my original research partner, Dr Adele Mueller. For this chapter, I am indebted to St. Thomas University for financing a Conference Travel Grant to the 8th International *Equality, Diversity and Inclusion Conference* in Tel Aviv, Israel (2015), and previous course releases for three years for research. I thank Marguerite Cassin for supporting my paper and the concept of the book, and for 40 years of being a supportive colleague; my greatest appreciation goes to Sylvia Hale for supporting my interest in this collection and for discussing in-depth research issues that arose in my own work and in relation to that of several authors; thanks to Eddie Ng, who introduced me to the Routledge Research Book Director, David Varley, and supported my efforts to locate a publisher; great thanks to Research Assistant Sarah Kallar, who has done excellent work on the literature searches and summarized many first generation-related articles; and most centrally, Christopher Adam has been a committed copyeditor for the entire collection, without whose contributions this collection would not have been possible: thank you, thank you!

Note

1 This paper was presented at the 8th Equality, Diversity and Inclusion International Conference, Recanati Business School, Tel Aviv University, Israel, 6–8 July 2015. Material from the institutional ethnography appeared as an Abstract, 'Working Class Atlantic Canadian Women University Graduates: Career Strategy, Migration and Cultural Capital' on the website of the *8th International Equality, Diversity and Inclusion Conference, 'Dealing with Diverse Identities'*, www.edi-conference.org.

References

Canadian Broadcasting Corporation (CBC). (2013) *Generation jobless, Doc Zone*. Canadian Broadcasting Corporation, Toronto, Canada.

Finnie R., Mueller R. E., Sweetman A., Usher A. (2010) New Perspectives on Access to Postsecondary Education. Education Matters: Insights on Education, Learning and Training in Canada, Statistics Canada Catalogue No. 81-004-XIE [Internet]. 7(1). Grayson, J. P. (1997) Academic achievement of first-generation students in a Canadian University. *Research in Higher Education*. 38 (6), 659–676.

Kamanzi, P. C., Bonin, S., Doray, P., Groleau, A., Murdoch, J., Mercier, P., Blanchard, C., Gallien, M. & Auclair, R. (2010) *Academic persistence among Canadian first-generation university students*. Research Note 9, Transitions Project, CIRST (Centre interuniversitaire de recherche sur la science et la technologie). Montréal, QC: University de Quebec à Montreal.

Karambelas, D. (2013) College in Canada more appealing than ever for Americans? *USA Today*. [28 July 2013].

King's College. (2015) *First generation students*. London, ON: King's University College at Western University. Available from: www.kings.uwo.ca/current-students/money-matters/financial-aid/first-generation-program/.

Lehman, W. (2009) University as vocational education: working-class students expectations for university. *British Journal of Sociology of Education*. 30 (2), 137–149.

Maritime Provinces Higher Education Commission (MPHEC). (2007) *The intentions of maritime university students following graduation: a survey of class of 2007 Maritime university students*. Fredericton, NB.

Maritime Provinces Higher Education Commission (MPHEC). (2009) *Two years on: a survey of class of 2007 Maritime university graduates: selected provincial statistics*. Available from: www.mphec.ca/resources/GFU2007in2009ProvEng.pdf.

McCarron, E. O. & Inkeles, K. K. (2006) The gap between educational aspirations and attainment for first generation college students and the role of parental involvement. *Journal of College Student Development*. 47 (5), 534–549.

NBJobs. (2017) *New Brunswick labour market outlook 2017–2026*. Available from: https: NBjobs.ca.

Organization of Economic Cooperation and Development (OECD). (2015) *Education policy outlook*. Canada.

Post-Secondary Education, Training and Labour, Government (PETAL). (2015) *Timely completion benefit. New Brunswick*. Available from: www2.gnb.ca/content/gnb/en/services/services_renderer.200868.Timely_Completion_Benefit_-_New_Brunswick.html.

Post-Secondary Education, Training and Labour, Government (PETAL). (2016) *Free tuition program*. Available from: www2.gnb.ca/content/gnb/en/services/services_renderer.201421.Free_Tuition_Program.html.

Reimer, M. (2012) Accessing counseling services and achieving career goals for first-generation women university students. *The Canadian Journal of Career Development*. 11 (1), 5–17.

Reimer, M. & Mueller, A. (2006) Accessing the transition to careers for female undergraduates in the restructured university in New Brunswick. *Canadian and International Education*. 35 (1), 81–89.

Reimer, M. & Ste-Marie, M. (2011) Denied access: the focus on medicalized support services and 'depressed' women students in the corporate university. *Resources for Feminist Research*. 33 (3, 4): 137–160.

Smith, D. E. (1999) *Writing the social: critique, theory, and investigations*. Toronto: University of Toronto Press.

Smith, D. E. (2005) *Institutional ethnography: a sociology for people*. Toronto: University of Toronto Press.

Statistics Canada. (2012) *University tuition fees, 2012–2013*. Available from: www.statcan.gc.ca/daily-quotidien/120912/dq120912a-eng.htm.

Statistics Canada. (2017) *Education indicators in Canada: an international perspective 2017*, Report (81–604-X). Available from: www5.statcan.gc.ca/olc-cel/olc.action?objId=81–604-X&objType=2&lang=en&limit=0.

Stephens, N. M., Hamedani, M. Y. & Destin, M. (2014) Closing the social-class gap: a difference-education intervention improves first-generation students' academic performance and all students' college transition. *Psychological Science*. 25 (4), 943–953.

St. Thomas University. (2015) *STUworks: a new on campus work program for 1st and 2nd year students*. Available from: w3.stu.ca/stu/currentstudents/employment/News/154596.

Terenzini, P. T., Springer, L., Yaeger, P. M., Pascarella, E. T. & Nora, A. (1996) First-generation college students: characteristics, experiences and cognitive development. *Research in Higher Education*. 37 (1), 1–22.

The O'Reilly Factor. (2013) [17 July 2013], New York: Fox News

Tudiver, N. (1999) *Universities for sale: resisting corporate control over Canadian higher education*. Toronto, ON: James Lorimer.

Turcotte, M. (2011) Intergenerational educational mobility: university completion in relation to parents' educational level. *Canadian Social Trends, No. 92, Catalogue No. 11–008-X, Statistics Canada*, Ottawa, Canada.

Tym, C., McMillion, R., Barone, S. & Webster, J. (2004) *First-generation college students: a literature review*. Round Rock, TX: Research and Analytic Services, Texas Guaranteed Student Loan Corporation.

Wente, M. (2013) Fries with that BA? The declining value of a degree. *The Globe and Mail*. Available from: www.theglobeandmail.com/opinion/fries-with-that-ba-the-declining-value-of-a-degree/article10869374/. [9 April 2013].

2 Gendered Choices in Post-Secondary Education—Math and Science or Liberal Arts?

A Study of Women Students from Rural Newfoundland[1]

Monique Bourgeois

Introduction

In 2004, the newly elected Progressive Conservative provincial government in Newfoundland and Labrador proposed a new approach to governance for promoting economic self-reliance in the province (Government of Newfoundland and Labrador, 2004). The proposal recognized that offshore petroleum developments were no longer able to deliver sufficient revenues to meet provincial needs. The new approach would be to emphasize education for the emerging knowledge economy. In his Speech from the Throne, Premier Danny Williams stated,

> My Government believes, as do economic leaders and innovators, that the time has come for Newfoundland and Labrador to set its sights on other opportunities in the knowledge economy. The fuel of the new economy is knowledge ... My Government will make world-class education among its highest priorities.
>
> (Government of Newfoundland and Labrador, 2004, para. 17)

A key theme in human capital theory in the 1960s was that the education of all individuals, women and men, is essential to generate individual and collective economic wealth (Gaskell & Rubenson, 2004; Porter, 1993; Taylor et al., 1997). By the 1980s, neo-liberal governments, such as the Mulroney administration in Canada and the Reagan administration in the USA, began to blame inadequacies in publicly funded education systems for shortfalls in economic advancement. If, as human capital theory claimed, more education could contribute to a strong economy and social progress, then evidence of a weak economy and persistent social problems must be the result of an inadequate education system [see Bourgeois (2009), for further discussion].

Dissatisfaction with the ability of a publicly funded education system to generate wealth after the 1970s prompted reforms in educational systems across many western industrialized countries, including Canada. There was a marked shift in emphasis from publicly funded education as a social good to education as a private investment (Porter, 1993, p. 38). Neo-liberal public policies emphasized privatization of business enterprise in the form of selling off crown corporations (Marquardt, 1998) and for-profit corporate takeover of formerly public-sector social services, including education. According to the neo-liberal view, welfare states are unable to maintain public institutions effectively. They are too costly and wasteful, and their 'clients' are too dependent (Brule, 2004). By contrast, neo-liberal thinkers hail the market as the 'inevitable and rationally superior alternative' (ibid., p. 248) because the market can distribute resources far more effectively based on supply and demand, and individual competition. Human capital theory sees people as self-interested, rational individuals who make informed decisions about how to maximize their personal economic utility. Individuals are thus expected to see education instrumentally, as a means to an end, as one that they must achieve for themselves, and as thus responsible for their own success or failure (Brule, 2004). What is private came to be defined as necessarily good and what is public as necessarily bad (Giroux, 2003).

The neo-liberal rhetoric around private enterprise and the needs of the global knowledge economy has had a profound impact on policy formation with respect to post-secondary education. According to Slaughter (1998), universities in developed countries, including Canada, increasingly instituted policies that encouraged university-corporate partnerships and a general reorienting of higher education to focus on economic activity, with a strong preference for supporting departments and colleges with direct relevance to the market. Declining federal funding for post-secondary educational institutions gave further impetus to the push to develop corporate partnership funding for education. The result has been an increasing emphasis on the market exchange value of post-secondary education centred around technical training and skill development (Hyslop et al., 2006, p. 13).

From this perspective, liberal education, learning that is not primarily oriented towards the needs of industry, increasingly came to be characterized in the rhetoric of federal and provincial governments, and indeed in the mass media, as irrelevant (Hart, 1992). In the federal budget of 2009, the Conservative Government introduced a new stipulation that scholarships funded through the Social Sciences and Humanities Research Council of Canada (SSHRC) had to be primarily directed towards business-related degree programmes (Usher, 2009). The Newfoundland and Labrador Government White Paper of 2005 similarly declared, 'To close productivity gaps, we must close skills gaps and that, in part, means creating a provincial public post-secondary system that is more responsive to needs and more regionally relevant' (p. 11).

In addition to prioritizing fields related to industry needs, neo-liberal policies also strongly encourage more student enrolment but at a lower cost to the state (Slaughter, 1998). This involved raising tuition fees and a shift from reliance on government grants to student loans (Slaughter, 1998, p. 46). Overall, neo-liberal policies have meant that students pay a much higher portion of the risks and costs associated with university attendance, corporations play a growing role in shaping university policy and university funding is tied more and more to graduate employment 'outcomes' (Anisef et al., 2001, p. 49). The Province of Newfoundland and Labrador began to modify this policy in 2007 to convert a portion of provincial loans to a non-repayable, upfront needs-based grant. In August 2015, all provincial student loans were replaced entirely by non-repayable grants. The goal was to encourage more lower-income and rural students to attend university.

Rural Newfoundland Women in University

In line with neo-liberal views, the White Paper of 2005 advocates increasing women's post-secondary enrolment specifically in high-income science and technology-related fields, as a key mechanism to reduce long-standing income inequality between women and men (see Bourgeois, 2009). Across Canada, there has long been a persistent gap between the earnings, wealth and employment levels of women and men, a gap exacerbated in Newfoundland and Labrador, where family incomes are generally lower than the Canadian average (Bourgeois & Kirby, 2012). The White Paper recommends that the government encourage educational institutions in the province to ensure that their recruitment strategies support women's participation in engineering, applied sciences, technology and skilled trades programmes, and that institutions focus more scholarship opportunities on women in these areas. Additionally, the White Paper suggests that the provincial government improve women's representation in decision-making positions, and work with the federal government, business and industry, to enhance apprenticeships for women (p. 31).

The White Paper also identifies rural Newfoundlanders as experiencing barriers to participation in post-secondary education because their families are generally less well off financially than those of other students. The paper notes that low family incomes, combined with the higher costs associated with distance from university, can deter students from pursuing post-secondary education, regardless of interests and abilities. Rural students, in addition, have higher attrition rates (p. 32).

The issue that this paper explores is how this neo-liberal emphasis on education for economic advancement impacts the choices and self-concept of women students who do not conform to this model. Women continue to be over-represented in liberal arts and humanities disciplines in Newfoundland and Labrador and in university generally. Rural women also choose university over other post-secondary options in technology and trades (Government of Newfoundland and Labrador, 2005; Hussey, 2007; Kirby & Sharpe, 2008; Thorne and Hussey, 2006). Few studies have explored why women leave rural communities at a higher rate than male counterparts and are significantly more successful in formal education.

The key questions explored in this paper are: How do women from rural Newfoundland see the meaning of their liberal arts degrees? Do they draw on neo-liberal ideologies, and in what ways? To what extent do they see themselves as rational individual actors out to maximize their economic self-interests through higher education? How does the rural context of their lives impact the choices they make and the meanings they ascribe to these choices?

Research Methodology

This research was conducted during 2006–2007, with eight rural Newfoundland women enrolled in third-year classes in the faculty of Arts at the St. John's campus of Memorial University. They were enrolled in diverse disciplines—three in anthropology and sociology, and the others in French, Folklore, English, Psychology and Classics. The women ranged in age from 20 to 50. Two were married with children, three were partnered with no children, one was an unmarried mother and two were single women without children. Six of the eight had at least one parent with post-secondary education. All came from small rural communities a long distance away from the city of St. John's, and all described their communities as financially stressed by the restructuring of resource-based industries and/or the moratorium on cod fishing.

University Education and Jobs for Rural Newfoundland Women

Consistent with neo-liberal theory, the eight women interviewed did associate their decision to enrol in university with future work opportunities but mostly in a vague and unfocussed way rather than citing specific career objectives. One of the two students whose parents had no post-secondary education stressed that both her parents pushed her, as a young woman, to get a university education:

> I guess they haven't been that well-off, like financially probably, because, you know, raising two kids and just on their incomes is not the greatest ... I think they want me to be something more than they were, just working the fishery or homecare ... They know, like everyone in [my community], they're just drinking, they're on welfare, they don't do nothing.

The other student from a low-income, single-parent family, herself a single parent, similarly stressed how her mother had long pushed her to get a 'professional' education, pressure she had long rebelled against until she began to seriously consider the limited economic options open to her and her daughter:

> I work a waitress job. Like, my education and that is redundant now it's so long ago, you know. And I want to see [my daughter]. I want to be around her and my grandkids. What if she's in BC how am I going to go see her with a minimum wage job? … [My] boss is expanding and stuff, but what if he decides one day that he doesn't want it any more. Where am I? I'm in a rural town that's getting smaller all the time. Like, where's my future? Where is my daughter's future?

These two accounts both conceptualize post-secondary education as an individual endeavour that can help overcome social problems like poverty, through upward mobility. However, the second student clearly prioritizes her financial and personal responsibility for her daughter, along with care for her now elderly mother who had long struggled as a single parent to raise six children. She spoke further about her hopes that a degree in sociology, while itself perhaps not of much use as a career credential, would help her get into Social Work, and thus eventually into a career that would fulfil her goal of making a positive difference in the world.

The oldest informant, a 50-year-old woman, reflected on the economic insecurity of herself and her husband as owners of a small business in a rural community, especially as illness was pushing her husband into semi-retirement:

> I don't know how long I want to do [the business] … But I know that I have to start preparing myself because if I wait for something to happen, it's not going to … Maybe one day I wouldn't be able to do it anymore or maybe my husband can't do it anymore or maybe he would die or I would die … and then you think, well, do you want to do this the rest of your life? In ten years I will be 60 years old. Do I just wanna do that or do I wanna do exciting things in the summer …?

For her, going to university was both a backup plan, should she be unable to continue running her business, and an opportunity to explore some potentially more exciting opportunities in the future.

A third older student, who had been taking university courses on a part-time basis, received a promotion from a secretarial to a coordinator position at her workplace, on the condition that she completes her degree. Continuing her studies thus became an explicit means to achieve promotion, although this had not been her primary motivation for initially taking courses. Each of these women discussed university education as a way to have a career and a secure financial future. Yet at the same time they spoke of the intrinsic value of education and the importance of 'being educated' and 'doing well'. Higher education is a lifestyle choice in the context of their lives as middle- and working-class women, single mothers and working wives and mothers, looking to create a secure future for themselves and their families in uncertain times.

University is for Women

The young woman noted earlier, from a poor family whose parents had no post-secondary education, made explicit the gendered character of parental expectations for their children on finishing high school. Her parents pushed her to attend university, even though they did not encourage her brother. The difference seems to be embedded in their assumptions about job opportunities open to women and men. Her brother moved to Alberta to work as a roofer and was hoping to be accepted into the military. He was openly disdainful of university as 'a waste of time' and 'a waste of money', and he openly ridiculed her for going. The perceived post-high-school options available to women like her, however, were far more limited than those open to young men, and it is this that made university more valuable and desirable for women. This informant told me that she knew of some other young women from her rural home community who attended university, but no men.

A broader literature on the relationship between migration and formal education in the Maritimes (Corbett, 2007; Pinhorn, 2002) supports the view that young men from single-industry towns are predisposed to reject post-secondary education because they conceptualize themselves rather as being 'born and bred' for such industries as fishing or coal mining. The power of this representation of male identity as manual working men persists even in the absence of a stable industry. In Pinhorn's study of rural Newfoundland, young men viewed life in the military as particularly appealing because they saw it as involving outdoor activities similar to the ones they engage in as youth, such as hunting. As my informant expressed it,

> I think it's like different for guys and girls in [my community] … hunting's a big thing. Guys will go out and catch rabbits in the back of their house because there's so much woods, or they go cutting wood in the winter, and stuff.

When I asked her what women did in her home community, she described more passive indoor kinds of activities:

> I guess like what you would consider just housework probably ... there's a fire hall in the community that's like the centre of activity. Sometimes like they'll have darts leagues and card games, and that's basically it.

For this student, her home community appears to offer limited options for work and leisure for women, which makes the option of leaving rural Newfoundland appealing. Another young student echoed this view that there is nothing for her to do in her home community. She described at length the view of the deadening and demoralizing lives of young women her age who stayed behind in the community:

> I don't know, the chicks I knew, like pregnant and just like, doing nothing at home, it just burns me out ... different strokes for different folks, you know what I mean? Like, some people wanna just live in [my home community] the rest of their life and, like marry the local hero [laughs]. Like, I don't know, it's crazy [laughs] ... because it's like, I can't even fathom being there myself. But, like lots of girls I know are still there are just working part-time at Canadian Tire, having boyfriends and going to the local pub and getting drunk with, like old men. Like God, You know what I mean? Just really, really outrageous, like. I just can't imagine.

This quote reveals her view that the only opportunity for young women in her home community is to become the wives of the men who also remain there. They have babies at a young age, work part-time in local shops and drink for entertainment at the local bar with 'old men'. This was a vision that had no appeal for her. It offered no way to do anything meaningful to make the world a better place.

The three older students among my informants concurred in describing a gendered division of space in rural Newfoundland. Their male partners appear to have taken minimal or no share of responsibility for care giving for children. They worked in the stereotypically male occupations of seasonal farming, auto-repair and bricklaying, while the women themselves had worked in traditionally female jobs. They each noted that all their sisters had gone to university, but not all their brothers.

These accounts of families and communities differentiated along gender lines challenge the suggestion that gender ideologies are weakening, along with the restructuring of rural Newfoundland economies (Bates, 2006; Davis, 1993, 2000; Felt & Sinclair, 1992). Rigid differences along gendered lines seem to persist among today's youth and adults, regardless of socio-economic background. If policymakers hope to increase the participation of rural students in post-secondary education, they will need to engage with dominant constructions of rural manhood and womanhood that act as barriers to further study. These constructions also act as barriers to social and economic development of rural areas because women who leave for further education may well not wish to return to their rural home communities.

The Choice of a Liberal Arts Education

The tone of the Government's White Paper of 2005 implies that selecting a liberal arts education is the wrong choice, being less marketable than a degree in science or technology. Women, it suggests, need to be encouraged, through outreach programmes and financial incentives, to choose careers in male-dominated fields like science and technology, and this will work to close the gender-wage gap.

The realities that influence women's decision-making, however, are more complicated than the White Paper assumes. All the students in my study were well aware of how widely others disparage their liberal arts education as useless:

> Even in the Muse [Memorial student newspaper] ... they had this Editorial about two homeless people burning Arts degrees to keep warm, right? Like, people - it's just a common kinda view - everybody says it, you know what I mean?

Even the women themselves expressed some acceptance of the idea of the worthlessness of an Arts degree. When I asked the student majoring in Classics if getting a job after graduation was important in her choice of a major, she said,

> I'm doing Classics, I mean, unless I decide to go on and do my Masters' ... this is what people ask. They're like 'Oh, you're doing Classics. What the hell are you going to do with that when you graduate?' ... I mean ... that could be said for a lot of the Arts degrees actually.

All the women, with the exception of the one who had been offered job promotion already, were considering earning additional credentials as a librarian, teacher or social worker—still stereotypically female kinds of service work but offering the prospect of professional status in their home communities, and potentially a stable and secure middle-class income.

If Arts degrees are viewed as worthless in the job market, possibly requiring additional credentials, then why do women students continue to pursue such degrees? I argue that these women are not simply behaving irrationally. Their decisions are based on more than the potential economic gains that may result from education. What these women choose to study depends upon their perceived abilities, age, class, marital status and family situations. All of these factors affect women's perspectives on money, their choice of major and timing of their education. Policies will need to address these gendered ideas in the families and communities that shape women's engagement with post-secondary education.

Women's Academic Choices: I am No Good at Math!

Each of the women in my study rejected studying math and science as uninteresting and/or too difficult. Two younger single students each explicitly rejected the idea of studying mathematics as insufficiently interesting, even though they succeeded in the subject area in school:

> I didn't really like my first year [at Memorial]. Like I didn't like the math courses I had to take. I did advanced math in high school and stuff, but I never ever really enjoyed it, and … I'm not too much into math … I don't find it enjoyable in any sense.
>
> I can't see myself coming in here and doing a math degree … it must be an interest thing, because, like, I'm not interested in sciences enough to do that. Like, I've gone back and spoken to people and they've said, 'You're doing an arts degree? An' I said Yeah, and they go, 'Why aren't you doing a science degree. You had good enough marks to do a science degree', but I don't know [laughs]. You know … if that's not what you're interested in, that's not what you're interested in. So, I think it was just basically an interest thing.

Three other women spoke of math and science being too difficult to pursue in university—that it was too hard to maintain the required high grade point average to continue to study biology or that it would be too difficult to catch up after being out of school for many years. This included the 50-year-old student, who told me,

> I decided that I wanted … that I really like psychology. I've done seven psychs [courses], actually, but then I thought, 'Okay, then that means I have to go back and do math'. Which puts me at a disadvantage from a lot of young people coming out … Like, I would have to go and do extra math and stuff and I just don't know if I have the confidence to tackle that or the fight to do it or the 'what it takes' … I just don't know if I can do that. So I wanted something that geared away from that.

Another younger student who had taken a few years out of university expressed her disappointment about having failed Economics in first-year university, likely because she was scared of the class, the teaching methods of the professor and the subject matter. She told me,

> I think it was my first year in university … and I was out of high school for almost two years so I wasn't used to studying, so it was hard, and I don't know, it just scared me because they were writing all these

> charts on the board and I just didn't understand it, and yeah, it was a really big class. I think it just scared me, for the most part.

Rural Education and Gendered Academic Subject Inclinations

In addition to experiences in gendered communities, other realities of math and science education in rural communities contributed to the difficulties women experienced in university studies. One student recounted how half the students in her grade-11 math class failed the subject because her regular teacher became ill, and the school could not find a qualified substitute. After this she lost interest in studying math. Instead, she developed a keen interest in art, nurtured by one of the few rural community college visual arts programmes that happened to be located in her community.

Another student who intended to study business at university was required to rethink her decision after she failed first-year Economics. She also linked her poor performance at university to her experience of schooling in rural Newfoundland, combined with her parents being barely literate and hence unable to help her. As she described her struggle with studying English in school,

> They stick you into Academic English and ... then you get a paper back [with comments like] 'run-on sentences' and all this, and like, 'your sentences are not complete sentences', but they never would teach all that. Like, our school didn't teach people what a noun was, verbs, and you probably heard this from other people, like ... it's a big thing out in rural Newfoundland, like, they don't teach you proper things. So I think the education systems are really different from, like St. Johns to [my community].

As a result of her struggles with learning English in school, she found academic work at university very difficult, seeking help through student services and the Writing Centre offered at Memorial University.

A third student wanted to study biology but switched to psychology when she could not achieve the high grades in math and science that she was accustomed to receive in high school. She explained that, unlike students from high schools in St. John's, her rural school had not taught calculus and did not expose students to any laboratory work in chemistry, physics or biology:

> I just didn't have any exposure to it. We never did labs in high school. And maybe the other kids didn't either, but I just found I wasn't able to apply the knowledge from the classroom to the lab. Maybe that was me. Maybe I was intimidated. Maybe it wasn't the environment,

> because I was quite young ... but then, I couldn't deal with not doing well, especially when other people were, because I thought if they can get a 90, I can get a 90, so the problem was with me.

As this comment 'the problem was with me' shows, this student internalized her lower grades in university biology as personal inadequacy, despite the fact that she was learning material that she had not been exposed to previously in school. It was a huge blow to her ego, she explained, when she got a 65 in biology, after she had done all the course homework and the practices. On the advice of her brother, she switched to psychology, a subject in which she could get grades in the upper 80s and 90s.

Consideration of the quality of rural schooling needs to be taken into account by policymakers if they hope to achieve an accessible post-secondary educational system. It will not be sufficient, as described in Chapter 7 of the White Paper, 'Strategies for Helping Students', to focus on sharing student services between Memorial University and the College of the North Atlantic. There is a deeper need to address shortcomings in rural schools, particularly in areas of math and science teaching for girls.

Liberal Arts as Positive Choices

While all the women articulated a sense of math and sciences as uninteresting and/or difficult, they spoke very positively of their eventual choices to major in liberal arts as a continuing interest that arose directly out of their experiences as women from rural Newfoundland. One woman who had switched her major three times finally decided on English because it had always been a passion fostered through experiences of reading with her mother and aunts as a child. Each night, she told me, her mother would read a number of stories to her, and in addition, her mother and aunts would have tea together weekly and informally exchange books:

> Mom ... and a couple of our family members who are from other smaller communities, when they all go to my Aunt's house, they would all meet up, like on Sunday evenings, it's a tradition to go to my Aunt's house and have a cup of tea, and when they go, they'll, uh, one of them will bring in a bag of books and that's what they'd do. They trade off books and whatever ... it's like their own little private book club.

This student's experience of these gatherings to share tea and books echoes a broader literature on women's lives in rural Newfoundland that describe the salience and prevalence of exclusively female social relations. It was this experience of all-female gatherings focussed around reading, coupled with her mother's habit of reading nightly with her, that shaped her decision to study English at university.

An older student likewise saw her choice to study psychology as well suited to her experiences as a girl in rural Newfoundland and the kind of person she perceived herself to be:

> People have always said to me, you know, you're a people person. People talk to me, I mean, they joke about me in the office being, you know, 'you should do counselling if you're gonna do psychology' because ... I mean, I have everyone in my office.

When asked to elaborate how she thought she came to be a people person, she told me that she had always seemed to be curious about other people and to want to care for them:

> I was always that way even as a child ... If I saw somebody that was left out of a group–I would always drag some child home from school every year in class that nobody else would play with.

This desire to care for others translated into caring for sick or hurt animals that she sometimes found outside near the barn. She told me that she would bring them in and try to nurse them back to health.

The older, single-parent student I interviewed similarly described herself as a caring person who wants to make a difference. She was the only student who said that she enrolled in university to work towards a specific career, that of social worker. She told me that this desire came out of her experiences of growing up and her desire to live a 'down to earth' life:

> I know that everything I've experienced, um, there's times when you think that people don't understand, that you're the only one ... But everybody feels ... That is down to earth, that's average, it's life. Like, uh, the average person doesn't have more money than what they know what to do with, or they don't have these big beautiful paid homes, or you know, they have issues, they have problems, they have things they have to deal with and I think that gives you a better sense of fulfilment if you address things, you know, from the level of the average person, like, the down to earth people, the real people.

Literature on the topic of women and academic subject choice points to the pervasiveness of women's disassociation from male-dominated subjects like 'math and science, and preference for 'caring' subjects, perceived to be based in liberal arts disciplines, and the complexity of this issue (Calabrese et al., 2006; Davis & Steiger, 1994;

Mendick, 2005; Montgomery, 2004; Mura et al., 1987; Tripp-Knowles, 1999). A review of the White Paper needs to be conducted to re-conceptualize post-secondary education in ways other than its contribution to success in business. Governments and institutions of higher education need to encourage women who want to study liberal arts subjects, and help them visualize and achieve career goals. This is important, given the confusion that students expressed about career options, and whether a degree in liberal arts would be sufficient to find adequate employment.

The focus on social concerns expressed by many of the women students in this study points to a very different construction of the value of post-secondary education evident in neo-liberal ideology. Post-secondary education policy needs to consider community development and social concerns, such as equity. A liberal arts education, long associated with the goal of social justice, should be part of education policy. The 'social' need not be taken out of social concerns.

University for Happiness: Place, Family and Academic Subject Choice

Rural place shapes women's decisions to enrol in post-secondary education and their academic subject preferences. All the women interviewed for this study listed happiness as a priority in deciding what to study. Studying something that did not interest them would not make them happy, and they were not willing to sacrifice happiness for an educational pathway that might get them a job quickly after graduation. One student who had taken several years out of school before enrolling in university told me she had considered a skilled trade:

> There's a friend of my Mother's who's a welder and she said it was very rewarding … and she really enjoyed it … and it was a great skill to have and that the pay was excellent. You didn't have to go to school for very long, you know, you get out there and you're part of the workforce right off the bat. You were guaranteed a job, basically. So, I did consider doing that, but I don't know if I would be happy … I mean, yes, you wouldn't have to worry about money, but, you know …

Thus, students in this study rated doing something that is interesting and that makes one happy as more important than doing something for its perceived relevance to the job market. They seemed willing to sacrifice some money for happiness, given that they recognized it might be difficult to have both simultaneously. This suggests a gendered, non-instrumental approach to post-secondary education (Tett, 2000, p. 189). Five of the eight women I interviewed said explicitly that prioritizing what makes one happy was a value passed down by their parents. The student who changed from majoring in Social Work to Sociology stated,

> My Mom is always like that, 'Do whatever makes you happy', but a lot of other people were like, 'oh, No'. I know so may people who did Social Work and they burned out by the time they were thirty-five.

Similarly, another student stated adamantly that, while it was important that she eventually be able to get a job with her degree, she wanted to be happy in her job above everything and that her family would be disappointed in her if she did otherwise:

> If I didn't follow up on what I really wanted to do ... they would be happier if I did that, than if I was stuck in a dead end job that I frigging hated and was, you know, sucking the life out of me [chuckling]. They wouldn't be happy with that.

The prioritizing of happiness was evident even among students who came from families that struggled financially. One such student talked about studying for a degree in law but eventually chose a major in folklore:

> I like legal things, so ... I know you make great money ... I think it's more being happy. Yeah, I don't think money ... to me, I do work hard but to me, I just want to be happy ... What makes me happy is learning. It's not like, buying designer clothes or going on big fancy trips or going out. Like, I enjoy all that stuff, but I'm happy with just, like, a computer and a word processor and typing.

The oldest student included in the study also prioritized being happy over material wealth, and this involved being 'down to earth', working with real people with everyday issues. This, she said, she learned from her mother, a hard-working, single parent. Women differed in their views of what would bring them happiness. For one, it was the academic life of learning and writing. For another, it was giving something back to others. While they recognized the necessity of money in order to live, they did not see material wealth of itself as a life goal. These cultural values, embedded in rural life in Newfoundland, are not considered in the government White Paper, which conceives of rural places only as geographic and financial barriers to participation in business success.

Conclusion

This research shows how gender intersects with place, and other aspects of identity, including age, social class, family and marital status, to shape the way rural women engage with liberal arts education. In contrast to the portrayal of rural students in the government's White Paper, the women interviewed in this study were not all from families that struggle financially, and none of the women see their post-secondary education solely in economic terms. While women with financially stressed backgrounds and older women with family responsibilities spoke of their education in terms of upward mobility and unfulfilled potential, economic considerations are just one component of their experience. The choices that women from rural Newfoundland make with respect to enrolling in university studies and the selection of discipline of study reflect broader features of their lives as women.

All the women said that they believed their degrees in liberal arts would not be sufficient to secure the kind of work they wanted, without further professional study. Their choices do not conform to the neo-liberal model of rational, profit-maximizing individuals, yet their choices are nonetheless carefully considered and intelligent. Their choices are rooted in the context of their lives as diverse women from diverse rural backgrounds, informed by their gendered perceptions of their abilities and interests, and the constraints of age, class, marital status and family supports and responsibilities. All eight women described how their gendered experiences of growing up in rural communities, as well as their limited exposure to math and science subjects in rural schools, shaped their subject preferences.

This research suggests that the primary educational objectives laid out in the White Paper, those of promoting individual economic success in the global knowledge economy, need to be re-conceptualized. The White Paper's strategy for achieving gender equity, based on pressuring women to specialize in math and science in order to compete better in male-dominated professions, unfairly places the onus for achieving gender equity on individual women's choices. As Paige Porter (1993) argues, such a strategy individualizes the problem of equity and reduces its solution to individuals making the 'right choice' of post-secondary education. In effect, it downloads responsibility for achieving equity to individual women, and confines their choices to those that the government defines as instrumentally rational. This approach is consistent with neo-liberal ideology. Individuals are enjoined to adapt to the 'new times', with the implication that those not doing so will need to change (Leathwood, 2006, p. 47). As Leathwood suggests, a deficit discourse underlies this way of thinking, a discourse that constructs those who do not conform to policy conceptualizations of post-secondary education as responsible for their own individual failure to achieve equality.

Note

1 A previous version of this article was published earlier as Bourgeois, M. & Kirby, D. (2012). Post-secondary education and rural women enrolled in liberal arts undergraduate degrees. *Canadian Journal of Higher Education, 42* (3), 143–169. The work is based on research conducted as part of the author's master's thesis (Bourgeois, 2009).

References

Anisef, P., Axelrod, P. & Lin, Z. (2001) Against all odds?: The enduring value of a liberal education in universities, professions, and the labour market. *The Canadian Journal of Higher Education*. 31 (2), 47–77.

Axelrod, P. (2002) *Values in conflict: the university, the marketplace and the trials of liberal education*. Montreal, QC: McGill-Queen's University Press.

Bates, J. (2006) Gendered spaces of industrial restructuring in resource peripheries: the case of the Corner Brook region, Newfoundland. *Journal of Economic and Social Geography*. 97 (2), 126–137.

Bourgeois, M. (2009) *The significance of post-secondary education in Newfoundland: a comparison between the provincial government's white paper on public post-secondary education (2005) and rural women enrolled in liberal arts undergraduate degrees*. [Master's thesis]. Available from: http://collections.mun.ca/cdm/ref/collection/theses4/id/95326.

Bourgeois, M. & Kirby, D. (2012) Post-secondary education and rural women enrolled in liberal arts undergraduate degrees. *Canadian Journal of Higher Education*. 42 (3), 143–169.

Brule, E. (2004) Going to market: neo-liberalism and the social construction of the university student as an autonomous consumer. In: Reimer, M. (ed.). *Inside corporate U: women in the academy speak out* (pp. 247–264). Toronto: Sumach.

Burbules, N. & Torres, C. A. (2000) *Globalization and education: critical perspectives*. New York: Routledge.

Calabrese Barton, A. & Brickhouse, N. (2006) Engaging girls in science. In: Skelton, C., Francis, B. & Smulyan, L. (eds.). *The Sage handbook of gender and education* (pp. 221–235). London: Sage.

Corbett, M. (2007) *Learning to leave: the irony of schooling in a coastal community*. Black Point, NS: Fernwood Publishing.

Davenport, P. (2002) Universities in the knowledge economy. In: Laidler, D. E. W. (ed.). *Renovating the ivory tower: Canadian universities and the knowledge economy* (pp. 39–54). Toronto: C. D. Howe Institute.

Davis, D. L. (1993) When men become women: gender antagonism and the changing sexual geography of work in Newfoundland. *Sex Roles*. 29 (7/8), 457–475.

Davis, D. L. (2000) Gendered cultures of conflict and discontent: living 'the crisis' in a Newfoundland community. *Women's Studies International Forum*. 23 (3), 343–353.

Davis, F. & Steiger, A. (1994) Self-confidence in women's education: a feminist critique. In: Bourne, P., Masters, P., Amin, N., Gonick, M. & Gribowski, L. (eds.). *Feminism and education: a Canadian perspective volume 2* (pp. 143–160). Toronto: Centre for Women's Studies in Education.

Felt, L. & Sinclair, P. (1995) *Living on the edge: the Great Northern Peninsula of Newfoundland*. St. John's, NL: ISER Books.

Gaskell, J. & Rubenson, K. (eds.). (2004) *Educational outcomes for the Canadian workplace: new frameworks for policy and research*. Toronto: University of Toronto Press.

Giroux, H. (2003) Selling out higher education. *Policy Futures in Education*. 1 (1), 179–200.

Government of Newfoundland and Labrador. (2004) *Minister launches white paper on public post-secondary education*. Available from: www.releases.gov.nl.ca/releases/2004/edu/0629n01.htm. [18 May 2009].

Government of Newfoundland and Labrador. (2005) *Foundation for success: white paper on public post-secondary education*. Available from: www.aesl.gov.nl.ca/postsecondary/skillstaskforce/whitepaper05.pdf. [29 May 2018].

Hart, M. U. (1992) *Working and educating for life: feminist and international perspectives on adult education*. London & New York: Routledge.

Hussey, L. (2007) *Fact book 2007*. Memorial University of Newfoundland Centre for Institutional Analysis and Planning. Available from: www.mun.ca/ciap/FACT_BOOK_2007_final.pdf. [15 February 2009].

Hyslop-Margison, E. J. & Sears, A. M. (2006) *Neo-liberalism, globalization and human capital learning: reclaiming education for democratic citizenship*. Dordrecht: Springer.

Kirby, D. & Sharpe, D. (2008) *July 2008 project update: CURA transition study*. Available from: www.ucs.mun.ca/~dkirby/CURA%20Transition%20Study%20Update.pdf. [14 July 2008].

Laidler, D. (2000) Renovating the ivory tower: an introductory essay. In: Laidler, D. (ed.). *Renovating the ivory tower: Canadian universities and the knowledge economy* (pp. 1–38). Toronto: C.D. Howe Institute.

Leathwood, C. (2006) Gendered constructions of lifelong learning and the learner in the UK policy context. In: Leathwood, C. & Francis, B. (eds.). *Gender and lifelong learning: critical feminist engagements* (pp. 40–53). London: Routledge.

Marquardt, R. (1995) *Enter at your own risk: Canadian youth and the labour market*. Toronto: Between the Lines.

Mendick, H. (2005) A beautiful myth? The gendering of being/doing 'good at maths'. *Gender and Education*. 17 (2), 203–219.

Montgomery, L. M. (2004) 'It's just what I like': explaining persistent patterns of gendered stratification in the life choices of college students. *International Journal of Qualitative Studies in Education*. 17 (6), 785–802.

Mura, R., Kimball, M. & Cloutier, R. (1987) Girls and science programs: two steps forward, one step back. In: Gaskell, J. S. & McLaren, A. T. (eds.). *Women and education: a Canadian perspective* (pp. 133–149). Calgary: Detselig.

Olssen, M. & Peters, M. (2005) Neoliberalism, higher education and the knowledge economy: from the free market to knowledge capitalism. *Journal of Education Policy*. 20 (3), 313–345.

Peters, M. A. & Besley, A. C. (2006) *Building knowledge cultures: education and development in the age of knowledge capitalism*. Lanham: Rowman and Littlefield.

Pinhorn, L. (2002) *Post-high school aspirations of rural Newfoundland and Labrador youth years after the cod moratorium: a new generation*. Available from: ProQuest Dissertations & Theses (AAT MQ73625).

Porter, P. (1993) *Place and persistence in the lives of Newfoundland women*. Aldershot: Avebury.

Porter, P. & Vidovich, L. (2000) Globalization and higher education policy. *Education Theory*. 50 (4), 449–465.

Skolnik, M. (2005) Reflections on the difficulty of balancing the university's economic and non-economic objectives in periods when its economic role is highly valued. In: Jones, G. A., McCarney, P. L. & Skolnik, M. L. (eds.). *Creating knowledge, strengthening nations* (pp. 106–126). Toronto: University of Toronto Press.

Slaughter, S. (1998) Federal policy and supply-side institutional resource allocation at public research universities. *Review of Higher Education*. 21, 209–244.

Taylor, S., Rizvi, F., Lingard, B. & Henry, M. (1997) *Education policy and the politics of change*. London & New York: Routledge.

Tett, L. (2000) 'I'm working class and proud of it'—gendered experiences of non-traditional participants in higher education. *Gender and Education*. 12 (2), 183–194.

Thorne, T. & Hussey, L. (2006) *Fact book 2006*. Available from: www.mun.ca/ciap/Analysis/Factbook/FACT_BOOK_2006.pdf. [14 May 2018].

Tripp-Knowles, P. (1999) Women and post-secondary science education: a case for curriculum transformation. In: Stalker, J. & Prentice, S. (eds.). *The illusion of inclusion: women in post-secondary education* (pp. 146–153). Halifax: Fernwood.

Usher, A. (2009) *News release: The 2009 federal budget: an EPI commentary*. Available from: www.educationalpolicy.org/PR/PR_090127_budget.html [Accessed 13 June 2009].

3 Postgraduate Transitions in Transforming China

Exploring Lived Experiences of First Generation Female Students in Two Chinese Universities[1]

Yixi Lu

Introduction

Since the late 1970s, the People's Republic of China (PRC) has undergone major transformations. The economic reforms have brought spectacular economic growth and dramatic change in social stratification and social structure, including increasing economic disparity and social inequality. The dramatic social and economic transformation during the past 35 years has resulted in a profound restructuring in China's higher education system and job market, which has brought tremendous impacts on university students' transition process from school to work. There has been a growing public concern about the increasingly challenging job market for university graduates (Bai, 2006; Education Online, 2006, 2016a; Wang, 2009). Although the authoritative statistics on the employment rate of university graduates are not adequately available in China[2], several related issues, such as an unsatisfying wage for their first employment, increasing difficulty in finding jobs or satisfactory jobs and education-job mismatch, have been recognized as social problems in recent years (Economic Daily, 2009; Hui, 2010).

There has been extensive discussion and debate on the reasons for intensive postgraduate employment pressure on college graduates since the early 2000s (Bai, 2006; Reuters, 2011; Wang, 2009; Wang & Moffatt, 2008). The expansion of higher education enrolment, along with the decreasing standards of higher education as well as the capacity and structure of the labour market, has been widely recognized as the most important reasons. Since the late 1990s, the policy drive to make higher education more widely available has led to a dramatic growth in graduate numbers. The number of college graduates has increased from 1.14 million in 2001 to 7.95 million in 2017, and this number was 6.11 million in 2009 when the empirical data was collected for this study (Education Online, 2016a). This dramatic and constant increase in college graduates for more than a decade results in tremendous pressure on the capacity of labour markets to absorb such a large number of college graduates into the workforce. Increasing educational opportunities for all Chinese youth is one of the main incentives of higher education expansion; however, this may not necessarily lead to more equal access to higher education among different social classes (Mare, 1980), and more access to higher education does not guarantee equal educational outcomes. Essentially, the current higher education system and educational outcomes affecting the situation of social inequality in China deserve both academic and public attention.

Taking an intersectional perspective, this chapter aims to examine the effect of gender and class by exploring the social and economic barriers and challenges faced by the first generation female university students (FGFUSs) in the process of their postgraduate transition. Theoretically, the study adopts Bourdieu's concepts of habitus and capital as a conceptual and analytical framework. Empirically, by using the first-hand qualitative data from the interview survey conducted in two universities in Northwest China, Xi'an Jiaotong University and Lanzhou University, this study not only reveals how social inequality has been reproduced through these FGFUSs' university experience and the barriers they have faced during postgraduate transition, but also explores the strategies they used to achieve their post-university transitions. The interviews were conducted in 2009, which was the worst period of time during a global economic recession that started at the end of 2007 in the USA, becoming globalized and exacerbated in 2008 and 2009. This economic recession worsened the already pessimistic employment situation for university graduates.

Inequalities in Educational and Employment Opportunities: Gender and Class

Main Changes in Higher Education in China

A policy of higher education expansion began to be implemented in 1999. The gross rate of post-secondary enrolment grew from 9.8 per cent in 1996 to approximately 40 per cent in 2015 (Bai, 2006; Education Online, 2016b). Between 2000 and 2014, the average annual growth rate of post-secondary enrolment has been 10.7 per cent, and by the end of 2014 the population of students enrolled in post-secondary institutions in China had reached 35.59 million, with the total number of post-secondary institutions increasing from 1,071 in 1999 to 2,824 in 2014 (Ministry of Education, 2015). Meanwhile, a job assignment system designed to guarantee university graduates tenured positions since the 1950s was abolished in 2000. In this context, university graduates' employment rate has declined significantly since the early 2000s and reached the lowest point in 2008 and 2009, when the financial crisis broke out in the USA in 2007 and spread globally. Meanwhile, there has been a trend of a decreasing wage premium for university graduates (Knight et al., 2017).

Along with the expansion of higher education and increasing public concern over postgraduate employment, university tuitions have increased significantly. From 1949 to 1988, post-secondary students were provided with a tuition waver, living allowance and free dormitory accommodation. In the 1990s, the government started to charge post-secondary tuition and fees. The average annual tuition increased significantly from CN¥800 (Chinese yuan, approximately USD 100) in 1995 to approximately CN¥5000 (approximately USD 715) between 2006 and 2009 (China News, 2013). After a tuition freeze was implemented during 2006–2011, there was another increase (Cang, 2014). Tuition prices vary in terms of disciplines, types of post-secondary institutions and provinces; no authoritative statistics can be found, so only estimated averages were collected from news reports and research. Researchers also noticed decreases in the proportion of higher education funds from government appropriations and increases in the proportion of tuition and fees (Dong & Wan, 2012). This increasing individual responsibility of financing higher education constrains socioeconomically disadvantaged students' accessibility to higher education in spite of the expansion.

The third major reform was to abolish the planning system for allocating post-secondary graduates to work positions. Before the 1990s, all the college graduates would be assigned a tenured position by the government, and this job assignment system was purposefully designed to support a planned economy. Along with the establishment of a market economy in China, a desire for self-seeking employment was growing. The constraints of the job assignment system were abolished in 2000. Presently, the vast majority of post-secondary graduates find jobs based on mutual agreements between them and employers, with little intervention from the government. Consequently, on the one hand, the graduate receives much more freedom in searching for jobs; on the other hand, with the expansion of higher education, competition in the job market became increasingly fierce. These changes have shaped the social settings of the school to work transition processes experienced by Chinese college graduates, in which they face inequalities and compete for better socioeconomic status (SES).

Inequalities: Rural-Urban Division, Income Gap and Gender Inequality

To understand the intersectional effect of class and gender inequality, this paper contextualizes the structural barriers faced by the FGFUS by introducing how rural-urban division, income gap and gender are interplayed in shaping the socioeconomic inequalities in China. Primarily, structural inequality in China has been derived from the interplay of rural-urban division, income gap and gender inequality. In 1958, a rigid household registration (*Hukou*) institution was promulgated to control the movement of people between administrative regions and between urban and rural areas. Compared to urban residents, rural residents benefit much less from economic growth, public education and healthcare. In 2014, this *Hukou* distinction between urban and rural residents was called to an end institutionally, but it will take years to develop an observable effect on the rural-urban division. Since 2000 the rural household's net income has been only 30–36 per cent of an urban household's disposable income (Figure 3.1). Figure 3.2 shows that the tuition-income ratio for urban residents has increased from approximately 18 per cent in 1995 to 65 per cent in 2001, and this ratio for rural residents increased even more drastically, from roughly 50 per cent in 1995 to 190 per cent in 2001. The overall trend suggests that in the era of rapid higher educational expansion, the dramatic growth of tuition-income ratio resulted in a tremendous economic barrier for young people from disadvantaged family backgrounds, especially those from rural areas, in accessing higher education.

Consequently, there has been a definite gap between urban and rural access to higher education. In 2005, high school graduates from urban areas were 1.44 times more likely to have access to higher education than those from rural areas (Qiao, 2010). The proportion of students from rural areas has declined as the ranking of Chinese post-secondary institutions has risen (Ma, 2012). Since the higher education expansion, the enrolment rate of students from disadvantaged family backgrounds

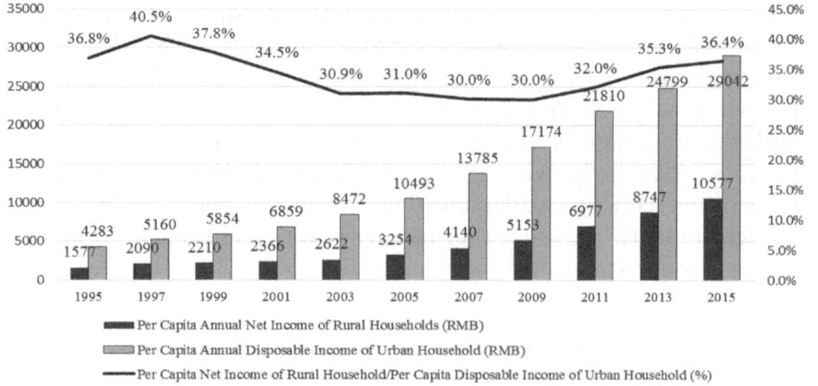

Figure 3.1 Per capita income gap between urban and rural households.
Source: National Bureau of Statistics of China, 'China Statistical Yearbook 1996–2016', www.stats.gov.cn/tjsj/ndsj/.

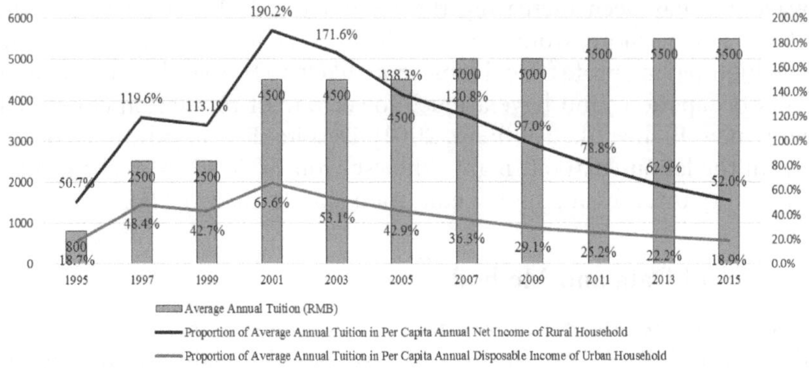

Figure 3.2 Proportion of average annual postsecondary education tuition in per capita annual incomes of rural and urban households.

Source: National Bureau of Statistics of China, 'China Statistical Yearbook 1996–2016'; Estimated average tuition numbers were collected from various news reports and research (Cang 2014; China News 2013).

at elite universities has considerably declined (Wu, 2010). Studies have also found that students from families of high SES are much more likely to enrol in 'popular' programmes that are favourable in the job market but charge higher tuitions, such as finance, IT and engineering (Zhong & Lu, 2003). The massive increase in post-secondary graduates greatly lowers their credentials' competitiveness in the job market, but some relative advantages can be signified by degrees from highly ranked universities and in popular majors, which are dominated by students from socioeconomically advantaged families (Ye, 2012). Several studies have demonstrated that coming from rural areas and low SES families increases the probability of postgraduate unemployment (Xie et al., 2010).

In addition to the urban-rural division and income gap, gender also has significant influence on education and employment opportunities. Since the 1980s researchers have observed increases in both women's education level and their proportion in post-secondary institutions (Xie et al., 2010). However, the gender inequality in education still largely exists especially when intersecting with rural *Hukou* status (Dong et al., 2008). Female rural residents accounted for 50.5 per cent of the entire no-schooling population in 2010, and that was 2.5 times the population of male rural residents who had no schooling (National Bureau of Statistics of China, 2010). Compared to Chinese men, Chinese women have approximately 9 per cent less share in the population who have received post-secondary education (54.3 per cent vs. 45.7 per cent). Although after the college expansion, the gender gap in accessing higher education has disappeared (Yeung, 2013), female university graduates are still much less likely to find a job upon graduation, their educational returns are lower compared to their male counterparts and the gender wage gap has been increasing throughout the 2000s (Gao & Smyth, 2015). Furthermore, women are less likely to be found in administrative and high-paying professional jobs, more likely to be found in clerical and sales occupations and have a much lower rate of promotion compared with men (Bian et al., 2000; Fu, 2001). Despite their disadvantaged status in the labour market, many Chinese women decide to resist gender inequality by accessing higher education (Lin & Bian, 1991).

Sources of Data and Method

The main interest of this research was to investigate university students from low SES families who are supposed to gain upward mobility through higher education. In order to access this population, Xi'an Jiaotong University in Shaanxi province and Lanzhou University in Gansu province were chosen as the research sites. Both universities are located in the north-western region of China, which has long been characterized as less developed, with harsh weather and environment, and many students reported that low educational and living costs were one of the main reasons for them to choose one of the two universities. Also, both universities are nationally well-known and prestigious 'key-point' universities[3], despite being located in relatively remote provinces. These features of the two research sites allowed for a greater access to the student population of interest.

The data was collected through semi-structured interviews conducted from May to July 2009. As mentioned earlier, 2009 was one of the most difficult years for new university graduates seeking employment, due to fierce competition resulting from rapid expansion of higher education, as well as the economic depression caused by financial crisis starting in 2008. According to an optimistic estimation, the initial employment rate[4] of new post-secondary graduates in 2009 was 74 per cent (News China, 2010), which was among the lowest rate between 2000 and 2015. The structural barriers and inequalities became even more intensified for university students from disadvantaged SES backgrounds.

To identify the graduating student with a disadvantaged SES background, the selection criteria for participant recruitment included: (1) they were to graduate from an undergraduate programme in July 2009; (2) they were the only one receiving university education in their immediate family; (3) they were recipients of student loans or subsidies or lived in a rural area before university. Recruitment advertising was sent through student organizations in both universities. Initially, 40 undergraduate students from Xi'an Jiaotong University and Lanzhou University agreed to participate in the research, 35 participants met the three criteria and 20 were female university students who made up the sample in this article.

Table 3.1 Distribution of the First Generation Female Student Sample in Demographic Characteristics and SES

	n	%
University		
Xi'an Jiaotong University	8	40%
Lanzhou University	12	60%
Total	**20**	**100%**
Major		
Sciences and engineering	0	0%
Social sciences and humanities	20	100%
Business, management and finance	0	0%
Total	**20**	**100%**
Postgraduate status		
Have found a job	3	15%
Still looking for a job	7	35%
Received admission from a graduate programme	6	30%
Preparing to apply for a graduate programme	4	20%
Total	**20**	**100%**
Residential area before university		
Urban area	5	25%
Rural area	15	75%
Total	**20**	**100%**
Annual family income		
10,000 *Chinese yuan* and below	12	60%
10,001–15,000 *Chinese yuan*	7	35%
15,001–20,000 *Chinese yuan*	1	5%
20,001 *Chinese yuan* and above	0	0%
Total	**20**	**100%**
Father's occupation		
Owner and white-collar worker[4]	0	0%
Worker and staff	4	20%
Peasant	15	75%
Unemployed	1	5%
Total	**20**	**100%**
Mother's occupation		
Owner and white-collar worker	0	0%
Worker and staff	2	10%
Peasant	12	60%
Unemployed	6	30%
Total	**20**	**100%**
Highest education level of two parents		
Elementary education or less	6	30%
Some or completed junior high school	10	50%
Some or completed senior high school	4	20%
Post-secondary education	0	0%
Total	**20**	**100%**

Table 3.1 presents a profile of this sample in terms of their demographic characteristics and SES. It is expected that with a focus on low SES students, the sample consists of 75 per cent of participants from rural areas, 60 per cent of participants' family income was below 10,000 Chinese Yuan per year, 75 per cent of them whose father was a peasant, 30 per cent of them whose mother was unemployed and 80 per cent of them whose parents received no more than junior high school education. More importantly, among these FGFUSs, only 45 per cent were able to achieve postgraduate transition by either finding a job (15 per cent) or receiving admission from a graduate programme (30 per cent). The majority of them (55 per cent) were either still looking for job (35 per cent) or preparing to apply for graduate study next year (20 per cent).

Bourdieu's Concepts of Habitus and Capital

Bourdieu's concept of habitus is 'a system of durable, transposable dispositions, structures predisposed to function as structuring forces, that is, as principles which generate and organize practices and representations' (Bourdieu, 1990, p. 53). According to Bourdieu, habitus results from early socialization experiences in which external structures are internalized, and as a result, the internalized dispositions continue to set the broad parameters and boundaries of people's practices in a stratified social world through further socialization. Thus, on one hand, habitus sets structural limits for actions; on the other hand, habitus generates perceptions, aspirations and practices that correspond to the structures of earlier socialization. For Bourdieu, habitus is a generator of behaviours. The trajectory of individual life transition depends on the social constraints of the habitus or the internalized self-regulation it entails, as well as the ability of that person to use different forms of capital in his/her capacity.

According to Bourdieu (1986), capital is the set of usable resources and powers that an individual possesses, and it is effective in a given social space that enables one to obtain specific profits through participation and contest in it. Capital comes in four principal types: economic capital (material and financial resources at one's disposal), social capital (resources accrued by virtue of membership in a group representing one's social networks), cultural capital (cultural resources rooted in social origin, such as language ability, knowledge, information and tastes, that are linked to educational and occupational aspiration) and symbolic capital (resources based on honour, prestige or recognition as an authoritative embodiment of cultural value) (Bourdieu, 1986; Bourdieu & Wacquant, 1992).

Bourdieu's concept of cultural capital is closely related to habitus. According to him, cultural capital can exist in three forms: the embodied state, that is, in the form of long-lasting dispositions of the mind and body, such as habitus, aptitudes, tastes and competencies; the objectified state in the form of cultural goods, that is, pictures, books or instruments; and the institutionalized state, a form of objectification that can be seen in the case of educational qualification, the academic certificate of cultural competence that confers on its holder a conventional, constant and legally guaranteed value with respect to culture (Bourdieu, 1986).

For Bourdieu, certain problematic circumstances are the precondition of developing and practising rational strategic agency. Bourdieu defines those circumstances as the situation of crisis, which disrupts the immediate adjustment of habitus to social structures. The adjustment of habitus may be enabled in social transformation and life transition processes where actors are experiencing uncertainties, tensions, risks, confusions and alternatives. This chapter is especially concerned with such a problematic circumstance, in which the FGFUS in China are experiencing an increasingly challenging and uncertain process of school to work transition in the context of constant reforms in higher education, transformation of economic structure and labour market, increasing difficulties in finding a satisfactory job and globally weak economic progress.

Bourdieu also suggests that the 'convertibility of capitals' is a situation where one type of capital can be transformed into other types of capital 'in accordance with a principle which is the equivalent of the principle of the conservation of energy, profits in one area are necessarily paid for by cost in another' (Bourdieu, 1986). The convertibility of four types of capital leaves room for the development of individual strategic agency that is influencing and influenced by the domination of habitus in problematic circumstances.

In addition to capital and habitus, Bourdieu's understanding of class also takes into account other stratifying factors, such as gender, race or ethnicity, place of residence and age. In *Distinction*, Bourdieu (1984) considers them important factors affecting the fundamental 'material conditions of existence' (pp. 102–109). As he specifies, 'the volume and composition of capital give specific form and value to the determinations which the other factors (age, sex, place of residence, etc.) impose on practices' (Bourdieu, 1984, p. 107). Thus, as theoretical tools, Bourdieu's concepts of capital and habitus also enable in-depth and systematic understanding of the inequality, structural barriers and discrimination experienced by these female students, as well as their strategies in resisting and overcoming their disadvantages.

Thus, Bourdieu's conceptions of habitus and forms of capital provide an effective analytical tool to explain the processes and patterns of these students' postgraduate experiences and decisions, to examine the role of habitus in limiting their abilities to achieve upward mobility and to explore the possibility of self-empowerment by practising strategic agency despite structural barriers and limitations.

Findings

The Triple-Disadvantaged: The Female Student from a Poor Rural Family

Ping was born to a peasant family in a village. She had two younger brothers and an older sister. She had to overcome tremendous barriers that might have prevented her from pursuing higher education. Ping was a top student in her junior high school, but her parents still tried to stop her from getting into senior high school and university afterward. Due to poverty, they couldn't afford to send all their kids for higher education. However, rather than providing the limited resource to the child who had the best academic performance, they gave such preference to their sons. Ping's older sister gave up her chance of higher education as her parents convinced her to work sooner in order to help out the family financially, but Ping fought hard for her educational right by even threatening to commit suicide. She was finally able to continue partially because her brothers' academic performances were not good enough to get into senior high school. Despite her victory in this battle, she started feeling guilty, 'not filial' to her parents, because she didn't 'comply with' her 'fate' to 'relieve financial burden on her parents' by 'going to a vocational school' and making money for her family, just like her brothers and sister.

Some traditional gender roles are much more valued in rural areas than urban areas. In rural China, boys are still highly privileged in resource distribution, especially when such resource is in short supply (Hannum et al., 2009). The gendered structure in Ping's family and community determined that her brothers had the privilege to receive more resources from the family, and Ping had to fight for an equal opportunity in relation to education from her parents. Because of her disobedience of the gender role assigned to her, she felt ashamed for not being able to provide financial support for her parents, even though her parents' original plan of supporting their sons' education might impose a similar amount of 'financial burden' on her family.

Ping's disadvantaged family SES and guilt for her family pushed her to study hard for scholarships, to work part-time jobs to support her own education and her family financially, and to set a goal of 'making lots of money' in order to please her parents rather than pursue her own dream. Ping described it this way:

> My dream was actually to be a scholar, to travel, to read and learn … but I have to make more money for my family. I never asked for money from my parents … I worked from the first to the last year. … I had a scholarship for two years, but I couldn't keep it because my GPA dropped when I worked, so I got student loans. All my brothers

> and sister are making money for the family now, I felt really bad that I couldn't.

According to her narrative, through years of cultivation of university culture, Ping had developed an aspiration—'to be a scholar, to travel, to read and learn'—but her action and motivation were largely limited by her class habitus. Her regret for disobeying her parents and understanding of the hardship caused by poverty made her give up her personal dream and set a primary goal of improving her family's SES. With an intention to change her entire family's SES through her education, Ping planned to invest tremendous time and energy into acquiring cultural capital and social capital and converting them into economic success in the future. She described her plan as follows:

> I have been admitted in a graduate program at [XX] University. I will learn as much as I can and build social networks. ... Then I will find a job, work hard, save up money. Eventually, I want to start my own business ... make lots of money. I want my family to be the richest one in our village [laughter], so my parents, brothers and sister don't have to ask for help from anyone else.

However, her disadvantaged family background brought her challenges in accumulating useful cultural and social capital in university. On the one hand, she had difficulties in studying computer science and English, as she never saw a computer before university and the English education she received before failed to match the university standard. She claimed she was 'like a blind person when looking at the computer screen', was 'like a mute when trying to speak English' and the only thing she was good at was studying as hard as she could. She failed her first computer course and did poorly in English; her solution was to memorize everything in the textbook, and eventually she passed the exam with a decent mark. On the other hand, she had problems in building important social networks. She only felt 'comfortable to talk to students from similar family background' as her own and found that 'those city girls don't seem to like' her and 'shared no same interests' with her, so she only managed to make one friend during university.

She 'was not good at developing good relationships with professors', and because of her 'quietness' in her department and lack of recognition and recommendation from the professors, she lost her opportunity to continue graduate study in her department, where she was eligible to be admitted with the exemption of the graduate examination. Even though she was able to pursue graduate study in another university through examination, she was fully aware of her inability of accumulating social capital, which is important for her future school-to-work transition.

Ping's experience and postgraduate transition process reveal a triple-disadvantaged situation. First, as female students, the traditional gender role greatly reduces their opportunities to receive higher education, especially in rural China where male privilege is still the dominant value, and whoever resists this value is viewed as having a stigma and morally flawed. Second, as students from low SES families, their academic performance can be greatly affected by lack of economic support, as they have to support their higher education and sometimes even help their family financially by working part-time jobs while studying full time. Third, due to the disparity between rural and urban education as well as the cultural difference between rural and urban upbringing, students from rural areas found themselves in disadvantaged positions in obtaining cultural capital in university even though they were able to pass the college entrance exam with high marks. Rural students tend to have weaker practical English skills due to lack of well-trained English teachers in rural areas, and they are more likely to have little computer knowledge prior to university as there are not enough resources to provide related courses or training in rural areas. Moreover, rural female students' habitus may constrain their ability to acquire useful social capital in university. The feeling of dislocation in university limited their motivation and ability to establish good relationships with students from higher SES or with authority figures such as professors.

Incompatible Habitus, Traditional Gender Role and Gender Discrimination in the Job Market

For first generation female students, university can be a pathway to upward mobility, but many of them have recognized that more social and cultural capital is needed to achieve upward mobility than merely a university degree, so they may decide to prolong their education in order to collect more social and cultural capital by pursuing graduate study, just like Ping. However, some may decide that higher education was incompatible with their dispositions and habitus.

A common theme among the FGFUS's narratives was that they were either convinced that 'university education can change many things' before getting into university or forced to go to university by their parents, who expected their children 'to be an urban resident' or 'become rich one day'. However, after almost four years of university life, they came to the realization that university is not the pathway naturally leading to higher SES, and they feel regret for getting into university and planned to return to their original class lifestyle. For example, according to Mei's narrative,

> I don't know what kind of job I can look for, I knew nothing about university when I came, I don't belong here. ... As long as I can feed

> myself, I'll be fine, if they recruit secretaries or staff, I will submit my resume ... University is not for me. ... I would rather be a housewife ... My father said, I should go to university, so I can stay in the city ... Honestly, I don't mind going back if I can find a happy life there.

Mei's narrative is an unexpected response from a university student, but it is a representation of her habitus in class and gender. Even though she has received higher education, her habitus has restrictively structured her motivations and actions to allow her to comfortably give up the academic pathway to upward mobility and easily accept a traditional gender role as a stay-at-home mother dependent upon her husband. Mei's father was able to motivate her to pursue higher education with a prospect of better life, but due to lack of knowledge about higher education to informatively support such a prospect, Mei found her habitus became increasingly incompatible with university life and the academic pathway to upward mobility.

Furthermore, due to encountering tremendous gender bias and discrimination in the labour market, female students find themselves in a much more disadvantaged position than male students, some even start considering to actually retreat to the traditional gender role. As Yan stated,

> I went to a job interview with my boyfriend, he got that job, I didn't. That's unfair. They recruited 10, only one is a girl, and that girl is an athlete in university. They might think girls are not physically tough enough for travelling? It's difficult to find a job, even more difficult for girls. ... You can find recruitment ads explicitly saying that they prefer guys.

When being asked why it is, Yan replied,

> They [employers] may think girls want to work close to family, or follow their boyfriends; we cannot decide where to work on our own. Also, girls will get married, have a kid, then we need maternity leave, they don't like that. Guys don't need to think much, just the job ... like my boyfriend, he decided to accept that job without telling me anything, but I have to find a job in the same city, or we will have to break up.

Jing would be a graduate student in a couple of months, but she also felt the social pressure to adopt a traditional gender role. Her family and friends have been constantly telling her to 'find a husband with a promising future', but she believes only a higher degree would help her find a decent job in this job market.

Female university students have observed a phenomenon that they in general face more difficulties and barriers in the job search than male students, regardless of what major they are in. The socially accepted gender role and male-dominated gender structure play important roles here. Women are stereotyped as physically vulnerable to travel around, financially and emotionally attached to men, and not committed to work. Such gender bias leads to strong gender discrimination and gender inequality in the job market, and as a result, the traditional gender role and stereotype become accepted, realized and propagated by this structural barrier in the job market. Consequently, marrying a 'guy' with a 'promising future' becomes an ultimate goal of pursuing higher education, or the female disadvantage in job market is only to be compensated by more education.

Conversion between Cultural Capital and Social Capital

When female students don't have a privileged family background that provide them with adequate economic, social and cultural capital to achieve their postgraduate goals, some of them decided to invest considerable amount of time and energy to convert what they have into the capital they need.

Rui was a first generation university student from a city, but she described her family background as 'poor'. She has a younger brother and a younger sister who will try to get into university in the next couple of years. To reduce the financial burden on her parents, she relied on student loans and scholarships to continue her higher education, but she still inherited some important cultural assets, mainly because she was staying with her grandparents a lot when she was a child and her parents were busy with work. Her grandpa's interest in Chinese traditional literature and operas brought her traditional values, such as 'benevolence, righteousness, propriety, wisdom, sincerity' and to be 'gentle, kind, respectful, frugal and humble'; even though such a value system has been weakened in modern China, it is still representative of favourable virtues in Chinese society. Influenced by her family, she developed a great interest in reading.

Rui gave an example of how she converted her cultural capital into social capital:

> As Confucius said, 'three persons walk together, I can always find a teacher among them'[5], so choosing friends whom you can learn from is important. We have university blogs, I would like to search for students who are kind, have merits and outstanding achievements ... I followed their posts, comment, and learn a lot from them. Gradually, we get to know each other, then we may become close friends in real life. ... Many of them are the responsible person of campus clubs or student organizations. A friend of mine helped me

> find a summer internship at CCTV (China Central Television). That was great experience, very helpful for me to get my job.

According to Rui, she has made this value system embedded in her mind and practice to be part of her cultural capital. Most importantly, she invested time and energy into building friendships with outstanding strangers, turned them into her close friends and accumulated social capital. Her social capital helped her to obtain more cultural capital through an internship at the national TV station. This impressive cultural capital greatly increased her opportunity in finding a satisfactory job.

In addition to friend networks, as a member of Communist Party of China (CPC), Rui was actually privileged in having access to positions in the public sector. Bourdieu (1986) defines social capital as 'the aggregate of the actual or potential resources which are linked to possession of a durable network of more or less institutionalized relationships of mutual acquaintance of recognition' (p. 21). Thus, friend networks can be viewed as non-institutionalized form of social capital. Bourdieu (1986) also suggests a type of institutionalized network that can be socially guaranteed by the application of a common name (e.g., name of a clan, a class, a tribe, a school, a party, etc.). CPC membership can be categorized as an institutionalized social capital, since the vast majority of the employers in the public sector in China prefer to recruit CPC members (Bian et al., 2001). Rui believed that her CPC membership and her sense of commitment and responsibility as a CPC member helped her find a satisfactory job.

In general, Rui inherited, internalized and accumulated the cultural capital, which is consistent with the dominant values and ideology in China. Such cultural capital inspired her to invest time and energy in acquiring effective social capital. She converted social capital into other types of cultural capital, which are crucial for her successful postgraduate transition. Rui's strategy is not uncommon for the first generation students who are motivated to climb up the social ladder, but not all of them are successful. Even though Rui was from a low SES family, and none of her parents or grandparents received any post-secondary education, her cultivation of traditional culture and reading habits through her grandparents' influence as well as her parents' encouragement allowed her to build an important foundation for practising such a strategy. It shows that accumulating relevant cultural capital actually provides room for strategic agency to act beyond the confinement of gender and class habitus. Among all the interviews, nine FGFUSs failed to accumulate adequate social and cultural capital to make the school to work transition, but they decided to postpone their transition through graduate study in order to invest more time and energy into collecting and converting relevant capital.

Conclusion

For most Chinese university students, especially those with disadvantaged backgrounds, university education is a necessary condition for upward mobility. However, in the process of social and economic transformation, they have to face a number of obstacles: the dramatic expansion of higher education, increasing difficulties in finding satisfactory jobs, education-job mismatch and increasingly competitive labour markets. When they start looking for jobs upon graduation, they realize that there is a considerable gap between their expected return on university education and the job searching experience in reality. A university degree may be important or even necessary, but it is definitely not sufficient for upward mobility. By using Bourdieu's conceptual framework of capital and habitus, this article provides in-depth analysis on how gender and SES affect university graduates' postgraduate transition process and how social inequality is reproduced through university experiences.

The qualitative analysis shows that among all the first generation female university graduates in this study, only 15 per cent of them had found a job, and 30 per cent have received admission from a graduate programme, which means that the majority of them (55 per cent) have not been able to achieve a postgraduate transition to work/career. They were either still job hunting or preparing to apply for a graduate programme for the next year. Getting into graduate programmes is a way to accumulate more cultural capital and a strategy to postpone the school to work transition or a backup plan after failing to find a job. From Bourdieu's perspective, two dispositions can be found: one disposition involves their realization of the incompatibility of individual class and gender habitus, which results in lowering expectation on educational return and stronger intention to retreat to their original class and gender habitus; the other disposition is to practise strategic agency by actively accumulating and converting cultural capital to other types of capital especially social capital and economic capital, in order to break out from the confinement of class and gender habitus and achieve upward mobility.

Although all the participants in this study were first generation female university graduates, their choice between the two dispositions is closely related to their socioeconomic background, original class habitus, as well as gender stereotypes at both individual and structural levels. Despite being able to access university education, their opportunity of achieving upward mobility is still greatly limited. The successful ones like Rui were able to accumulate some cultural capital through the cultural influence and affirmative actions of family members and actively convert the cultural capital into social capital and upgraded cultural capital. However, most of the female students with disadvantaged family backgrounds tend to have family members with no ability or attempt to provide any cultural capital, which may help them to have a constructive university life and academic success. Some families, especially the ones in poor rural areas, even become an active inhibiting factor for the female student in accessing such cultural capital, due to rigid gender structure in the family and community. Furthermore many female students have a difficult time to make the school to work transition due to strong gender discrimination in the job market derived from the gender stereotypes against them. Therefore, many FGFUSs become triple-disadvantaged by the barriers set by poverty, traditional gender role and class habitus.

In general, this study has demonstrated that social inequality can be reproduced during the postgraduate transition despite students obtaining higher education in China. However, the existence of success stories also indicates that sufficient exploration and utilization of cultural capital may repress the reproduction of social inequality. A strong motivation to break away from one's original class and traditional gender role as well as the active practice of strategic agency in accumulating feasible cultural and social capital during university may enable self-empowerment of the female students who are in vulnerable and marginalized positions. The rarity of successful cases shows the lack of initial positive influence from family upbringing, but also indicates the lack of guidance from public education. Thus, this study suggests that the educational institutions, especially the higher education system, should provide relevant courses and services to help university students, especially those with disadvantaged backgrounds, to develop full awareness of the structural obstacles and inequalities in postgraduate transitions; then these students may make personalized strategies and plans to overcome the obstacles mainly by accumulating and converting the social and cultural capital that would facilitate their self-development.

This study has a couple of limitations regarding the research population and the sample. Due to the limitation of time and cost, this study only selected two key-point universities in China. First, it controls the influence of students' academic performance before university, but excludes the student population who are in non-key-point universities and colleges. Since the participants in this study reported tremendous difficulties in making successful postgraduate transitions, I suspect that students with less prestigious credentials from non-key-point universities may experience even more challenges in making such transitions. Second, only the FGFUSs who were specialized in humanities and social sciences were interviewed in this study, and it is reasonable to believe that students studying in other disciplines may have different experiences in postgraduate transitions, depending on the demand of the labour market. Focussing on a less heterogeneous student group can help in managing potential variations in the sample, but it also reduces the generalizability of the findings. Nevertheless, the findings and the theoretical tools utilized in the analysis can be further examined in future studies, which may focus on other student groups' postgraduate transition processes in China or other countries, especially the ones in marginalized and disadvantaged positions.

Notes

1 Most of the employment rates were obtained through mass media. Researchers questioned the accuracy of these numbers due to two major concerns; first, they might be self-reporting information provided by individual post-secondary institutions, which are likely to report a higher employment rate than there actually was; and second, the criteria used by different research agencies or levels of government to define employment rates might not be consistent (Hui, 2010).
2 'Key-point' is a title given to an educational institution by the Chinese government based on an evaluation of this institution's quality of teaching, students and other educational facilities and resources. The officially recognized key-point schools would receive substantial supports from the government.
3 The initial employment rate of new post-secondary graduates refers to the ratio between the graduating students who have formally arranged employment or postgraduate education before officially graduating at the end of July and the total graduating population.
4 White-collar worker here refers to a person who performs professional, managerial or administrative work.
5 A verse from the Analects of Confucius.

References

Bai, L. (2006) Graduate unemployment: dilemmas and challenges in China's move to mass higher education. *The China Quarterly*. 185, 128–144.

Bian, Y., Logan, J. R. & Shu, X. (2000) Wage and job inequalities in the working careers of men and women in Tianjin. In: Entwistle, B. & Henderson, G. E. (eds.). *Re-drawing boundaries: work, household, and gender in China* (pp. 111–133). Berkeley, CA: University of California Press.

Bian, Y., Shu, X. & Logan, R. J. (2001) Communist party membership and regime dynamics in China. *Social Forces*. 79 (3), 805–840.

Bourdieu, P. (1984) *Distinction: a social critique of the judgement of taste*. Trans. R. Nee, Cambridge, MA: Harvard University Press.

Bourdieu, P. (1986) The forms of capital. In: Richardson, J. (ed.). *Handbook of theory and research for the sociology of education* (pp. 241–258). New York: Greenwood Press.

Bourdieu, P. (1990) *The logic of practice*. Stanford: Stanford University Press.

Bourdieu, P. & Wacquant, L. (1992) *An invitation to reflexive sociology*. Chicago, IL: University of Chicago Press.

Cang, W. (2014) Tuition fees see first hike in 10 years. *China Daily*, 8 August 2014. Available from: www.chinadaily.com.cn/china/2014-08/08/content_18269714.htm.

China News. (2013) *Social Science Academy report: university tuition fees in China have increased 25 times*. 1 March 2013. Available from: www.chinanews.com/edu/2013/03-01/4607697.shtml [In Chinese].

Dong, H. & Wan, X. (2012) Higher education tuition and fees in China: implications and impacts on affordability and educational equity. *Current Issues in Education*. 15 (1), 1–10.

Dong, Q., Li, X., Yang, H. & Zhang, K. (2008) Gender inequality in rural education and poverty. *Chinese Sociology and Anthropology*. 40 (4), 64–78.

Economic Daily. (2009) *The postsecondary graduate employment rate has reached 68%*. 9 July 2009. Available from: http://paper.ce.cn/jjrb/html/2009-07/09/content_72399.htm [In Chinese].

Education Online. (2006) *College students' employment rate and opinions on employment, 2006*. Available from: www.eol.cn/jiuye_dy_4516/20060621/t20060621_184927.shtml/ [In Chinese].

Education Online. (2016a) *7.65 million college graduates' employment is facing structural difficulties*. Available from: www.eol.cn/html/c/2016gxbys/index.shtml [In Chinese].

Education Online. (2016b) *The gross rate of higher education enrolment in China has reached 40% in 2015*. Available from: http://gaokao.eol.cn/news/201604/t20160408_1384606.shtml [In Chinese].

Fu, Y. (2001) The survey: Chinese women's status in transformation. *Women of China/English Monthly*. 30 December 2001.

Gao, W. & Smyth, R. (2015) Education expansion and returns to schooling in urban China, 2001–2010: evidence from three waves of the China urban labour survey. *Journal of the Asia Pacific Economy*. 20 (2), 178–201.

Hannum, E., Kong, P. & Zhang, Y. (2009) Family sources of educational gender inequality in rural China: a critical assessment. *International Journal of Educational Development*. 29, 474–486.

Hui, T. (2010) An in-depth analysis of the postsecondary graduate employment rate. *Statistics and Practices*. 4, 25–44 [In Chinese].

Knight, J., Deng, Q. & Li, S. (2017) China's expansion of higher education: the labour market consequences of a supply shock. *China Economic Review*. 43, 127–141.

Lin, N. & Bian, Y. (1991) Getting ahead in urban China. *American Journal of Sociology*. 97, 657–688.

Ma, W. (2012) Why the rural poor get fewer opportunities to leading research universities. *Asia Pacific Education Review*. 13, 263–271.

Mare, R. D. (1980) Social backgrounds and educational continuation decisions. *Journal of American Statistical Association*. 75, 295–305.

Ministry of Education of the People's Republic of China. (2015) *The third party evaluation report on higher education 2015*. Available from: www.moe.edu.cn/jyb_xwfb/xw_fbh/moe_2069/xwfbh_2015n/xwfb_151204/151204_sfcl/201512/t20151204_222891.html [In Chinese].

National Bureau of Statistics of China. (2010) *The 2010 population census of PRC*. Available from: www.stats.gov.cn/tjsj/pcsj/rkpc/6rp/indexch.htm [In Chinese].

News China. (2010) *Ministry of Education: the initial employment rate of university graduates has reached 74%*. 2 March 2010. Available from: http://news.china.com.cn/edu/2010-03/02/content_19503212.htm [In Chinese].

Qiao, J. (2010) On the rural-urban disparity in access to higher education opportunities in China. *Chinese Education and Society*. 43 (4), 22–31.

Reuters. (2011) China says graduates should lower job expectations. *Entertainment News*. Available from: www.reuters.com/article/idINIndia-55925820110328.

Wang, H. (2009) The current graduate employment survey of the problem. *Higher Education Forum*. 8, 118–120.
Wang, W. & Moffatt, P. G. (2008) *Hukou* and graduates' job search in China. *Asian Economic Journal*. 22 (1), 1–23.
Wu, S. (2004) The comparative analysis of the students' cost about attending school and getting employment between public and private universities. *Education and Economics*. 2, 6–10.
Xie, Z., Wang, W. & Chen, X. (2010) A study of women's access to higher education in rural and urban China. *Chinese Education and Society*. 43 (4), 32–40.
Ye, H. (2012) College expansion and school-to-work transition in China, Ph.D. dissertation, The Hong Kong University of Science and Technology.
Yeung, J. W. (2013) Higher education expansion and social stratification in China. *Chinese Sociological Review*. 45 (4), 54–80.
Zhong, Y. & Lu, G. (2003) The equity effects of cost recovery in higher education. *Peking University Education Review*. 1 (2), 52–64.

4 Towards the Good Society

Expanding Women's Capabilities through Community Education and European Social Policy in Northern Ireland

Susan Hodgett

Background

This chapter considers life in Northern Ireland (NI) during the Troubles (BBC, 2017) and examines the positive role that community-based education played in improving the lives of women, an excluded social group. It does not discuss formal educational provisions provided by the state, rather, it provides incidences of innovative informal adult education in local communities, what Nita Freire, with reference to her husband Paulo's oeuvre, described as 'the act of seeking knowledge … reading the world, and of acting in it' (as cited in Strajn, 2016). The following case study and its attendant theory of human development (the belief in enlarging peoples' choices) sheds light upon policy interventions that increased women's autonomy in disadvantaged communities in NI supported by an emergent European Union (EU) social policy near century's end; a number of EU-funded community-based projects in high-conflict communities are considered. Given the United Kingdom's (UK) 2016 decision to leave the EU, questions are raised concerning whether such experimental interventions will prove possible in future.

Such uncertainties feed into wider apprehensions regarding the diminution of women's equality in working (and other) environments in the UK post-Brexit. In view of the fact that hard-won improvements (e.g., part-time/fixed-term/outsourced workers' rights, paid holidays, health and safety protection, unpaid parental leave, pension/agency workers' rights) were achieved through EU membership, such concerns seem appropriate. Anxieties about future maintenance of achieved equality legislation for women have been voiced by interest groups in the UK (Smethers, 2016). Yet in NI these worries remain largely unvoiced given the recent multiple political crises or scandals and the collapse of the local Assembly in 2017. Ironically though, apprehensions over the future status of women are acute given that, after Brexit, NI will be the only part of the UK to have a land border with the EU (with the Republic of Ireland). This fact, and fears over the implementation of a renewed 'hard' border on the island of Ireland, perpetuates concerns about a return to a province physically (and mentally) divided from its neighbours and suffering deteriorating socio-economic conditions. In the past, such conditions bred increased sectarianism and violence worsening overall quality of life. And, as our case study demonstrates, any reversal of hard-won progress for women should provoke significant disquiet.

The position of women in NI has historically been poor compared to other parts of the UK. Knight (1998, p. 40) has observed that this is likely not accidental as 'human life [and freedom] is always limited in ways characteristic of the basis of a given form of society'. One indicator of the reduced position for women in NI can be seen in female participation in the UK's local assemblies; in 1998, female representation in Scotland was 37 per cent, Wales 40 per cent and NI 12 per cent (Galligan, 2014). Nineteen years later statistics read Scotland 35 per cent, Wales 42 per cent and NI 30 per cent (Parliament UK, n.d.). Other indicators of disappointing female participation in the province show women holding few senior public or private-sector positions.[1] While it could be argued that representation for females has improved slowly, the troubles have continued to take their toll pushing women's issues far down public and governmental priorities. This situation has been sharply highlighted by the recent referendum result in the Republic of Ireland (May 2018), encouraging a change in the country's constitution facilitating the availability of abortion in future and overturning a constitutional amendment that outlawed it 35 years earlier. This turn of events ensures that NI remains the only part of the British Isles with reactionary laws on this subject making it singularly a place apart in the UK and Europe. Activists in NI have for years outlined the ways that women have been 'excluded and silenced' on a raft of issues, including reproductive rights, dealing with the past, agency (lack of control, fear and intimidation from paramilitary activity), domestic and sexual violence and mental health issues (Bloomer & Fegan, 2014; Ward, 2013).

This might be expected, it could be argued, given the scale and character of long term political conflict and domestic violence in earlier years wherein Monica McWilliams (1997, p. 80) noted 3,200 people were killed and 36,800 seriously injured, from a population of 1.6 million. The consequence was an 'insidious atmosphere of sectarianism and violence' where women coped with the death and injury of loved ones while enduring the 'destruction of normal family life'. During these blighted years women contended with multiple social problems: high unemployment, arrests under emergency legislation, trial by non-jury courts, appalling child-care provisions, community expectations of wives' or women's loyalty to prisoners, social isolation, financial strain, depression and anxiety. Meanwhile

McWilliams tells us 'those residing in ... troubled working-class areas ... had to live with the fear that their children could be caught up in cross-fire, killed or maimed by plastic bullets, or blown up in explosions'.

McWilliam's work has made a substantial contribution in identifying the less obvious difficulties of women's lives during this time and in this place. When dealing with sectarianism and male violence she presents a harrowing list of evidence, including murders of women, arson attacks against single mothers, incidences of rape used as a weapon and significantly 'the less public nature of the *private* violence that women ... experienced from men known to them' (McWilliams, 1997, p. 81) [italics added]. Such insights into 'an acceptable level of violence'[2] against women are often overlooked in accounts of the troubles; in particular, the experience of women living with men holding guns (legal or otherwise) and the implications for threatening or violent behaviour in the home. McWilliam's research has been important because it addressed the 'interaction of militarism and masculinism in Northern Ireland', what some have dubbed armed patriarchy. Her accounts of how male *public* violence influenced aggression towards women in the *private* domain have been revelatory. Her contribution has been to demonstrate that 'violence ... against women [was] used to keep women in their place; to limit their opportunities to live, learn, work, and care as full human beings' (McWilliams, 1997, p. 89). And, as she notes wryly, '[i]n the competition for resources and attention between political terrorism and domestic terrorism in Northern Ireland, the former ... always win[s] out'; this, during a period, when police failed to record domestic violence incidents.[3] Such was the environment in which our case study took place, a landscape where 'normal' everyday life was often devoid of hope and where community-based education offered some women the possibility of welcome escape.

Education, Culture and Identity

According to Inglis (2004, p. 23),

> [i]t is a truth much forgotten that the point of education is to help ensure that the society which is home to all of us is capable of carrying on and will continue into a recognizable future. [It is important to know] how to keep the colossal show of a society on the historical road.

Keeping the colossal show of Northern Irish society on the historical road has proved challenging. It is beyond the scope of this paper to detail efforts to improve 'well-being', the state of being comfortable, healthy or happy in the province although it is addressed elsewhere (Doran & Hodgett, 2018; McAloney, 2014). Nonetheless, this chapter will demonstrate that education, and particularly community-based adult education, has played a significant role. Education can be an enabling environment, one where people may develop their potential and expand their choices to lead the kind of lives they have reason to value. Such aims, it remains true, prove difficult in a society with a culture deeply divided and an education system, to university level, riven by religion. NI's education system comprises 827 primary schools (4–11 years old) and 202 post-primary schools (12–18 years old) (Perry, 2016, pp. 9–10). Most are divided by religion, with post-primary schools apportioned between grammar[4] and secondary schools; a small number of religiously integrated schools serve approximately 5 per cent of the population. Schools in NI have differing governance with (Protestant) controlled schools at 39 per cent, (Catholic) maintained schools at 36 per cent, voluntary grammar schools at 15 per cent and others (mostly Irish medium) making up 1 per cent of institutions. Education at the two universities is not religiously segregated, although teacher training is. Most people, however, are educated along religiously separated lines reaching adulthood with little or no experience of those from a different background. All of this is to say that NI society remains fundamentally divided with the former First Minister acknowledging that the 'education system is a benign form of apartheid' (Belfast Telegraph, 2010). Divisions exist in other aspects of life too, including sport and housing. The *Irish News* noted that for '[a]lmost two decades after the signing of the Good Friday Agreement, ... more than 90 per cent of social housing in Northern Ireland remain[ed] segregated on grounds of religious background' (Morris, 2016). Protestant and Catholic communities are separated by a growing number of 'peace' walls[5] that maintain *active* sectarian segregation.

Such problems have far-reaching implications. Research on the impact of societal division shows children as young as three indicating preference for specific cultural events or symbols; by the age of seven, 34 per cent of children identified with either Catholic or Protestant communities (Connelly et al., 2002). By identifying with their own politico-religious community, 'us', children inevitably become suspicious of 'them'. McManus (2017, p. 411) has dubbed this process 'othering', arguing that 'there is a need to confront the othering processes [which] help[s] ... to generate ... division' even before children start school. Addressing such issues is a matter of social justice, and MacIntyre (cited in Knight, 1998, p. 40) has indicated that it is within the means of societies to improve realized human possibilities and freedom, if there is the genuine will to do so.

Halsey et al. (1997, p. 25) has told us that we should 'think of education in the modern, if not post-modern world, as a means to achieve a balance between equality, liberty, and community'. Under this rubric, one might argue that the formal education system in NI has failed and alternative means become necessary. Adults, we know, create the basis of our transmutable cultures; they embody our varied, robust or fragile, local communities. Their vision of the best that communities may be depends on their own education, and moreover helps shape the future 'Good Society'. And, as Hattersley (Inglis, 2004, p. 12) reminds us, a good society necessarily concerns notions of democratic government.

Education so becomes the context of a culture, playing a role in the making and handing down of history and civilization, and in the reduction of inequalities within the society it serves. It strives to produce its offspring, to paraphrase Inglis, as the citizen-consumer, each with a moral imagination and a picture of what it would be like to live in a society where everything went well; whose members are healthy, happy, fulfilled, loving and responsible (Inglis, 2004, p. 24). Successful education thereby becomes the proprietor of our collective social dreams and the keeper of our best community ambitions. In our search for utopia, our dominant values are passed on by the very processes of learning. In this way, we realize how we came to be who we are, who we might become in future and how we might possibly get there. Education *can be* the means of enlarging people's choices and the opening up of new perspectives. Moreover, and as MacIntyre (cited in Knight, 1998, p. 240) has reminded us, education is more than the simple acquisition of skills but also of the virtues; encouraging those in search of an excellent life to review 'what place should the goods of each of the practices in which I am engaged have in my life?' (work, family, etc.). In so doing, he notes, we must acknowledge the *communal*, remarking, 'what place should the goods of each of the practices in which we are engaged have in *our* common life? What is the best way of life for *our* community?'

Reflecting on community in NI, McManus (2017, p. 412) has noted that '[o]ne characteristic of the failed efforts [of] ... dealing with the legacy of the past has been the ability of both communities to view the conflict as having stemmed ... from the Other and an inability to see their own community's role and responsibilities within that'. His solution is clear: 'implementation of community-based education to address "cultural constructions of reality"—those beliefs and views that are central in defining how groups view themselves and others' (McManus, 2017, p. 412). The passing on of an education encompasses the passing on of a culture and as Sen (2005) declared culture matters. Notably, Taylor (2001) reveals that culture plays an important role in the definition of oneself, and in the context of the modern world, it fixes one somewhere. Self-definition, he argues, is an individual's situation in moral and social space, and in theory 'human beings could become whatever they wished or whatever they were capable of becoming' (Taylor, 2001, p. 141). Yet, such opportunities remain intimately associated with the capacity to participate in society and on the opportunities provided to do so. Such insights address the nature of the policy interventions we discuss later.

Capabilities and Human Development

In pursuing human freedom, peoples and communities, as well as individuals, need assistance. Sen (1999, p. 14) reflected this in his addition of 'capabilities', the power or ability to do something, to econometrics concentrating on the 'broader focus of the lives we can lead' in becoming 'fuller social persons'. Sen's concern for the processes and opportunities people have in their society and the unfreedoms that arise from inadequate processes are clear. If freedom is the building block of development, then the expansion of capabilities of persons to lead the kind of lives they value is crucial to development. He is correct that capabilities can be enhanced or reduced by public policies (Sen, 1999, p. 18). Individual freedoms thus become the mainstay of development and a central element of creativity and social efficacy, enhancing the ability of people to help themselves. Moreover, they reflect the 'agency aspect' of the individual; where an agent is one who acts and brings about change and 'whose achievements can be judged in terms of her own values and objectives', or autonomy. As we have already seen, autonomy, the ability to govern oneself, to have the moral independence to make your own choices, was considerably constrained for women during the Troubles (McWilliams, 1997).

The Capability Approach (CA) helps us to understand the profound importance of an individual's autonomy or agency and the power of a group of community members to improve their collective situations. Such concerns were central to Sen's work (1999) and his ideas underpinning the United Nation's Development Program (UNDP) and its Human Development Index (UNDP, n.d.). Foundational to both were concerns regarding enlarging people's choices,

> defined by [the CA as] choice of focus upon the moral significance of individuals' capability of achieving the kind of lives they have reason to value ... A person's capability to live a good life ... defined in terms of the set of valuable 'beings and doings' like being in good health or having loving relationships with others to which they have real access.
>
> (IEP, n.d.)

It is these motivations that connect our case study to theory. Development goes beyond measuring economic indicators but helps communities to articulate their preferences to enlarge their choices, freedoms and capabilities. Alkire (2005, p. 117) suggests that this includes the resources necessary to allow the ability to make appropriate choices along with poverty reduction and justice. The approach then is made up of people's valuable doings and beings (functionings) and freedom. It appreciates *all* changes in a person's quality of life (e.g., relationships, self-confidence, employment and literacy). Alkire (2005, pp. 118–119) is concerned with the *means* and *ends* involved in achieving these while acknowledging the trade-offs and public judgements involved.

Sen, like Taylor, recognizes that the state is a moral agent in the *process* of development that enhances or negates individual and collective capabilities. Democratization is a process of production for *public good* in which education plays a fundamental role. In such a state, the public good, as West (2001, p. 1902) tells us, 'is one where individual autonomy, and particularly the autonomous right[s] of individuals to determine their own conceptions of the good' come to the fore. Materialism, self-rule and the welfarist or primary goods conception of the state prove insufficient. Rather, in this good society,

> Citizens ... enjoy certain fundamental human capabilities (thereby leaving to the citizens the choice whether or not to avail themselves of those capabilities)—including the capability to live a safe, well nourished, productive, educated, social, and politically and culturally participatory life of normal length.
>
> (West, 2001)

Education, in all its forms, is subject to public and social policy interventions. In our study we review how community education in NI 'use[d] public space for collective advancement' (Stromquist, 2014, p. 545) for women, considering Rodl's (2016, p. 84), and citing Bakhurst's, suggestion that 'the end of education ... [is] autonomy ... the power to determine what to do and think in the light of what there is reason to do and think'.

In conceptualizing ideas of human development and in interpreting Sen's ideas, Martha Nussbaum (2000, p. 79–80) has developed a list of ten significant life-enhancing capabilities. These include the right to life, notions like the importance of senses, imagination and thought and the significance of emotions to capability. Walker (2003, 2006) argues that there are two particular capabilities of Nussbaum's ten of importance to education being practical reason and affiliation. Practical reason turns to ideas of education and the good society and involves conceptualizing 'the good' in planning one's life. Affiliation, as a capability, involves living with and towards others, showing concern and compassion for them in appropriate situations, feeling empathy, aiming for justice, regarding friendship, demonstrating self-respect and offering dignity. Walker (2006) believes that these two educationally significant capabilities suffuse all others. This chapter is a tentative foray into the relevance of such capabilities, for women, within the informal educational setting of the

Community Infrastructure (CI) measure in NI funded and influenced by the EU.

Identity is made up of both universal components (moral commitments like religion, political ideology, etc.) and particular attachments (to groups or communities) (Braude, 1988). So, well-being is a complex web of people and place, of subjective feelings and views of how life is in that place. Education contributes to the improvement of our well-being in aiming for, as Nussbaum (2004, p. 1) puts it, a life that is truly human. And, following Walker, we acknowledge that 'education enhances humanity, agency and freedom; [moreover] it should not diminish lives'. Not diminishing lives has been a constant concern in Sen's reconceptualization of development. Moving from the normative to the evaluative approach has been his radical contribution to social science. Realizing that well-being is a tissue of interconnections that depends on an individual not being deprived of capabilities to achieve functionings like sufficient income, literacy, nourishment, education and good health is profound. Even in affluent countries, Sen shows us that being unemployed (or underemployed) is debilitating. It promotes social exclusion, loss of self-confidence and loss of self-reliance while damaging psychological and physical health. How we feel about how we live influences the quality of life we experience daily. So, participatory freedoms are primary in improving social arrangements, including education, and become the focus of redefining development and considering 'eudaimonia', the state of being comfortable, healthy or happy. Community education, as practised in the CI measure, is valuable because adult education itself is a means to enhance capabilities. It enhances not only individual capabilities but also collective capabilities through its aspiration to a different culture of increased autonomy, agency and freedom.

Sen (1999) is interested in the expansion of the capabilities of persons to lead the kind of lives they value and have reason to value. Development of the CA outlines how policy interventions can enhance the capabilities of the public (through free speech, civic participation and critical thinking) and allows, particularly women, to influence policy through effective use of their capabilities (Clark & Hodgett, 2018; Ibrahim & Tawari, 2014). Sen's conception of capability as freedom involves not only freedom as the means to choose amongst valuable alternatives but more, freedom as opportunity to make a choice, as well as the actual choices made. Sen (1999, p. 18) reminds us therefore that public policy is 'a two-way relationship' that makes, and remakes, modern social policies. This chapter examines a policy intervention that used informal adult education to broaden the capabilities of local people, especially women, in an identifiable historical context. It views the role of community education as both a *private good* to the individual and a *public good* to society.

Experience of community education in NI must to be seen within the broader UK context that Gravatt (2015, p. 15) described as undergoing 'unmanaged decline'. Deeming a 'crisis in adult education', Stanistreet (2014) lambasts government in the UK for ensuring that education is only for the young, while headlines record 'adults abandon[ing] further education' amidst growing concerns over social inequality.[6] In NI abandonment of adult community education by government was offset (for a time) by EU Structural Funds estimated to be £1 billion between 2002 and 2012 (Stewart, 2014, p. 1). During this time evidence can be found of improved human flourishing despite dire social and political circumstances (Hodgett, 2008).

Sen's ideas on human flourishing[7] relate to the European Social Model,[8] within the building of a local *Community Infrastructure* to support the voluntary sector in NI. This initiative supported sixty-one community-based projects at a time when the province experienced severe civil unrest and a per capita GDP of less than 75 per cent of EU average.

The CI measure, established in 1993, was an attempt at working to achieve local development in the province influenced by membership of the EU. Its most interesting feature was the involvement of the voluntary sector in policymaking, economic development and education. Its success was its willingness to acknowledge divisions reflecting Sen's belief that agency, through collective action, could relate the person to multiple levels of government (micro, meso and macro). This experiment, part of a larger NI peace process, was an effort to expand participatory communities' capabilities and to effect development. NI was divided on sectarian lines, with religious and political groups engaged in othering and reinforcing single-community advantage. Yet this policy intervention, and its community-based education, sought to develop mutual interests across these divides, beyond community sectarianism, and to achieve a universal humanitarianism by creating conjoined community interests.

Policy Study: Communities and Capabilities

CI was set within a difficult culture but achieved developmental success, making people *feel better* about themselves and their communities. Its accomplishment was to find a narrative to this end. In NI policymaking contributes to quality of life situations, with well-being measured against ill-being. Undertaking a cultural discourse among deprived communities was a challenge for policymakers who had to find a language to communicate with both communities. CI proved significant because it understood the importance of stories individuals tell in building their communities. In a region divided by sectarianism discourse itself proved problematic. Terms like 'poverty', 'community' and 'state' had divergent cultural, social and political connotations for Catholic and Protestant communities. Government sought agreed policy measures bridging competing demands based on *individual agency*. By persuading local activists to work together in partnerships and networks, they promoted discussion, agreed targets and overcame oppositional views of public administration. This allowed a

> dialectical process by which individual identities [were] established in relation to others in society—by human *bargaining* on the one hand and by human *attachments* on the other.
>
> (Dean, 2003, p. 3.) [Italics added]

Community-based organizations had a surfeit of *local* attachment. Nonetheless, by encouraging cooperative behaviour, government facilitated capability expansion. In terms of the CA, they sought what Ibrahim (2006, p. 397), in her work on Egypt, envisaged as 'self-help', achieved through acting together to expand and exercise new *collective capabilities*. In this way, government supported and protected local communities and challenged views on improving everyday quality of life and widening capability sets. This was an unusual approach for the British government, which more often used objective measurements of well-being based on income. Yet Europe strongly encouraged *subjective* views of well-being, after the Commission called for a social model to promote well-being, cohesiveness and a high quality of life (UNHD, 1990). Such experiments reflected social indicators influenced from Brussels, which academics at the time argued 'developed joint social policy standards and the role and structures of relevant interest groups' (Falkner, 1998, p. 2). These European interventions proved significant to the NI peace process.[9]

Projects and policies influenced by such ideas bridged the gap between the local and the universal perspectives of the world. Interpretive approaches were used by the CI measure during the EU-sponsored conference on the intervention (DHSS, 1999). Here, storytelling demonstrated insights into the competing repertories of community life in NI, as well as the outcomes of several of the projects funded. This concern for, and promotion of, a narrative in individual and collective contributions to public policy was extraordinary. Interventions were usually evaluated using numeric data on job creation, time contributed, people involved or projects undertaken. Using a storytelling method for CI relied on Weber's notions of 'verstehen', of uncovering subjective meanings to pursue the concepts and values used by individuals on their personal understanding of society. In search of an evaluation method that would more accurately represent the impact of the measure itself, storytelling showcases demonstrated what projects had done, what people had learned and how communities had benefited. The EU conference considered the valuable beings and doings that had been achieved, and looked for examples of freedom enhanced and capability expanded, particularly for women.

This was also a major concern for the CA. Nussbaum (2004, p. 199), for example, considered how disadvantaged women can be better heard through Socratic dialogue and by using international agreements as templates for domestic political processes. Indeed, she used 'narrative ... [as] a method of civic education ... to ... imagine the problems, to see the human issues involved in what might otherwise read as bare statistics, and to show the connection between one problem and another' (Nussbaum, 2004, p. 202). Such approaches, Nussbaum believed, were imperative to understand what it *feels like* to live (Nussbaum, 2004, p. 203). What it felt like for women in NI was rarely addressed in academic literature; nonetheless it was vitally important.

Expanding Capabilities in NI

From 1972 to 1998 and 2002 to 2007, NI was governed from Westminster by local civil servants seeking greater legitimacy in the decision-making process. In 1989 NI received Objective One Area status under the first EU Structural Funds aimed at 'increas[ing] the social and economic cohesion of the European Community through ... economic development' (HMSO, 1993). Funding was to build and sustain a CI (investment in voluntary and community activity) and to achieve economic development. Programming addressed how people felt about place, their quality of life and well-being (Hodgett, 1998, 2008). Its purpose was to involve new groups of people in working with government, using community development for economic regeneration.

The educational processes in projects offered opportunities to disadvantaged communities, and sought to improve their freedoms, commodities and capacities. Sixty-one projects were funded (1994–1999) totalling £11.5 million (DFP, 2003). Each project's criteria were set by the local administration but influenced by the EU around: group support and networking, community resources and facilities, social exclusion, integrated area partnership building, independent advice-giving, contribution to policy formation and capacity building. These aims sit easily with Sen's motivations of removing unfreedoms and giving people access to improved well-being. Each project was to contribute to community development using

> [a] set of methods which can broaden vision and capacity for social change ... a way of working which is informed by certain principles which seek to encourage communities—people who live in the same areas or who have something else in common—to tackle for themselves the problems which they face and identify to be important,

> and which aim to empower them to change things by developing their own skills, knowledge and experience and ... by working in partnership with other groups and with statutory agencies ... the task and the process is important.
>
> (DHSS, 1996, p. 9) [Italics added]

Using Sen's terms, this measure was about improving functionings and human agency and had Frierian motivations. It worked to broaden vision, increase freedoms and attain valuable beings and doings. It tackled community problems through empowerment by developing skills, autonomy, knowledge and experience, thereby improving people's functionings, what they have and can do in their life and their (community's) capacity to function. This, it might be argued, is the main purpose of the process of education. Certainly, the measure fulfilled Sen's criteria of agency freedom (one's freedom to bring about achievements that one values) and well-being freedom (one's freedom to achieve those things that are constitutive of one's well-being). It thereby fulfilled two core functions of education (Walker, 2006).

The community development approach understood the importance of quantitative methods and the need for qualitative assessment. Specific *quality of life indicators* were used, including economic activity, material gains, anti-poverty measures, *education*, transport, safety, policing and community life (DHSS, 1999). Yet NI government sought to reflect people's feelings, their well-being and their meanings and understandings, and acknowledged that while less tangible things can be easily measured, they may be less important (DHSS, 1996).

So CI attempted two objectives, the first being a 'sectoral approach' to fund the wider voluntary sector. The second intention was to establish support networks and government-funded organizations like the Community Development and Health Network (CDHN), a province-wide organization linking 400 members involved in health. The network undertook a research project to 'identify the *enabling* and the constraining factors of integrating a community development approach into health and social services. ... [and] mainstreaming community development ... into statutory bodies' [italics added]. This experiment expanded capabilities to *learn*, and improved the participant's level of education.

The CDHN found CI vital in allowing people to develop alliances for peer education, peer support, and to influence the policy environment; all valuable commodities. It formed a productive relationship with the local Rural Community Network and the body representative of the voluntary sector, the Northern Ireland Council for Voluntary Action. Through working in cooperation with like-minded organizations, lobbying and *training* on 'tools of practice' (research methods, evaluation techniques and means of assessing community health), the network increased resources available to activists, promoted awareness of policy and enlarged the number of people involved in policymaking. Increased confidence, increased capacities, skills development, in the view of the network, contributed to improving health attitudes and activities, what Walker called stories of educational practice.

The CDHN saw its role as a pressure on government to involve citizens by creating a community education package for activists, making them better informed about the health service and improving their functioning so they could work together. Their influence on policy can be seen in the altered means of policymaking from a local health board—that drafted by civil servants—to one subcontracted to CDHN. More transparent methods of consultation evolved involving health stakeholders quality-assured by a panel from local voluntary organizations. This measure achieved Sen's aim of promoting well-being freedom, where groups of individuals had, through *peer education*, achieved an improved capability set. Such processes reflect Nussbaum's capability *affiliation,* the use of intellect, imagination and the feeling of particularity *in situ*.

CDHN commented that it had a larger public voice in health consultations, through community arts projects, a photographic competition for disabled people and other means. They noted too changed priorities for the NI Department of Health (from heart disease and cancer to poverty, mental health issues and poor education). CI projects involved local people in active citizenship through running a family support programme, an environmental scheme, an after-schools club and community centres. Each might be construed as effective community education or active lifelong learning.

Like the 1990 UNDP Report so influenced by Sen (UNDP, 1990), this European project was focussed on how development enlarges people's choices. The measure used community development to include new groups in the policy formation process including women. One centre in a working-class area of Belfast helped women become more politically aware and assertive developing links with the Northern Ireland Assembly and the new Women's Coalition Party.[10] Women who were doubly disadvantaged, being working-class and religiously segregated, creatively used funds to engage with others from across the political divide to learn Irish. Unorthodox female cooperation challenged the macho male culture in the working-class communities around them. Informal learning garnered appreciation, and understanding of the capabilities and commodities of 'other' women's lives across the sectarian divide. We see many of Nussbaum's ten capabilities including compassion and a quest for justice. We identify emotions and senses engaged in overcoming bigotry and prejudice, and a freeing of the imagination. These Belfast women used affiliation to promote the 'human powers of practical reason and sociability' (Nussbaum, as cited in Walker, 2006).

Such empowerment of women may, or may not, be maintained. In NI over the last 30 years, women and their priorities have often been *missing* from government and public policy. The consequence has frequently been the acceptance of a macho, male-dominated, violence-riven culture. Even so, when government failed to put aside ring-fenced money for the women's sector, lobbying ensured that the Office of the First and Deputy First Minister found funds to which they could apply. This demonstrates Sen's desire to promote women 'as active agents of change' (Sen, 1999, p. 189).

This measure helped women in NI's most deprived and violent areas understand that their treatment was less than equal. It asserted their agency in playing a fuller role in their local communities. This was important because the society we get is shaped by what we think of ourselves, and, particularly for women, by what 'amount of self-esteem you are led to have by your society [and] what your society tells you about the opportunities that are likely to be open to you' (Walker, 2006). For women in NI burdened with a slow-to-change patriarchal society the

> attraction of the capability approach ... is that, as a social practice, education is fundamentally about what we each learn to be, as much as about what knowledge we acquire. It is then, above all, a domain of activity which requires thinking and judgment not only about what has been done but as a guide to future action.
>
> (Walker, 2006)

Conclusion

The CI measure was successful despite the odds in difficult social and political circumstances. There were complexities in implementing some of the projects between the public, private and voluntary sectors. There were challenges too in promoting acceptance of an intersubjective narrative between the religious communities and the sustainability of projects. At the outset, the measure was ill thought-out and lacked clarity, which, perversely, may have been advantageous as civil servants practised pragmatism. Evidence of active citizenship continuing from the measure can be seen in the NI Department of Social Development's *Partners for Change* document in policies implemented across all government departments (DSD, 2001). The NI Programme for Building Sustainable Development 2000–2006 promoted urban and social revitalization, and a new task force was set up for the promotion of the Voluntary Sector (DSD, 2001). Many of the individual measures of the European Union's Peace and Reconciliation Programs arose from this measure.

This policy experiment was effective under difficult conditions. The peace process built upon its positivity, particularly regarding the involvement of people condemned to the margins of society. While the measure brought together local civil servants, the voluntary sector and EU bureaucrats, most importantly, it offered a positive narrative of the stories we tell ourselves about ourselves encouraging *community imagining* and *communal learning.* CI contributed to modern democracy through supporting the autonomy of many, especially women. Autonomy, or using Sen's term, agency, requires collective decision-making and the extensive involvement of citizens in public affairs and participative democracy. This contributes to political freedoms (Sen, 1999, p. 148) and the achievement of political rights that proved to be significant to the wider peace process. This measure helped improve the basic freedom and capabilities of women and their political and liberal rights, and expressed their *claims to political attention.* Nussbaum (2000, p. 36–39) has told us that capabilities are significantly close to ideas of human rights (political liberties, the freedom of association, the free choice of occupation) but that, fundamentally, they challenge definitions of development based only on wealth, poverty or economics. Rather, the CA offers increased precision and supplementation of traditional human rights. So that

> by focusing from the start on what people are actually able to do and to be, [the CA] is well placed to foreground and address inequalities that women suffer inside the family: inequalities in resources and opportunities, educational deprivations, the failure of work to be recognized as work, insults to bodily integrity.
>
> (ibid)

Such insight was fundamental. This measure moved the NI government towards achievement of eudaimonia or improved human flourishing in the establishment of a functioning peace process. It proved popular with, and beneficial to, women, helping to secure their autonomy and agency in an unstable and violent NI. This achievement was remarkable given the time and the place, for as Walker & Loots (2016, p. 261) have shown, transformative gender equality is often lost in the process between setting policy goals and later policy evaluation.

This study was an effective experiment in public policy lending weight to Sen's claim that freedom-orientated diversity enhances cultural capabilities. The importance of such experiments is clear. Looking forward to the best that might be achieved in the creation of human development, Flores-Crespo (2004, p. 4) suggests that the CA effectively 'recaptures the humanistic view of education' by exploring the links between education and freedom. In this endeavour, Nussbaum notes, there are *three capacities essential to the cultivation of humanity*: first, the critical examination of oneself to produce better citizens in emotion and thought, and, second, viewing ourselves as citizens of the world and aspiring to global standards of mutual respect. Finally, having

> [t]he ability to think what it might be like to be in the shoes of a person different from oneself, to be an intelligent reader of that person's story, and to understand the emotions and wishes and desires that someone so placed might have.
>
> (Flores-Crespo, 2004, p. 11)

To facilitate citizens in achieving this narrative imagination, Unterhalter (2003, p. 4) has suggested that governments should 'establish and sustain the conditions for each and every individual, irrespective of gender, ethnicity, race or regional location, to achieve valued outcomes'. Sen also believes that, in seeking human freedom, government should promote cultural 'liberty' rather than 'captivity' (Sen, 2005). Within this aim, education must play a necessary role aspiring to a life of the highest possible *public good*. In thinking of eudaimonia, MacIntyre (as cited in Knight, 1998, pp. 240–243) wrote that each individual in considering the use of goods and practices in their own lives will inevitably realize that they cannot address questions on human flourishing alone. He argues,

> [o]ur primary shared and common good is found in the activity of *communal learning* through which we together become able to order goods, both in our individual lives and in the political society. Such practice learning is a kind of learning that takes place in and through activity, and in and through reflection upon that activity, in the course of both communal and individual deliberation.
>
> [Italics added]

In creating the 'good society', government must establish more opportunities for such *communal learning* and *community imagining* taking place. In so doing, they eschew the ridiculous notion that education is limited to the preparation of workers for the capitalist economy. Such beliefs prove ludicrous, for, as Wilson Strydom (2016, p. 160) has pointed out, '[e]ducation plays a central role in human development, both as a capability in and of itself, and as an enabler or multiplier in the realisation of other capabilities'. Solava Ibrahim (2006, p. 413) has written of the importance of considering the role of the CA in improving the lives of women beyond NI. In particular, she remarks on its contribution to 'the process of self-help [as] a means for poor communities to widen their collective freedoms and to use their collective agency to achieve sustainable improvements in their individual and communal wellbeings'. Her Egyptian research has much to say to women in NI today, amidst a depleted and oft-threatened peace process.

In conclusion, West (2001, p. 1903) has argued that it is no less than the responsibility of liberal states, as a minimum obligation, to 'secure the minimal material preconditions of the basic human capabilities to be a basic constitutional duty'. Furthermore, she suggests that '[a]ll states, particularly liberal states, ought to regard their obligation to secure the preconditions of basic human capabilities as fundamental and … required by justice'. For a good society, West reminds us, is both liberal and just, 'one in which the state is not just permitted, but … obligated to ensure, on behalf of its [all its] citizens, that the … material preconditions of our fundamental human capabilities are met.'

Our theory, the CA, has shown us that 'the deeper meaning of gender equality is not adequately stipulated … through an exclusive focus on simple quantifiable indicators, while neglecting … the qualitative, every day, lived experiences of people' (Walker & Loots, 2016, p. 261). We have seen that the CI measure leant towards qualitative evaluation by taking account of the way women's lives were lived and could be improved. Yet recent work in South Africa indicates that other considerations should play a part in future developments. In conceptualizing gender equality for the future, and as expanded opportunities, Walker and Loots outline *two new* ways of seeing: first, an *evaluative* application of the CA (considering which capabilities are expanded, for whom and to what extent) and, second, a *prospective analysis* (considering which actions are likely to generate a greater stream of expanded capabilities) (Walker & Loots, 2016, p. 263). Such matters need to be considered as NI moves forward and as any possible future administration sets new priorities. More detailed arguments regarding the contribution that the CA might make in NI have been outlined in detail elsewhere (Doran & Hodgett, 2018).

NI is currently overwhelmed by multiple serious political crises while bereft of a functioning government or a clear path to the future. The EU is undergoing its own immediate challenge with the loss of its third biggest budget contributor as the UK moves towards Brexit. At the same time, in the new millennium, academics have criticized the earlier view that EU social policy has matured and solidified as the union has enlarged. Recently, Lendvai & Stubbs (2015, p. 447) have suggested that EU social policy in the twenty-first century might be better conceived as mere window dressing or a convenient fiction. Such observations proffer multiple questions about the odds of maintaining earlier generous, liberal social policies into the new millennium and, so, supporting the position of women in Europe, particularly its liminal fringes.

At this moment in history, using the CA to focus on women and their individual and collective capabilities, in this place, shines light on improvements that must be nurtured, fought for and maintained. This takes place against a background of looming storm clouds in the regional economy and difficult political imperatives. Researchers in NI (Bloomer et al., 2016) have already noted the crucial importance of community education initiatives in freeing and securing women's choices on social policy. This, allied to Macintyre's observation that effective politics must necessarily include local reflection upon political structures, social and cultural traditions to assess human norms and *human good* (as cited in Knight, 1998, p. 246) indicate that deliberate planning will be needed to secure the freedom and autonomy of women in NI into the second decade of the millennium.

In the end, expanding women's capabilities through social and public policy and community education demonstrates the absolute imperative of aspiring to, and achieving, eudaimonia for *all* citizens, thereby helping to attain greater societal well-being and improved quality of life. Such actions display an important signifier of 'progress in achievement [and] ... progress in our conception and recognition of what the highest perfection is' (MacIntyre, as cited in Knight, 1998, p. 110).

Acknowledgements

The author would like to thank Prof. Basim Massallam (Cambridge University) and Prof. Fred Inglis (University of Warwick) for their helpful comments on an earlier version of this work.

Notes

1 The NI Assembly (2017) quotes female representation as MPs 11%, Local Council 25%, Chair of Public Bodies 22%, Permanent Secretaries (Senior Civil Service) 0%, Senior Judges 0%, Boards of NI top 100 companies 15%. Available from: www.assemblyresearchmatters.org/2017/03/08/representation-women-public-life-northern-ireland-stand-now/.
2 This phrase was used about the level of violence (in general) in NI by the British Home Secretary in 1971. Available from: http://cain.ulst.ac.uk/othelem/glossary.htm.
3 Domestic violence has only been recorded by the police since 2004, and the pattern is upward. Available from: www.womensaidni.org/assets/uploads/2012/01/domestic-violence/domestic-violence-statistics/domestic_abuse_incidents_and_crimes_in_northern_ireland_2004-05_to_2014-15.pdf. [30 July 2017].
4 For information on grammar schools, see www.bbc.co.uk/news/education-34538222.
5 History and definition of Peace Walls. Available from: https://northernireland.foundation/sharedfuture/research/peace-walls/. [30 July 2017].
6 See http://news.bbc.co.uk/1/hi/education/6184145.stm.
7 Notions of Human Flourishing broaden concentration on economy, income and wealth to include factors like illiteracy, ill health and poor education. In relation to NI at the time the 1996 Adult Literacy Survey (Department for the Economy, 2000) indicated that 24% of the adult population performed badly, 21% of children left secondary education without qualifications (Hansard, 2004) and 24% of young people (18–25) had poor literacy or numeracy skills. To 2014, NI continued to be rated 19th of 24 countries on OECD numeracy and literacy league tables. Yet educational underperformance was not the only problem. Health and well-being in NI proved problematic with the Health and Social Wellbeing Survey (NISRA, 2001) finding 38% of men and women with long-standing illness or disability. By 2014/15, conditions remained much the same, with two-fifths of adults in NI reporting long-standing illness (DHSSPS, 2015, p. 7). The province continues to

have 'the world's highest recorded rates of Post-Traumatic Stress Disorder' with 40% of the population effected by conflict-related trauma experiences (Doran & Hodgett, 2018) and higher rates of suicide than Great Britain. Between 1984 and 1993, NI suicide rates for males were estimated at 15.5% (Largey et al., 2009); by 2005, this had risen to 18.5 compared to 9.4 in England (standardized rates per 100,000 population) (ONS, 2014). At the same time NI unemployment rates varied between 9% and 14% against the UK average of some 9% (Denman & McDonald, 1996, p. 6).

8 European Social Model to 'create a more equal society: ending poverty and poverty wages, guaranteeing fundamental human rights, essential services and an income that enables every individual to live in dignity' through creating social rights, social protection, social dialogue, social and employment regulation and state responsibility for full employment. Available from: www.etuc.org/european-social-model. [2 August 2017].

9 Available from: www.irishnews.com/opinion/letterstotheeditor/2016/09/12/news/eu-made-a-hugely-important-contribution-to-peace-process-688692/.

10 Northern Ireland Women's Coalition (NIWC), a political party established in NI in 1996 to secure the representation of women in peace negotiations. As advocates for peace and human rights, the NIWC was successful in engaging women in politics and campaigning against sectarian violence, but following electoral losses in 2003, the NICW formally disbanded in 2006. Available from: www.britannica.com/topic/Northern-Ireland-Womens-Coalition. [28 August 2017].

References

Alkire, S. (2005) Why the capability approach? *Journal of Human Development.* 6 (1), 115–135.

Belfast Telegraph. (2010) *Separate schools 'benign apartheid'.* Available from: www.belfasttelegraph.co.uk/news/northern-ireland/separate-schools-benign-apartheid-28565119.html [Accessed 28 July, 2017].

Bloomer, F. & Fegan, E. (2014) Critiquing recent abortion law and policy in Northern Ireland. *Critical Social Policy.* 34 (1), 109–120.

Bloomer, F., O'Dowd, K. & Macleod, C. (2016) Breaking the silence on abortion: the role of adult community abortion education in fostering resistance to norms. *Culture, Health & Sexuality.* 17 (7), 1–14.

Clark, D. A. & Hodgett, S. (2018) The integrated capabilities framework: exploring multiculturalism and wellbeing in participatory settings. In: Clark, D. A., Biggeri, M. & Frediani, A. (eds.). *Sen's capability approach, empowerment and participation: frameworks, methods and application.* London: Palgrave Macmillan.

Connelly, P., Smith, A. & Kelly, B. (2002) *Too young to notice? The cultural and political awareness of 3–6 years olds in Northern Ireland.* Belfast: Community Relations Council.

Dean, H. (2003) Discursive repertories and the negotiation of wellbeing: reflections in the WED framework. *Working Paper 04*, ESRC Research Group on Wellbeing in Developing Countries.

Denman, J. & McDonald, P. (1996) *Unemployment statistics from 1881 to the present day.* Central Statistical Office. Available from: file:///C:/Users/Susan's%20PC/Downloads/unemploymentbackto1881_tcm77-267536.pdf [Accessed 8 August 2017].

Department for the Economy. (2000) *Adult literacy in Northern Ireland—Full report 1996*. Available from: www.economy-ni.gov.uk/publications/adult-literacy-northern-ireland-full-report-1996 [Accessed 28 May 2018].
Department of Health and Social Services. (1996) *Monitoring and evaluation of community development in Northern Ireland, Belfast*. Belfast, NI: Department of Health and Social Services.
Department of Health and Social Services. (1999) *The story of community infrastructure in Northern Ireland: developing indicators for monitoring and evaluation of the community infrastructure measure*. Belfast, NI: Department of Health and Social Services.
Department of Finance and Personnel. (2003) *Northern Ireland statistics* [Accessed 8 December 2003].
Department of Health, Social Services and Public Safety NI. (2015) *Health survey Northern Ireland first results 2014/15*. Available from: www.health-ni.gov.uk/sites/default/files/publications/dhssps/hsni-first-results-14-15.pdf [Accessed 8 August 2017].
Department of Social Development. (2001) *Partners for change: government's strategy for support of the voluntary and community sector 2001–4*. Belfast, NI: Department of Social Development.
Doran, P. & Hodgett, S. (2018) Wellbeing and post conflict in Northern Ireland. In: Bache, I. & Scott, K. (eds.). *The politics of wellbeing*. London: Palgrave Macmillan.
Falkner, G. (1998) *EU social policy in the 1990s: towards a corporatist policy community*. Abingdon: Routledge.
Flores-Crespo, P. (2004) *Situating education in the human capabilities approach*. Paper presented at the Fourth International Conference on the Capability Approach: Enhancing Human Security, University of Pavia, Italy.
Hattersley, R. (2004) Education and the good society. In: Inglis, F. (ed.). *Education and the good society* (pp. 1–11). Basingstoke, UK: Palgrave Macmillan.
Galligan, Y. (2014) Women in politics. *Knowledge exchange seminar series, Northern Ireland Assembly*. Available from: www.niassembly.gov.uk/globalassets/Documents/RaISe/knowledge_exchange/briefing_papers/series3/galligan200314.pdf [Accessed 26 July 2017].
Gravatt, J. (2015) Unmanaged decline. *Adults Learning*. 26 (2), 15–17. National Institute for Adult and Continuing Education, Leicester. Available from: www.learningandwork.org.uk/wp-content/uploads/2017/01/Adults-Learning-April-2015.pdf [Accessed 1 July 2017].
Halsey, A. H., Lauder, H., Brown, P. & Wells, A. S. (eds.). (1997) *Education: culture, economy, society*. Oxford: Oxford University Press.
Hansard. (2004) *House of commons, Wed. 30 June 2004, column 266*. Available from: https://publications.parliament.uk/pa/cm200304/cmhansrd/vo040630/debtext/40630-01.htm#40630-01_spmin0 [Accessed 28 August 2017].
Hodgett, S. (1998) *Community infrastructure: the Northern Ireland voluntary sector and European regional policy*. Belfast: Northern Ireland Council for Voluntary Action.
Hodgett, S. (2008) Sen, culture and expanding participatory capabilities in Northern Ireland. *Journal of Human Development*. 9 (2), 165–183.
Her Majesty's Stationery Office. (1993) *Northern Ireland Structural Funds Plan*. Belfast.

Internet Encyclopedia of Philosophy. (n.d.) Available from: www.iep.utm.edu/sen-cap/ [Accessed 25 July 2017].

Ibrahim, S. (2006) From individual to collective capabilities: the capability approach as a conceptual framework for self-help. *Journal of Human Development*. 7 (3), 397–416.

Ibrahim, S. & Tiwari, M. (2014) *The capability approach: from theory to practice*. Basingstoke: Palgrave Macmillan.

Knight, K. (1998) *The MacIntyre reader*. Cambridge: Polity Press.

Largey, M., Kelly, C. & Stevenson, M. (2009) A Study of suicide rates in Northern Ireland 1984–2002. *Ulster Medical Journal*. 78 (1), 16–20. Available from: http://pure.qub.ac.uk/ws/files/547603/A%20study%20of%20suicide%20rates%20in%20northern%20ireland%201984-2002%20-%20Ulster%20Med%20%20J%202009%20-%20Stevenson%20MR.pdf [Accessed 6 August, 2017].

Lendvai, N. & Stubbs, P. (2015) Europeanization, welfare and variegated austerity capitalisms—Hungary and Croatia. *Social Policy and Administration*. 49 (4), 445–465.

McAloney, K. (2014) 'Mixed' religion relationships and wellbeing in Northern Ireland. *Journal of Religion and Health*. 53 (4), 1036–1045.

McManus, C. (2017) Dealing with the legacy of ethnic conflict: confronting 'othering' through transformative adult education. *Ethnopolitics*. 16 (4), 411–429.

McWilliams, M. (1997) Violence against women and political conflict: the Northern Ireland experience. *Critical Criminology*. 8 (1), 78–92.

Morris, A. (2016) Over 90% of social housing in NI still segregated. *Irish News*. 20 February 2016. Available from: www.irishnews.com/news/2016/02/20/news/over-90-of-social-housing-in-ni-still-segregated-423726/ [Accessed 6 August, 2017].

Northern Ireland Statistics and Research Agency (NIRSA). (2001) Available from: www.nisra.gov.uk/whatsnew/wellbeing/general_health/health%20and%20ill-health.pdf [Accessed 14 December 2005].

Nussbaum, M. (2000) *Women and human development. The capabilities approach*. Cambridge: Cambridge University Press.

Nussbaum, M. (2004) On hearing women's voices: a reply to Susan Okin. *Philosophy and Public Affairs*. 32 (2), 193–205.

Organization for National Statistics (ONS). (2014) *Suicides in the UK: 2014 registrations*. Available from: www.ons.gov.uk/peoplepopulationandcommunity/birthsdeathsandmarriages/deaths/bulletins/suicidesintheunitedkingdom/2014registrations#uk-suicides [Accessed 27 January 2017].

Parliament UK. (n.d.) *Research briefings: women in parliament and government*. Available from: http://researchbriefings.parliament.uk/ResearchBriefing/Summary/SN01250 [Accessed 26 July 2017].

Perry, C. (2016) *Education system in Northern Ireland*. Research and Information Service Briefing Paper, Northern Ireland Assembly. Available from: www.niassembly.gov.uk/globalassets/documents/raise/publications/2016-2021/2016/education/4416.pdf.

Rodl, S. (2016) Education and autonomy. *Journal of Philosophy of Education*. 50 (1), 84–97.

Sen, A. (1999) *Development as freedom*. Oxford: Oxford University Press.

Sen, A. (2005) *Culture and captivity*. Fifth Annual Conference of the Human Development and Capability Association, UNESCO, Paris [Accessed 11 September 2005].

Smethers, S. (2016) *What Brexit means ... for women's rights*. Available from: www.politics.co.uk/comment-analysis/2016/07/12/what-brexit-means-for-women-s-rights [Accessed 26 July 1917].

Stanistreet, P. (2014) *The crisis in adult education*. Robert Owen Centre for Educational Change, University of Glasgow. Available from: http://robertowencentre.academicblogs.co.uk/the-crisis-in-adult-education/ [Accessed 15 August 2017].

Stewart, J. (2014) *European funding streams: education*. Northern Ireland Assembly, Research and Information Briefing Note. Available from: www.niassembly.gov.uk/globalassets/documents/raise/publications/2014/education/2214.pdf [Accessed 1 July 2017].

Strajn, D. (2016) Book review: Paulo Freire: the global legacy. *International Review of Education*. 62, 389–391.

Stromquist, N. (2014) Freire, literacy and emancipatory gender learning. *International Review of Education*. 60 (4), 545–558.

Taylor, C. (2001) Modernity and identity. In: Scott, J. & Keates, D. *Schools of thought: 25 years of interpretive social science*. Princeton, NJ: Princeton University Press.

United Nations Development Program. (1990) *Human development report*. New York: Oxford University Press.

United Nations Development Program. (2005) *Human development reports*. Available from: http:/hdr.undp.org/hd/ [Accessed 15 December].

United Nations Human Development. (1990) *United Nations human development report 1990*. Available from: http://hdr.undp.org/sites/default/files/reports/219/hdr_1990_en_complete_nostats.pdf.

Unterhalter, E. (2003) *Education, capabilities and social justice*. Paper commissioned for the EFA Global Monitoring Report 2003/4, The Leap to Equality. pp. 1–11.

Walker, M. (2003) Framing social justice in education: what does the capabilities approach offer? *British Journal of Educational Studies*. 51 (2), 168–187.

Walker, M. (2006) Towards a capability based theory of social justice in education. *Journal of Education Policy*. 21 (2), 163–185.

Walker, M. & Loots, S. (2016) A capabilities-based gender equality policy for higher education: conceptual and methodological considerations. *Journal of Human Development and Capabilities*. 7 (2), 260–277.

Ward, M. (2013) *Excluded and silenced: women in Northern Ireland after the peace process*. Available from: www.opendemocracy.net/5050/margaret-ward/excluded-and-silenced-women-in-northern-ireland-after-peace-process [Accessed 26 July 2017].

Wilson Strydom, M. (2016) A capabilities list for equitable transitions to university: a top-down and bottom-up approach. *Journal of Human Development and Capabilities*. 17 (2), 145–160.

West, R. (2001) Rights, capabilities and the good society. *Fordham Law Review*. 69 (5), 1901–1932. Georgetown University Law Center.

5 Considering Gender and Economic Development Policy

Gender Relations, Engagement and Institutional Practice

A. Marguerite Cassin

Introduction

Industrial decline in rural communities nationally and internationally is widespread and well researched (Renkow, 2003; Ryser & Halseth, 2010; Schaeffer & Loveridge, 2000). While attention has focussed on loss of industrial jobs that are primarily done by men and the consequences, a more recent study has paid attention to changes in women's circumstances and the family (Latimer & Oberhauser, 2004; McDonald et al., 2012; Sherman, 2009).

The pattern of decline, typically triggered by the loss of industrial enterprises on which rural communities depended, means that well-paid jobs disappear; population declines; infrastructure maintenance and replacement is compromised and community facilities and resources are threatened by drastic reduction in municipal tax revenues; demand for social services, income supports and policing increases; political power shifts; and government services are closed and centralized. A way of life, often described as traditional or conservative in terms of family formation and gender roles, is changed as it was, 'in a heartbeat'.

What is striking about research, official explanation from businesses and government, and public media descriptions about these transformations is that the lack of determination of or seeming interest in agency, that is, how things come to 'happen'. These industrial shifts are attributed to and explained by changes outside the local place (Government of Canada, 2018; Government of New Brunswick, 2012, 2016). Changes in market, technology, transportation, investment, production costs and more that are objective are determined elsewhere and explain local action. Change, it is asserted, is the one constant, and generally signifies human progress.

And yet, of course, there is agency. It is a matter of learning how to discover and explore how things happen. Public and business economic development policy and practice are important sites of social action to consider when we start to ask about agency. In this chapter I am interested in public economic development policy and how to explore gender relations and economic development.

This chapter is about methods of thinking and investigation into public economic development policy and practice for how it shapes and affects gender relations. It considers how public policy on economic development is objective (objectified) and profoundly gendered at the same time. It illustrates this primarily from a field study I conducted in 2013 as part of research conducted with colleague Tamara Krawchenko on rural demography and development[1] in the midst of rural industrial decline in northern New Brunswick.

The empirical findings are generally in keeping with the literature: the decline of industrial jobs disrupts established patterns of family formation; men seek 'manly work' in national and international projects; initiatives to increase women's access to industrial jobs are unsuccessful; more women are encouraged to seek post-secondary education; community attachment and affiliation decreases; job loss and population decline includes men and women in administrative, professional and managerial jobs as well as men in industrial occupations; economic priority shifts to replacement industries with an immediate focus on tourism; capacity in the institution of the public service in the region is reduced and limited at a time when services are needed; men's and women's civil participation and engagement shifts; municipal governing is severely stressed; and political power is shifted away from the region. There is an overall decline in community confidence and capacity, and challenges to fostering equality-oriented gender relations. Exploring gender relations highlights the ways in which the absence of gender content in economic policy alignment has a deleterious effect on gender equality seeking.

As a way of seeing, institutional ethnography points to an ongoing research agenda in which institutional relations (in business, government, the not-for-profit sector and civil society) are explicitly examined for how they are empirically part of putting together sequences of social action that are fed into everyday life and that shape experience. The question generally raised is can economic development policy and programmes be initiated and supported in such a way that we 'can do better' at equality, inclusion and distributed prosperity?

In the case of economic development policy and gender relations, the findings raise questions about the current focus and structuring of regional economic development policy for themes of productivity and individual business development at least in northern New Brunswick and speculatively more generally in Atlantic Canada. The focus policy and strategy formed on the basis of neo-liberal economic thinking has been the subject of extensive discussion generally (Cassin & Krawchenko, 2013) and, in the context of this paper, specific ideas have been explored by Foster (2016), Krawchenko (2014) and Cassin and Krawchenko (2013).

In rural Atlantic Canadian cultures, there is considerable collectivism in communities and gender relations. This is often expressed in an orientation to social enterprise, which generally combines both business and social goals. While Atlantic Canada economic development agencies have a mandate in local economic development, it is underdeveloped. This chapter suggests that a useful application of social and economic policy analysis is one that is informed by institutional ethnography and focusses on opening agency in local economies. In this respect the first question might be 'can (and if so how can) a vibrant (local) economy be built on social enterprise?'

Public Policy Analysis and Institutional Ethnography

There is active, sustained and engaged interest in researching public policy in most of the professional and social science disciplines. My late colleague Peter Aucoin cheerfully and routinely pointed out that policy is, after all, applied social science (Aucoin et al., 2004; Doern & Aucoin, 1971). Policy oriented research is publicly supported and fostered by national research-granting councils internationally, and academic journals are full of publications critiquing public policy. The approach to policy critique generally used in the social sciences and professional disciplines is to single out a policy statement (formulation); identify some domain of implementation; and report upon results or outcomes through research, secondary measurement, programme evaluation or related tools. While these approaches may offer important insights and indications of policy impact, they say nothing about policy regimes, if and how they work and how they might work better. In fact they leave the domain of policy implementation a 'black box'.

In practice, public policy formulation is the statement of intention (Pross, 1980) and is underpinned or conceptualized in a process that combines politics, opinion from across many settings, including 'stakeholders', evidence from academic disciplines, public servant policy specialists and a notion of public good. It is historically situated, and in our world has extensive sources of influence. Once written and adopted, it is an authorized foundation for action. But policy has no reality until it is organized and made administrable through some actionable form that is generally referred to as a programme and allocated resources. The design and implementation of programmes to implement policy can take many forms (administrative, services, grants and contributions, legal, funding for arms-length organizations, regulatory and compliance directed). In implementation, policies become the domain of the institution of the public service and the legal system and judiciary. In these contexts, policy is institutionalized and organized through principles of administrative process, norms of work organization, due process and equality, management and regimes of accountability. It becomes assigned work for public servants or employees' organizations implementing policy. These people are governed in their work variously by public service and professional codes of conduct as well as employee relations.

Policy is primarily conducted in institutional contexts. Policy is implemented through institutional practices and forms institutionalized relationships. Dorothy Smith (1987), making use of work from Marx and Engels as well as phenomenology, has argued that these institutional practices are stabilized in text (and now electronically) and form extended sequences of social action that connect people to one another and organize their institutional participation and compliance over time and space irrespective of their explicit knowledge, understanding or engagement. Smith problematizes this lack of apparent connection between how we 'rule' and how we experience our world as the 'everyday world as problematic' (Smith, 1987, pp. 19–24). It is a matter for empirical investigation. She identifies these institutional practices as forming modern social relations (Smith, 1987) and central to understanding ruling in contemporary liberal democracies.

In her work she devises and recommends a method of research that is directed to tracking and explicating social relations related to topics of interest. That is, she recommends empirically investigating and specifying the sequences of social action that together form a social phenomenon of interest. This includes or in fact focusses upon opening the 'black box' that is largely taken for granted in popular academic policy-oriented research.

Smith calls her research method institutional ethnography. Institutional ethnography is an exploration of social relations: extended sequences of social action across live action as well as document-based institutional practices. It calls attention to the significance of institutionalized practices, including routine forms and sequences of administrative action in shaping and creating our experience of everyday life and our lack of knowledge of how it comes about. Institutional ethnography seeks to empirically specify and connect everyday life and our experience to institutional relations. The point is when we know how it works, we are in a better position to do better.

Economic Engine and Integrated Economic Development: Industrial Northern New Brunswick

For decades, northern New Brunswick was characterized at the economic engine of New Brunswick. The robust industrial economy meant well paid, often unionized jobs with benefits and pensions in the mills and forest-harvesting and skilled jobs in the small- and medium-sized woodworking and chemical businesses that developed around the main production businesses (Government of New Brunswick, 2012; University of New Brunswick, 2005).

The industrial jobs were largely 'men's work'. The businesses were able to draw their bilingual labour force from generations of men with skills learned from fathers and uncles and in communities from neighbours. These businesses also had supervisory, administrative, management and professional jobs for a predominantly male workforce, and some jobs for women, often in human resources/personnel. The administrative work provided women 'traditional women's work' in clerical and administrative support jobs. This business cluster also provided the basis for legal and accounting firms and businesses supplying business materials and services.

These businesses and their work forces grew and supported a number of local towns and two municipalities on this breathtakingly beautiful land on the Restigouche River and surrounds. This created a business climate for service industry, vehicle, construction, consumer and related businesses. As a result of the property tax base and voluntary contributions from businesses and the communities, the municipal governments in the towns and municipalities were able to provide excellent municipal services and highly used public recreation programmes and facilities (including competition-level pool, ice and field-based athletic facilities) that facilitated an engaged sports climate. The strength of the economy and character of jobs also supported the development of golf clubs, specialized exercise facilities and arts programmes, including art galleries and art education (University of New Brunswick, 2005).

The contribution of taxes to the higher levels of government was seen by residents as giving the region both political power and government services. Informants in the field study noted that at least one Member of the Legislative Assembly (MLA) from the region was Minister of Finance, and often they had two ministers in the cabinet (Cassin & Krawchenko, 2013). Bilingualism, supported by provincial and federal governments, brought projects, services and benefits to these communities. The region had excellent provincial and federal government services, including schools, social services, health facilities and infrastructure, including essential business, relevant water, rail and road transportation and a post-secondary education in the form of a community college (which provided training and education related to industry attracting men and education for ancillary health care occupations and administration attracting women) (New Brunswick Community College, 2015).

Economic Development Policy and Operating Agencies

Government-funded economic development agencies offering various financial supports, know-how and advice to businesses, and leading public projects in support of development and embedded in economic development policy are now ubiquitous in public services across liberal democracies. The Atlantic Canada Opportunities Agency (ACOA) is the Government of Canada regional development authority for Atlantic Canada (ACOA, 2018). The growth and integrated and coherent character of the economy of northern New Brunswick as an economic engine was in part attributable to the success of rural economic development policy and programme design and implementation by ACOA.

Local economic development support began with a federally funded Industrial Commission in 1967–1969, and various programmes of support have continued.[2] Enterprise Restigouche (ER), a local development agency for Restigouche County, has been the most stable and consistent organization anchoring economic development support. While it began ACOA's mandate for community and economic development, there were changes in funding, policy priorities and organization over time so that they became a partner of the federal government (ACOA provided 60 per cent core funding), with the New Brunswick Government (Economic Development, 31 per cent), local government and some member organizations making up the rest of the funding. The ER had a Board of Directors comprised of people from the community as well as the funding partners. The agency staff worked with business as well as sectors overall. Overall the business development officers from the Agency saw their focus as helping businesses grow, and their work was making sure that businesses had viable, well-researched business plans in place that identified what businesses needed. The other dimension of their work was to identify sources of money and support and to understand the requirements of those sources. This meant that they could anticipate needs; coordinate opportunities; and work with businesses, communities, municipal officials and staff, other development officers in other agencies and departments, programme managers (e.g., Agriculture) and departments not represented in the community (e.g., Industry Canada) from senior levels of government. The long-term nature of the Agency meant that staff built up expertise in business, business sectors and the community. Over time they also built knowledge and connections to researchers, consultants and scientists who had expertise in relation to various dimensions of community and economic development. The agency built up a team of experts who were sector specialists in Restigouche County and northern New Brunswick. These sector specialists knew all businesses in the area as well as the state of technology and emerging science. With the business development officers, the specialists advised and networked businesses, anticipated changes and made expansion, replacement and sustainability work. As an Agency they were in a position to advise businesses, groups and government based on experience, networks and knowledge of place. They could mobilize resources and transfer knowledge. There was huge institutional capacity in the agency because of the continuity, relationships, knowledge, experience and understanding of place and the overall connections to government and industries. The Agency staff took the position that they worked for their client in a professional, independent and non-partisan way. ER was a local, horizontal intergovernmental agency that facilitated and organized relationships in business and development.

Conservative/Traditional Communities, Including Gender Relations

The overall consequence of the configuration of business, government, politics, civil society and history formed these communities into culture of what is characterized as conservative or traditional rural industrial communities (McDonald et al., 2012). Family formation and labour force participation normative to gender segregation in work (both paid and domestic) and community participation and overall post-secondary education were confined to the local community college with a smaller number of people going to university. Extended family-supported families with young children and ageing parents and relatives saw themselves as relying on one another, based on the interviews in the field study. While of course there were individual men and women who defied gender norms and entered nontraditional occupations, moved away or opted to enter into altered domestic arrangements, the culture of family affiliation as the centre of community and connection to place and way of life was persistent and valued. From the point of view of institutional relations, it is important to see that these gender relations and community affiliation were a consequence of personal choice and preference and shaped by the institutionalized social, educational and economic policy design and implementation and business practice at the same time. Policy analysis and research as well as change then also involve all of these elements, and it is important to take this into consideration as we explore development.

Economic Decline: Mayor's Message

This description of the region was reliable until the beginning of the decline of the industrial economy post 2005 and changed with the collapse of all the major industrial employers by 2010. I conducted our field study and institutional ethnography in the winter of 2013. Coincidentally, I started the field research the day ER closed.

When preparing to conduct the fieldwork in Northern New Brunswick, we wrote city mayors to arrange interviews. One mayor sent a written email reply in which he summarized the circumstances of the city, the strategy and the problems. The email is reproduced without attribution in Appendix 1. His account is used here as a guide to a brief overview and policy analysis of decline.

Economic Policy and Implementation in Crisis

The mayor, in his email (Appendix 1), seeks a clear strategy in trying to protect the assets of his and other communities so that the region is viable for investment. He is perfectly expressing aspirations for industry replacement and the preservation of the network of small- and medium-sized manufacturing businesses that formed the secondary level of the economy.

At the time of the field study, the clear strength for future capacity building and economic development was the locally situated public servants working in economic development at all levels of government who knew the communities, counties and region well and were committed to the place. They were an impressive group of men and women who had families in these communities and contributed to the communities beyond their jobs. In the economic development field they were very experienced at working with local community organizations and agencies, had extensive corporate experience and had built up relationships and could successfully call upon cooperation from different offices across government. They know the programmes and services and worked well with their counterparts in central administration as well as in other field offices. They were very experienced working with politicians, working through changes in programmes and assessing the needs of businesses. Their work and experience meant that they saw both the local circumstances and the larger regional, provincial, national and international contexts. Principally, they were experts in building, advancing and maintaining relationships, which in the crisis context was critical for the region. Their views, skills and knowledge are particularly important in view of the scale and rate of change in the region. Their work and coherence were central to finding economic resilience and a replacement path to redevelop the economy.

In some fundamental ways, economic development is always local, concrete and engaged with businesses and communities whether this is local or global. ACOA and ER were horizontal agencies whose main operating objective is to connect businesses and communities to one another and to governments and resources. At the time of the field study there was a huge stream of development proposals. The approach of field staff to proposals was not to reject or screen proposals but to bring people in business, government and community together. They were trying to attract investment money, bring business scrutiny to proposals and leverage public funds through partnerships. That is, they were searching for what would work. ACOA (or any economic development agency) cannot create communities or entrepreneurs; the field officers need to get out and learn about the community and the mechanisms for how it works, know the larger picture and look for opportunities for the community and provide support as possible.

At the same time that field officers worked on these approaches, other public policy kicked in. Reorganization, budget restraint and efficiency approaches (generally referred to as New Public Administration) were mobilized to rationalize the economic development resources in northern New Brunswick. ER was closed and a new regional structure was announced by the province that separated established patterns of connection and cooperation and established new field offices. The Community Business Development Corporation (CBDC) and ACOA, the longest standing economic and community development agencies, were detached from provincial initials (such as NB for New Brunswick). New policy tools were set in place and regional planning commissions formed to foster municipal cooperation. While many of the economic development staff went to the reforming agencies, the coherence and coordinating approach to development was undermined at best and lost at worst.

In these changes, economic policy shifted from seeking new development to tourism, local development and municipal reform as the economic development focus.

How can we explain and account for such action? Economic policy is informed and ordered by key concepts, largely coming from economics. One example is productivity, a concept that was adopted some time ago to measure, compare and strategize economic activity (Foster, 2013, 2016). In economics, productivity as a construct and measure is open to debate, revision and change. However, once adopted within public policy, the construct as defined becomes stable and institutionalized, treated as fact and used to make decisions across contexts. It becomes what is known as a policy operational tool. So then, when productivity (and other key constructs), for example, is used to create and measure an economic forecast (Conference Board of Canada, 2018; Government of New Brunswick, 2018), the foregoing discussion about process and implementation is superseded as the forecasting is entered into budget assessment and rationalized in larger programme and policy priorities. This is a routine practice in policy and budget planning in the public sector.

The consequence is that any expectation of a coherent strategy for economic recovery was rendered impossible in the restructuring and the shift to less ambitious supports for economic development adopted. During the field study, field officers and former field officers generally offered a view that they needed to find locally based solutions because the support from older forms of policy had collapsed. Field officers were working to consider what opportunities might be networked around the 'ships contract' (construction of frigates for Canada (Conference Board of Canada, 2018) that was anticipated and did materialize). Given directions, it seems unlikely this will be developed successfully. The new orientation directed people in communities and public servants in economic development to find opportunities and do development themselves and to abandon any expectation of large-scale assistance from higher levels of government.

Research Findings

Chasing Manly Work, Finding Work, Population Reduction, Family Formation, Education, Politics

Population decline as a consequence of job loss was immediate. Men who could retire with pensions did so. Young and middle-aged men laid off from industrial jobs sought the same work nationally (Alberta and Newfoundland) and internationally. Patterns emerged quickly. Younger men working in other parts of Canada moved. Men with established families commuted. Women lost their administrative, managerial and professional jobs, followed their husbands, stayed home to work at what was available while their men 'worked away' or sought new employment beyond the region. Younger and unattached women were likely to seek post-secondary education[3] either by moving away to a university or enrolling in community college. The community college offerings continued to train in health care support work and, more recently, have added agricultural assistant work in anticipation of the aspirations the province has in the area of cannabis production (Opportunities New Brunswick, 2018). The economic dislocation brought family and social change immediately. Young women and men did (can) not form their relationships and families with the same affiliation to community and place. There are also gender related losses that are not immediately clear. With the economic collapse, the early and possible future engagement of women in the trades and industrial jobs in this geography is also ended.

Job losses are not confined to industrial jobs and administration. Managerial and professional job losses have meant that people with these backgrounds and job skills have also left the communities and also the region in search of work, taking families with them. Professionals (lawyers and accountants) have moved and consolidated practices as work has declined. Moreover, young people who are leaving the community to seek educations for these sorts of jobs no longer have expectations to return.

The political power of the region was seen to have declined precipitously by informants in the field study. Evidence was seen as unequivocal. The region no longer had a minister in cabinet, MLAs were ignored and decisions including budget reductions were made without consideration about the impact on the region. The long contribution of this region to the province was seen as not mattering in the current climate.

Community Confidence, Criminality and Social Challenges, Vitality, Leadership

The loss of workers from all occupations has wide-ranging community impacts on the cities and towns of the region. The people leaving or left are no longer available to volunteer in recreation, community events, on community and economic development boards and in other forms of civic engagement, including Chambers of Commerce, municipal government and tourism councils. While new people who remain in the community do step forward and are willing, they lack the experience and often the skills to serve, particularly in the governing boards for the agencies.

Existing community leaders see the remaining youth population as poorly educated and motivated. Residents and businesses see increasing crime, mostly vandalism and theft, fuelled in their opinion by inactivity, lack of attachment to the community, absence of goals and separation from rather than integration into the life of community and economy. This creates challenges for police and policing. The increase in this form of criminality is limiting the capacity to solve crimes and creating a decline in confidence in the police to protect the community. In addition, residents believe that this criminal activity is further fostered by the low risk of being caught. This aspect of social problems is publicly displayed in boarded up businesses (discussed earlier) and houses. Overall, this is seen by people as a display of loss of civic pride, decline in the capacity of the community and increased lack of attachment to place. There are other social challenges. High unemployment brings the advent of broader spread poverty, reliance on transfer payments and illiteracy that is thought to be new. Community initiatives, particularly from libraries (in the case of literacy) and related social initiatives were developing at the time of the field interviews. However, these are not the same as broad spread civic engagement in governing.

In the midst of population decline and economic development challenges, residents perceive that there were increasingly evident labour shortages. Jobs for teachers, librarians, social workers, counsellors, nurses and other health professionals do not get filled. It is hard to get people to come to the towns and cities in the region, and it was anticipated that this would worsen with limited budgets and decreasing vitality. It is expected to be increasingly hard to attract people (Conference Board of Canada, 2018). This is in part a consequence that the population is ageing. People leaving the community are young. This increases reliance on pension and transfer payments in the community and demand for healthcare, eldercare and social services (notably areas where women work) at a time when these services are being rationalized.

While there was significant government presence in the region, that presence had been declining. This was having a number of unanticipated and cumulative consequences. Administration changes were also contributing to decline. For example, the Law Courts were closed in some communities and moved to other places in the region. When the communities lose courts, they also lose lawyers; judges do not travel to the communities. This undermines coherence in both the legal system and communities and fosters competition rather than cooperation. The loss of the wider workforce of managers and professionals was seen as contributing to a decline in both volunteerism and the kind of work volunteers can do. Similarly, the people seeking political office have narrowed and changed with the composition of the population and their occupations. This raises serious issues related to community capacity and it is something that concerns all the economic development specialists.

The economic change means that there are more poor children and families in the community. There is a food bank that the students at the Community College support through fund raising. There is also a growing problem of lack of functional literacy across the population. One inspiring project is a literacy programme sponsored by the library. With funding from Human Resources and Skills Development Canada, outreach to children in low-income neighbourhoods in one community began in 2008. To date they have made 350 visits to homes to tutor children (with volunteer retired teachers) and attract them to the library. The programme was seen to be having an impact on the community and was seen by the police as encouraging family life, contributing to a decrease in family violence and invigorating the neighbourhoods.

These projects and the topics are about gender relations in the community, and we can see the differential engagement and the changes that are directly and indirectly a consequence of economic shifts.

Tourism, Municipal Government and Community Development Initiatives

Municipal government is crucially important to communities both in the present and planning for and creating the future. Northern New Brunswick is challenged on all three dimensions (economic development, tourism and maintaining government services). In addition, there are underlying issues of population decline, social cohesion and solidarity and infrastructure, including transportation. In some respects, the intensity of the need for good governance in municipal government and professional strength in the municipal public service is a shift from earlier times of a robust economy, better tax base and greater presence of senior levels of government bringing investment, field staff and support. In previous circumstances there was more institutional capacity, direct and indirect support from business and more diversity in the people who sought public office and participated in the array of organizations that compose civil society. While these were central dimensions of resilience, today there is limited and declining capacity.

During the field study, the electoral cycle, the experience, goals and vision of elected officials and their understanding of community and public life were widely recognized by professional economic development staff as a barrier to developing the long view and the sort of knowledge and capacity to work on long-term issues. This makes the advisory job of public servants very challenging because they cannot rely on elected officials to bring a background of experience working institutionally or confidence in a base of knowledge built up in previous administrations. The recently formed Regional Commission introduced a new form of local governance in which all the mayors in the region participate, and their mandate allows them to address pervasive, commonly held, long-term issues related to infrastructure, including solid waste, security and planning.

While regional and cooperative perspectives are important, and this is policy in economic development at senior levels of government, it is difficult not to feel losses and be competitive in local circumstances where adjustment is taking place. For example, as there is a declining population and services are reducing and regionalized, one city in particular was perceived as being favoured and becoming a regional centre. It is challenging for mayors and elected officials to focus on cooperation and regional, provincial and national viewpoints when their electors are suffering and want elected people to alleviate pressing issues in the community. This is happening at a time when there are more women participating in all aspects of municipal government (employees, volunteers and politicians), but they lack mentors and experience that generally is relied on to innovate.

A municipal council in one community had been working on a tourism plan over three successive councils. In spite of funded research and professional advice, it was challenging to get a coherent plan and commitment to a clear direction. The Appalachian Mountains, presence of the interprovincial bridge and city's proximity to more strongly developed tourism on the east coast of New Brunswick were seen as assets. There was support for tourism in the city and county in the provincial tourism promotion (Tourism New Brunswick, 2018). One of the biggest challenges reported was political volatility. Politicians get elected by criticizing incumbents, and this makes them predisposed to insist on their own or at least different approaches from those of their predecessors.

The other challenge is more material and is described as 'flow'. The communities lacked a major tourist attraction that would hold visitors. Work being done to develop the waterfront and build tourism infrastructure is being supported by the economic development agencies. There was an impressive event calendar, particularly of festivals. Many of the municipal governments had staff dedicated to coordinating tourism initiatives, including developing and building festivals and events and developing four-season tourism. In one community, the civic centre, which has conference and sports facilities, including two Olympic-sized ice surfaces and an Olympic-sized pool, are important assets to build events, meetings and conferences around. The festivals and sports events are activities that rely upon and have attracted a core of committed volunteers. However even these activities are beginning to suffer from lack of volunteers because, as people who have been active retire, they are away more and others are burned out. There is difficulty attracting new, younger volunteers and current staff and volunteers quipped good-naturedly that volunteers are hard to find but complainers are easy to find. In tourism work, relationships are critical, and tourism initiatives are supported by organizations like the sea cadets and reserves, the Downtown Tourism Associations, Chambers of Commerce and Lion's Clubs.

Tourism does not produce well-paid jobs with pensions. It is not in any way a replacement for an industrial economy. It does increase women's participation (Moscardo, 2008; Sinclair, 1997; Swain, 1995) and provides small business and service opportunities.

This is a challenging time to be a municipal politician in the cities and municipalities in the region. The Mayor in his email (Appendix 1) clearly laid out their issues: population decline generally and the character of population decline in particular, industry collapse and job losses, new economic development initiatives, preserving transportation links, provincial and federal reorganization, centralization and regionalization in the face of deficit reduction. He also identified the push/pull of changing priorities in senior governments. It is clear that there is a broad consensus from the field study that citizens cannot rely on the senior levels of government to have policy that shares the same interests as the communities in the region. In this respect the decline in political power is consequential for all communities in the region, as well as local government and locally based initiatives.

Social Enterprise and Local Development

The CBDCs are a provincial, regional and national network of not-for-profit development corporations that support small business and offer loans and access to microcredit. The CBDCs focus on rural areas and have 41 centres in Atlantic Canada. Their funding comes from a mix of departments. Most CBDCs are active in a variety of initiatives that foster small business and the workforce for small business. Campbellton, one of the cities in the CDBC region, is the largest in the country with 20 staff, and had a wide variety of initiatives and projects, which included education, literacy, essential skills and participation in a national research project. Development officers (formerly field staff at ER) and those at ACOA suggested during the research that proposals to CBDC (and also ACOA regional field offices) at the time of the research showed a strong interest in and orientation to social enterprises. Generally we refer to social enterprises as not-for-profit economic-oriented organizations that mix social and business goals; examples include but are not limited to coops (Mountain Equipment Coop, food cooperatives), special purpose employment projects like those directed to employing persons with special needs, agricultural farm to table service and more conventional businesses with social goals. These sorts of business models tend to have more equality orientations. If development shifts to a community base, it is likely that the ideas that come from communities will orient to social enterprises.

Economic Policy and Gendered Futures

Women overall are not as experienced and in the economic development occupations or in politics, but their participation was increasing at the time of the fieldwork. It is also clear that gender relations were changing within the community, economy, home and overall. The economic development emphasis on community and local tools offers some possible consideration of gender and economic recovery in the region. There is overall increasing interest in social enterprise. One example is the CBDC, a provincial, regional and national network that not only supports small business but are most active in other things that foster a workforce for small business. In the field study, the institutional analysis suggests that commitments to place and attachment are not respected (and currently largely cannot be respected) in economic policy responses. There is an overall decline in community confidence and capacity, and challenges to fostering equality-oriented gender relations. Exploring gender relations highlights the ways in which the absence of gender content in economic policy alignment has a deleterious effect on gender equality seeking.

At the same time of the successful initiatives in the midst of economic crisis, the collectivism in a culture might be a pathway to renewal. It is interesting to consider whether economic development agencies like ACOA, which do have community-based as well as business mandates, can be encouraged to ask and investigate questions like: Can vibrant economies be built on social enterprise? What would public policy and economic development look like if we were to foster these more inclusive practices? What would gender relations look like as those changes were pursued?

Acknowledgements

I am very grateful for the opportunity to do the original field work that is referenced and that gave Tamara Krawchenko and me a lot of opportunity to discuss ideas. I have been influenced by Tamara and Karen Foster in thinking about neo-liberal economic policy. For this chapter I am indebted to the School of Public Administration and Eryn Mackenzie, Forester MPA18, who has been Research Assistant for me this year as part of her Dalhousie Graduate Scholarship. I recognize her excellent recent literature searches, government document searches, comments on the literature, summaries of the current economic outlooks and discussions about her experience and 'single industry towns'. Her interest in this piece has been influential. Christopher Adam has been steadfast in helping with creating the final version of this chapter under considerable time pressure.

Notes

1 This research study was for Demography and Development that I did with research colleague Tamara Krawchenko. There were four case studies, one in each of the Atlantic Canada provinces. I conducted the studies in Nova Scotia and New Brunswick. Dr Krawchenko conducted the studies in Prince Edward Island and Newfoundland. The research was supported by a research grant from the Atlantic Canada Opportunities Agency and the Atlantic Provinces Research Initiative, Contribution Agreement APRI Project # 200761.

2 This account is drawn from my field study write-up (available from the author) and our report on this research *Agency at the local level: capturing community and economic development practices in rural Atlantic Canada*, Cassin & Krawchenko (2013), Dalhousie University. In this paper the community and the informants are not identified due to the topic focus and brevity of the discussion.

3 Dr Marilee Reimer's work in this volume offers another window into women going to university and then accessing administrative jobs they might have had before, but with their degrees have opportunities at longer career futures in administration and management.

References

Atlantic Canada Opportunities Agency (ACOA). (2018) *Departmental plan 2018–2019*. Ottawa: Author.

Aucoin, P., Smith, J. & Dinsdale, G. (2004) *Responsible government: clarifying essentials, dispelling myths and exploring change*. Ottawa: Canadian Centre for Management Development. Available from: http://publications.gc.ca/collections/Collection/SC94-107-2004E.pdf.

Cassin, M. & Krawchenko, T. (2013). *Agency at the local level: capturing community and economic development practices in rural Atlantic Canada*. Halifax, Nova Scotia: Atlantic Canada Opportunities Agency.

Conference Board of Canada. (2018) *Provincial outlook long term economic forecast: New Brunswick 2018*. Ottawa, ON.

Doern, G. B. & Aucoin, P. (1971) *The structures of policy-making in Canada*. Toronto: Macmillan of Canada.

Foster, K. (2013) Generation and discourse in working life stories. *British Journal of Sociology*. 64 (2), 195–215. doi:10.1111/1468–4446.12014.

Foster, K. R. (2016) *Productivity and prosperity: a historical sociology of productivist thought*. Toronto: University of Toronto Press.

Government of Canada. (2018) *New Brunswick labour market bulletin*. Ottawa: Ontario.

Government of New Brunswick. (2012) *New Brunswick regional profile: northeast economic region*. Fredericton: New Brunswick.

Government of New Brunswick. (2016) *New Brunswick's growth plan: why growth is imperative*. Fredericton: New Brunswick.

Government of New Brunswick. (2018) *2018–2019 economic outlook*. Department of Finance. Fredericton: New Brunswick.

Krawchenko, T. (2014). Bringing municipalities into rural community and economic development: cases from Atlantic Canada. *Journal of Rural and Community Development*. 9 (3), 78–96.

Latimer, M. & Oberhauser, A. M. (2004) Exploring gender and economic development in Appalachia. *Journal of Appalachian Studies*. 10 (3), 269–291.

McDonald, P., Mayes, R. & Pini, B. (2012) Mining work, family and community: a spatially-oriented approach to the impact of the Ravensthorpe Nickel Mine closure in remote Australia. *Journal of Industrial Relations*. 54 (1), 22–40. doi:10.1177/0022185611432382.

Moscardo, G. (2008) Community capacity building: an emerging challenge for tourism development. pp. 1–15 In: Moscardo, G. (ed.) *Building community capacity for tourism development*. Wallingford: CABI Publication.

New Brunswick Community College. (2015) *Five-year review report 2011–2016*. Bathurst: New Brunswick.

Opportunities New Brunswick. (2018) *Cannabis: building an industry*. Fredericton: New Brunswick.

Pross, A. P. (1980) *Duality and public policy: a conceptual framework for analyzing the policy system of Atlantic Canada*. Halifax, N.S. Institute of Public Affairs, Dalhousie University.

Renkow, M. (2003) Employment growth, worker mobility, and rural economic development. *American Journal of Agricultural Economics*. 85 (2), 503–513. doi:10.1111/1467–8276.00137.

Ryser, L. & Halseth, G. (2010) *Rural economic development: a review of the literature from industrialized economies*. Vol. 4. Oxford, UK. 510–531. doi:10.1111/j.1749–8198.2010.00321.x.

Schaeffer, P. V. & Loveridge, S. (2000) *Small town and rural economic development: a case studies approach*. Westport, CT: Praeger.

Sherman, J. (2009) Bend to avoid breaking: job loss, gender norms, and family stability in rural America. *Social Problems*. 56 (4), 599–620. doi:10.1525/sp.2009.56.4.599.

Sinclair, M. T. (1997) *Gender, work and tourism*. London: Routledge.

Smith, D. E. (1987) *The everyday world as problematic: a feminist sociology*. Boston, Toronto: Northeastern University Press.

Swain, M. B. (1995) Gender in tourism. *Annals of Tourism Research*. 22 (2), 247–266. doi:10.1016/0160–7383(94)00095-6.

Tourism New Brunswick. (2018) *Tourism growth strategy 2018–2025*. Fredericton: New Brunswick.

University of New Brunswick. (2005) *Ebb and flow: The rhythm of New Brunswick's economy*. Saint John: New Brunswick.

Appendix 1: One Mayor's Description of the Circumstances of his City, the Strategy and the Problems [Email]

Our role is to lead our Municipal Government here in NB, promote economic development and tourism and with government to maintain government services in our community.

In 2010 this area in Restigouche County (was) faced with many closure of Pulp mills, chemical plants, saw mills etc ... just in the forestry sector and the closure of a major textile plant result(ed) in the loss of 2000 direct jobs with a payroll loss of approx. $75,000,000

In regards to Economic Development the province (of) NB has made major changes with the reduction of our regional office in Restigouche while establishing the Regional Service Commissions which will appoint an ad hoc committee in promoting Economic Development and tourism.

The CBDC (Community Business Development Corporation) has helped develop many provincial and national training programs which promote job creation, the Regional Chamber of Commerce and the Campbellton Business Improvement Corporation promotes our downtown commercial business center which is very important to our community (which has a) double digit unemployment rate.

We coordinate many of our Economic Development Project with our Federal MP and our Provincial MLA as well as the Provincial Minister responsible for Economic Development.

Our many challenges now and in the next 5 years is to maintain our transportation system that includes CN and VIA Rail, our municipal road(s) and provincial highways. Developing our tourist infrastructure on the Campbellton Waterfront as we are the gateway into Atlantic Canada from Quebec, continu(ing) to develop new programs at our NBCC (Community College), maintain(ing) our health care system and (continuing to) promote our bilingual education system.

Our City Council and City Staff is very much involved with Economic Development / Tourism as well as the Government of NB and the Government of Canada with our other identified partners.

Our main concern today is our population that is getting older and our young people because of our un-employment situation are moving to other larger communities in NB or in Western Canada.

Hope this is satisfactory
Mayor (no attribution)
City of (no attribution)

Part 2

Equity in Education and Government

Making the change in work-life equity—does it really happen? An Introduction to Part 2

Liisa Timonen and Marilee Reimer

Work-life equity is a widely discussed and contradictory phenomenon, which is explored in Part 2 from the dimensions of a Finnish higher education and human resources project, women's public service employment in Canada and Australia and women as career science researchers in Switzerland. These three examples illustrate female work-life pathway builders. However, it is necessary to ask how equity is discussed during higher education; how women are employed; and, finally, when employed as talented researchers, how are women rewarded when performing highly?

The chapters in this section discuss the following key questions: Does the human resources master's project promote equity for women? What are the prevailing factors that hinder women's advancement and employment? How does work-life equity manifest itself in the challenging and ambitious field of academic research? These three selected discussions share case studies and statistics from widely different geographical contexts, from Australia to Canada to Switzerland to Finland. Even though the cases and statistics do not arise from joint research and are separate individual studies, they do provide interesting perspectives and raise new questions on work-life equity for other researchers to explore.

The first chapter ('*Reflections on Equity in the Finnish Working Life: A Case Study on Master's Students as Diversity and Inclusion Promoters*' by Liisa Timonen and Erja Turunen) discusses Finnish higher education from the perspectives of the selected master's programmes at two Finnish universities of applied sciences: Karelia University of Applied Sciences and Metropolia University of Applied Sciences (UAS). The master's programmes involved in this study represent three fields of education: business, engineering and healthcare, and they illustrate how diversity and inclusion management form an integral part of the education. In addition, a comparison of workplaces is made by considering students' final theses, in which they conduct participatory action research that reflects their own work-life practises with an aim of making changes in the workplace of the human resources master's students.

This first chapter provides a conceptual reflection into diversity and inclusion management, and shows how the Finnish UASs are systemically raising awareness on equity and supporting master's students' learning possibilities by developing joint courses and learning materials, and promoting student research in the field. However, there are challenges at the workplaces: first in applying diversity legislation in hiring practises, second in achieving inclusive community values, third in recognising and preventing workplace bullying and fourth in promoting positive aging. It takes time to transfer new knowledge and skills into workplace practises. Raising awareness and modifying the work-life management and teamwork practises takes time, but the writers see the master's programme graduates as future change-makers.

The second chapter ('Diversity and Inclusion in Institutional Development in Science and Engineering in Switzerland: A Bird's-Eye View' by Ursula Gut) discusses equity in the highly competitive academic research frame based on data from Swiss Forestry Research Institutes. It describes the world of a very competitive work community, which follows the criteria and standards of prestigious scientific research, with a focus on publishing papers in the journals with the highest possible ranking. The study shows clearly the male dominance in all leading roles: they are directors, department heads and group leaders many times more than women, who hold only a very small percentage of the leading roles. Men also control the hierarchical decision-making and most often have permanent employment, whereas women prevail in short-term contracts. Officially, the policy should support equality and even the rhetoric as the community emphasises equal opportunities, but reality is different, and female career building seems to be a very difficult path. It is noteworthy that male managers devised an equity strategy for women that both promotes the Forestry Institute's objective of raising the productivity of scientific publications and advancing women scientists into management.

Finally, in Chapter 3, Eddy Ng and Erica French ('Are We There Yet? Advancing Women at Work in Canada and Australia: Similar Goals, Different Policies') reflect on women's public service employment and compare gender equity legislation in Australia and Canada, the locations of two of the most successful public-sector employment programmes in the world. They point out how the legislation remains vague and misses the real-life impacts of employability and hiring practises, even though goodwill might be there. The statistics, in their turn, show how big the gap is between the official policies and employability in reality. The status of women has not risen remarkably, and neither has the strategic actions supporting women in managerial positions. In Australia, there is a faster decline in the pay gap in most major industrial groupings with women in executive leadership, yet the decline still is slow in both countries. Furthermore, the analyses show how the female advancement discussion and practises lack enforcement, and provide only very weak penalties for non-compliance.

Together these three chapters provide an overview into equity processes from the perspectives of an education programme and workplaces addressing women's career advancement. The entity points out many open questions for further development: Will the diversity and inclusion management training in education make the difference in the long run? Who would look after it and gauge the impacts? What are the key factors in labour legislation that hinder women's employability? How should and could we develop both the law and consequences supporting employability and career building in real-life situations? Finally, how can we ensure that women have equal opportunities in career building? Even though the problem has been recognised and discussed many times, there still has not been any remarkable change. How can we do it, and should we believe in education changing the world in the long run?

The 'Conclusion' (Marilee Reimer) provides an overview of how the chapters address the discourse on women, careers and diversity policy. The implications of this research for the advancement of women in the current policy context, theoretically and from a comparative perspective, are addressed.

6 Reflections on Equity in the Finnish Working Life

A Case Study on Master's Students as Diversity and Inclusion Promoters

Liisa Timonen and Erja Turunen

The theoretical background relies on diversity and inclusion management, which is explored from the conceptual and experiential perspectives. The key concepts are equity, diversity and inclusion, multiculturalism and ethical issues underlying the encountering. Encountering here refers to a situation-related process where 'me' and 'the other' meet in an interactive context (see Bruner, 1986; Kakkori & Huttunen, 2007).

The notions of equity as well as diversity management (DM) among work organisations are increasing. DM, when properly designed and implemented, can promote equity and bring about many desirable improvements in work organisations, such as higher job satisfaction, more solid and transparent talent and competence management, better use of resources and higher team spirit as well as an increase in the creation of more innovative products and solutions. It is suggested that DM can greatly contribute to gaining a competitive edge, if implemented successfully. In the end—and that is what business managers look for—diversity and inclusion policies may be a factor to higher returns on human capital investments.

Finnish Universities of Applied Sciences (UAS) are aiming at creating a working life oriented and fit for a purposeful curriculum development to enhance master's students' competences and skills in promoting equity and applying diversity and inclusion management tools in a meaningful way. We see master's degree students as key actors in developing working life and enhancing the understanding of equity and diversity as a great potential in organisational human capacity building.

Conceptual Background

Equity

We discuss equity in working life as an organisational culture that prevents discrimination and provides equal opportunities to all community members truly embracing diversity among the community. When equity is part of organisational culture, it actively prevents harassment, discrimination and bullying. Management and communication practices that are open and commonly accepted, followed up and developed actively support equal opportunities. Diversity and inclusion are crucial elements in equity. It is all about people, the members in and outside of the community. Diversity and inclusion management is one of the tools to promote equity in working life (Conley & Wright, 2011; European Commission, 2012; Kauppinen et al., 2013; Robertson, 2013).

Diversity

In this paper, diversity is explored as an opportunity to utilise the varied combination of human skills, talent, competences, characteristics and experiences in promoting equity and building profitable teams of expertise. Following Sippola (2007, p. 17; see also Nieto & Bode, 2008; Timonen & Kantelinen, 2013) we explore diversity as a wide concept: it concerns differences relating to age, gender, disability, race and ethnicity, and comprises all human characteristics and features, including capabilities, personality, education, religion, culture, language, lifestyle and marital status. Furthermore, diversity is apparent in perceptions, actions and working styles (Sippola, 2007, p. 17). Diversity is a complex and constantly changing concept depending on the interpreter: it is context related, relative, selective and multidimensional (Sippola, 2007, pp. 18–19).

Diversity and inclusion are embedded; it is crucial to see the variation of human resources (HR) as a potential. The aim is to look for the best possible ways to combine different expertise to promote organisational productivity and, at the same time, to increase team spirit, joy and well-being. Open and inclusive management practices may remarkably promote equity, which, in turn, is one of the cornerstones of creating a working community where the members have a feeling of belonging, communality and commitment.

Multiculturalism

DM calls for a profound understanding of multiculturalism in its wide sense. We prefer to discuss holistic multicultural understanding. When multicultural competence is seen as a holistic approach, the main emphasis is on understanding the principles of human equality and acceptance of each other's difference (Kaikkonen, 2001; Timonen, 2011). The understanding of difference and equality is a demanding and probably never ending process, that continues throughout our lifetime (see Buber, 1961). In order to build holistic multicultural understanding, one needs support. Related to multiculturalism, we discuss the complexity of the world and its sense of difference and reflect on teaching approaches supporting the master's student in her learning path.

Complexity of the World

The base of holistic multicultural understanding lies in a profound acceptance of diversity in our world. The concepts of culture, multiculturalism and transculturalism are useful in exploring the diversity. We discuss culture as a combination of different kinds of shared meanings on a personal level and in a group; however this combination is altering and dynamic (Nieto & Bode, 2008). To us, culture includes all the characteristic of human beings—age, sex, life history, health, hobbies and other interests, social background, talents and competences, sexuality, religion and nationality. Culture is always in transition as the members of each cultural group are in interaction with other groups and the media. The interaction and dialogue shape cultures again. Despite the transition, culture constitutes a context through which we are able to understand the others and ourselves. We need a mirror to reflect the reality around us, and culture gives us that mirror.

Multiculturalism goes beyond culture; it is the complexity of our lives and the world around us. Multiculturalism is everywhere; it is the expression of different kinds of cultural features and meanings within and between cultural groups. However, multiculturalism as a concept is somewhat unclear. It is often defined through the questions of power, majority and minority, wealth and politics (Hall & du Gay, 1996). While discussing this, we need to ask: Who is actually allowed to define culture and multiculturalism and who is allowed to set the rules for the discussion? How do the working organisations deal with these questions? The demand for tolerance, acceptance and appreciation is not self-evident; hence, these concepts need to be supported in the working community. This is one of the highly important issues in the master's degree education and needs to be enhanced by all the teachers.

Diversity is complex and cannot be defined in a simple way. Transculturalism fuses the concepts of culture and multiculturalism further and it is a part of the working communities, too, even though not usually clearly visible or acknowledged. Transculturalism is the interaction of different cultural groups in which all the groups are in transition and reforming new cultural hybrids (Welsch, 2009). Cultural hybrids are more or less open groups, which are typically in a constant change and challenging to define. The world around us is more and more complex; it is difficult to say what is authentic or original. Similarity and difference are in an ongoing dialogue; furthermore time and space seem to diminish globally. Difference and change are crucial parts in our lives—this is the diversity of our live worlds. Culture, multiculturalism and transculturalism form the basis of diversity. There is a deep need to accept the uniqueness and variations of characteristics in humanity—that forms a base for ethically coherent encountering of the other to promote equity.

Diversity: A Sense of Difference and Similarity

Besides understanding the concepts of culture, multiculturalism and transculturalism, the master's degree student also needs to explore how the world around us might cause us a sense of difference. Difference can be a sense of personal minority or majority, an idea about being different from the others or finding someone different from oneself. This distinction between the senses of difference is related to power, control, familiarity or strangeness. Whatever the base is, it reflects the interaction with the other. The sense of difference might be related to the challenging feelings in interaction, such as fear, disgust or suspicion, but also to the motivating feelings, such as interest, curiosity and friendship. Exploring the concept and idea of difference helps the student to strengthen her own identity and the motivating feelings of interaction. This is one of the key skills in building effective multicultural working teams to support the expressions of personal and professional identities in the working community.

The basic dimensions, 'self' and 'the other', are always present in defining and developing 'self' by mirroring it with 'the other'. Supporting identity requires understanding of self, otherness, equality and inequality, difference and diversity. Who am I? Who are you? and What is the world around us? are important questions for a student. Defining self is an ongoing dialogue between self, the other and the experiences of the world (Hall & du Gay, 1986; Timonen & Piironen, 2014). Identity supports self-awareness when the student feels belonging in some groups and experiences life in a somewhat meaningful way. One aim of multicultural education is to prevent the student from diminishing in a too narrow world and from relying on simplifications (Kaikkonen 2001; Kohonen, 2009; Taylor, 1991; Timonen & Piironen, 2014; see also Bruner, 1986).

We all live our lives within the society around us. Even though we might not always follow or accept the rules of that society, they guide us at least on an implicit level. Each society and working community has its own system of values, norms and rules, and we live exposed to them. The interaction between the community and an individual formulates our identities and shapes our feeling of the self. When we follow the rules, the cultural standards of our own community, we do not need to think if we are normal or not—the standard model of normal and accepted is inside us. We might also juxtapose these standards and make different kinds of choices, but it is more demanding than living as the majority does. Furthermore, there might be a polarisation of values, like simultaneous growth of tolerance and intolerance, a kind of a fight between certain values. The cultural standards are somewhat different in each community, and the student needs to understand this complexity and make mindful choices.

Language is one of the most important means to enable the interaction between people. It helps to make the cultural features explicit (see Timonen & Piironen, 2014). Furthermore, language gives us a path to our inner world and enables us to reflect the reality inside and around us. Language helps us to categorise and understand phenomena; this, in turn, supports inner talk and the learning processes. Language supports building at least some kind of an understanding about ourselves, our identities and the other. However, language itself is full of cultural meanings; with its vocabulary, structure and implicit as well as explicit meanings it reflects the cultural variations in different societies and communities. Language is both personal and social. Moreover, language is always bound to the outside world, it comes alive and acquires meaning when used; 'meaning-making' reflects the mind and the mind reflects the world (Bruner, 1986). The student needs to understand the diversity, complexity and cultural bonds of language.

DM from an Organisational Perspective

DM includes policies and actions that build and maintain an organisational culture where equity, justice and productivity go hand in hand. Each member of the organisation can feel that she is included and respected as an employee, colleague, customer or any other stakeholder role (Sippola & Kasurinen, 2014).

DM is part of corporate social responsibility that is regulated by the law in Finland. The normative regulations provide the guidelines for the working organisations to meet with the (minimum) standards of equity. Diversity can also be seen as richness in an organisation; it is one of the greatest factors contributing to the creation of new knowledge (Savileppä, 2012). For personnel, the sense of being able to be oneself, to be able to use one's full potential, is significant. Inclusive management is a new term used to refer to the strategic approach in which diversity and inclusion go hand in hand in management-forming policies that an organisation may adopt and implement.

When introducing the concept of DM to business decision-makers, the question often arises: How does this show in the bottom line? According to Sippola & Kasurinen (2014), diversity should be seen both as a resource, in which case it should be taken into consideration, and as capital, having many implications for leadership and management. A goal-oriented diversity initiative can bring about results, they claim.

An example of long-term and systematic diversity and inclusion work can be found in Sodexo, a US-based service company that operates worldwide. It is advised by practitioners that a goal-oriented diversity programme be designed and implemented using a holistic approach. One should distinguish the most relevant areas in the wide spectrum of diversity: What is most crucial in the light of our company's future that needs the most attention? Two to five key areas can be pointed out as focus areas. In the case of Sodexo, these are generations, culture and origins, gender and people with disabilities (Heschung, 2014).

Measuring the impact of diversity and inclusion initiatives is vital for success. The progress in implementing the chosen programmes and initiatives must be made visible throughout the organisation to gain further support from top management as well as to motivate those taking part, in any role. To be able to show trends, growth, development, improved job satisfaction and other progress, systematic follow-up and communication of results are needed. In addition to quantitative measurement, qualitative indicators are required. It is advised by the practitioners (Heschung, 2014) that creating such indicators together with managers and superiors adds personal commitment to the diversity and inclusion policies and their implementation.

The following questions can help in getting started in diversity and inclusion work in an organisation (Heschung, 2014):

> Who are your employees? Are they doing the right things? Are they treated in an equal way? Are the opportunities equal and in balance with the potential? How are their potential, skills and know-how being utilised now? Where are the gaps and what are the hindrances to a better use of human capital?

Recognition of the current situation is a starting point—DM assessment tools can be of help in the current state analysis. Planning of development programmes, that is, diversity and inclusion initiatives, is the next step. Which tools are available? Which tools need to be developed? In our case studies, we explored some of these questions from the master's students' perspective.

The Research Context

The research context is a DM project carried out by four Finnish UASs as part of a nationwide development programme for master's-level education, in 2014–2015. The programme was funded by the Finnish Ministry of Education and Culture. The researchers from the four partner UASs form a multidisciplinary team of expertise that is utilised in collecting and analyzing the data and in the final discussions of exploitation of the results. The master's degree students form a kind of living lab, where the action research is implemented as one part of the development programme.

The research is conducted among most of the master's degree programmes of Jyväskylä, Kajaani, Karelia and Metropolia UASs, yet the organisations involved in *this* case study are Karelia UAS and Metropolia UAS. The field of studies involved are business, culture and creative arts, social and healthcare, social sciences and engineering. The data is collected embedded into the studies and consists of students' learning assignments: reflective essays describing their own perceptions, experiences and working communities in the beginning of their master's studies. For this report, the data is enriched with four Master's Theses, two from Karelia UAS and two from Metropolia UAS, to cover the whole span of master's studies and provide the perspective of a graduating student.

The minimum of three years of work experience is a prerequisite for entering a UAS master's degree programme in Finland. This is one of the key elements making these students so special in terms of actually being able to change things, improve the current state of management and leadership and fulfil the aspiration we have for master's students. They are expected to renew and develop working life during their studies and to a greater degree when graduating.

Pragmatic and Constructive Approach

In our chapter we first reflect on the different conceptions the master's students have about diversity and inclusion as they show up in our data. Furthermore, we present snapshots where the learners reflect and analyze diversity and inclusion management in their own working communities. Based on these findings, we discuss the pedagogical approaches and the curriculum development in the master's degree programmes, keeping in mind how they support or should support the students' understanding of and skills in diversity and inclusion management. In discussion we explore what kinds of pedagogical skills and understanding the lecturers and instructors should have to be able to promote this important area of learning. In the end, we come up with some suggestions for further development based on the findings in the research.

Method and Categories

The research context is naturalistic, and the data is phenomenological (i.e., Cohen et al., 2007). The research was integrated into the courses regularly running, and no special arrangements related to the study were made. Instructions to students were given by professors, and data collection leans on the learning assignments of the courses. The instruction of the reflective essay was designed jointly by the researchers before the course implementations. The same instruction was used in all the UASs. Furthermore, all the students were asked for permission to use their learning assignments as research data. The reflective essays are personal and descriptive in their kind and they represent socially constructed reality.

The data collected in the project (in total, 150 student essays) provides rich information and varied views to diversity and inclusion. The students describe diversity and inclusion from their own perspectives and experiences gained in their own workplaces. The organisations represented are varied and comprise public and private organisations from many different fields. In this chapter, the discussion is limited to the data provided by 20 Karelia and Metropolia students. Besides the reflective essays, the data was enriched with four Master's Theses conducted by master's students during the action research. The sampling was purposive (Cohen et al., 2007); first, the data was limited to the UASs represented by the two researchers conducting this study, and, second, the data was sampled following the saturation point. The Master's Theses were picked up among those conducted during the project. The data was analysed until the categories and subcategories became clear enough. The language of the learning assignments and Master's Theses is Finnish. The researchers have translated the samples into English trying to preserve the original message, partly with the help of the English abstracts written by the students in question.

The data is analysed following the research questions explored in this chapter; this involved applying the content analysis approach (i.e., Cohen et al., 2007), and the essays were read and categorised. In this chapter we discuss the three main categories: concept of diversity, DM and perceptions of inclusion. These main categories are divided into subcategories as follows:

- Concepts of equity and diversity: regulatory diversity, normative diversity, cognitive diversity
- DM: the meaning of management, processes and tools
- Perceptions of inclusion: feeling of belonging, feeling of otherness

The categories and subcategories revealed themselves clearly from the data; however rich variation came up in the personal interpretation of the phenomena. In addition to these three main categories, to enrich the data and to gain a long-term perspective covering the whole master's education, we analysed the upcoming results of the DM project by summarising four cases, that is, Master's Theses. How do master's students promote equity in practice?

Master's Students' Perspectives on Equity and DM

Concepts of Equity and Diversity

Sippola (2007, p. 55) discusses diversity in the Finnish context from three perspectives: regulatory (e.g., laws and regulations), normative (e.g., values and norms) and cognitive (e.g., interpretations and frames of thought). The students' perceptions can be categorised by applying the Sippola approach.

First, the regulatory diversity was discussed as follows: the students described different laws and rules defining the questions of equality and discrimination in their workplaces. However, the issues were seen as complex and varied. This, in turn, supports the theoretical complexity of the concept of diversity: it is a blurred concept that is always context related, changing and interrelated with personal communication and interpretation (i.e., Sippola, 2007).

> We have rules for ensuring equality. I think it comes from the law. And we don't allow discrimination or bullying ... I think it is important also to our public image to make these rules visible.
>
> What I could not stand in diversity management ... at least discrimination in recruiting. And with this I mean not in a way you should recruit someone to fulfil some rules of integrating some minorities or ensure balance in sex ... you should always be able to recruit the best one for the job even if these principles would not come true.

The master's students recognised regulatory diversity but mainly from the perspective of legislation. The regulatory diversity was visible and openly discussed in some of the workplaces, but not in all.

Normative diversity was discussed from the perspectives of hierarchy and organisational values. Some of the master's students described their workplace as a multi-floor organ. Yet the approach of mixing and separating the groups varied.

> In a way, we have three floors in our hierarchy: on the first floor there are those doing the heavy physical work. They share a similar kind of background and they always work in pairs. On the second floor, there is the monitory staff who follow the processes. They do not have much in common but some of them share similar kinds of hobbies in their free time. And the highest level is the management. That is the most varied one. These floors are easily recognisable and they form separate teams.
>
> We have three groups of employers: assistants, officers and experts. However, each of our teams has employers from all these groups.

Some students mentioned that even though there is hierarchy at their workplaces, the boundaries between the groups are not too high and it is easy to communicate between the groups. However, some of the students saw that the position, group or team might work as a barrier for inter-group or interposition cooperation. One's position in the organisation as well as the nature of the position (permanent, temporary) were still seen as important dimensions of workplace equity and diversity.

Regarding values, the students strongly brought up respect and fair play. Norms and processes for bullying were discussed in many essays. Also, acceptance, tolerance and respect were brought up. The abilities required in encountering was seen as being the most important skills for all the members of the working community.

> I would not accept any kind of bullying. And we have rules and a process for that, should anything turn out. I would tell my boss right away if I noticed any bullying.
>
> I do not understand why there are conflicts because of different ways people think or because of different values ... We should be able to have tolerance with each other.
>
> I do not understand some persons at my working place. They are always negative and racist and speak aggressively about their colleagues. I try to avoid them.

Cognitive diversity was discussed in all the analysed papers. This part of the concept of diversity was recognised as the best and was described from many perspectives. The students brought up, for example, the following dimensions: age, education, sex, personal values, hobbies, cultural background, religion, working history, nationality, health, talent, life situation and communicative styles. Organisational cultures were also discussed.

> My work place has been changing to more diverse within time. We used to be more homogeneous but now we are varied in many ways ... I think this is due to the change in the working life/life in general.
>
> In my working field, the experts are more multicultural nowadays. Many come from the neighbouring countries and I think it is good.
>
> We have many older employees ... I am a bit concerned about their ability to have enough strength for the rest of their careers. That should be supported. Aging should be discussed much more. These people know a lot.
>
> When there was a merger, at first it was a battle between the local and common organisational cultures.

Diversity was also discussed from the perspectives of homogeneity and visibility, which might appear in a neutral, positive or negative form:

> We are not too diverse. Most of us come from quite a similar educational background, represent the same sex (men) and more or less even the age.
>
> In my working place the most cultural features come from the home regions of the employees. We can get a lot out of that (using the regional stereotypes).

> All of us are women. All of us need to speak Finnish but there are two bilingual persons and one who speaks another language as her mother language ... Most are quite the same age and the younger ones have higher educational backgrounds. I do not recognise visible diversity but the non-visible diversity is there ... life history, family, home town ... We don't talk about our values or religion ... One (of us) talks about her illnesses very openly.
>
> I have noticed that in case of mistakes, the more senior employees blame those coming from different language background even though the mistake wasn't her fault or could happen to anybody.

Again, diversity appears as a blurred concept: it can be visible or non-visible and even if it is non-visible, the students somehow can feel it is there. The personal interpretation formulates the individual understanding of the concept. It seems inequity is interconnected with the perception of difference.

Diversity Management

The master's students' perceptions of the second main category, DM, can be discussed in two subcategories: first, the significance of management and, second, processes and tools. It was the managers of an organisation who were seen as a key factor in utilising diversity in a positive way; if the management works, the organisation is or at least could be equal and successful. And when management works well, the employees feel safe, and work satisfaction remains high.

> I think that diversity management aims at commitment and sharing. It is important that everybody be committed. I see the manager as a coach supporting us ... All new employees are integrated [in]to the teams and the working community ... We have a good image and reputation ... Everybody can feel respected and it has nothing to do with your age, background, nationality ...
>
> Diversity management is basically encountering, recognition, respect and understanding ... Equality and trust are crucial.

Yet management, if not working, might promote inequality that is perceived to be a de-motivator for an employee and the whole community.

> If an employee feels treated in an unequal way without a reason, it affects his/her working morale and effectiveness. It also affects the whole working community and weakens the working atmosphere ... The same happens if someone gets non-reasoned glory ... Reasoning and good bases are always needed.

Processes and tools are the managers' way of dealing with the diversity prevalent in an organisation and involving everybody in teamwork and cooperation. The students brought up different kinds of questionnaires, barometers and instructions.

> We have an anonymous annual questionnaire about equality. It covers all the employers. Furthermore, there is an open channel for everybody to make an anonym[ous] announcement to the managers and directors, whenever they would notice any discrimination or bullying.
>
> We have annual work satisfaction barometers and some other questionnaires, too. They (human resources) are measuring and following it (diversity/inclusion).
>
> We have instructions for dealing with conflict situations and a model for a right-away action in case of any difficulty.

Meaningful team building and systemic interaction between the employees were seen as important and expected from managers. Team building can be supported in official and less official contexts. The students place emphasis on both of these channels.

> It is very important that managers can build trust and commitment. A constructive way to deal with difficult situations is important … to work with how to proceed rather than trying to find who is guilty or who has made mistakes.
>
> Different kinds of recreational events are also important. We do different things related to the well-being at work … It strengthens the team spirit, too.

Inclusion

The feeling of belongingness and communality was described as arising from the feeling of similarity. Sharing similar kinds of interests and free time activities, life situations, educational backgrounds, positions and/or values was mentioned as a bond between community members. The feeling of similarity seems to support the experience of being understood and accepted by others. The use of humour was seen as a channel to inclusion, however, only when the sense of humour was similar. Different senses of humour might cause the feeling of exclusion or even disgust.

> Humour is nice and brings joy to a day … We understand each other. However, somebody not knowing us might find it insulting.
>
> There are similar kinds of hobbies among many, fishing, motor sports and horses.

The feeling of difference, on the other hand, was not described from the other's perspective. The students did not see themselves as different; rather, it was 'the other', like a new member of the working community:

> We got a new employee. He was different from us, quiet, and not communicative ... We did not find him fitting in. It was difficult to work with him and our team was not the same anymore.

The understanding of equity related to perception of difference and otherness seems to be a challenge—the interpretation is one way, and it seems that the students rarely reflect the difference with a two-way analysis.

Equity in Practice: How Do Master's Students Promote It?

Research-based development, even action research, is a recommended approach for a Master's Thesis in master's degree programmes at Finnish UASs. The Master's Thesis is the most significant part of one's studies, counting for a half or a third of the whole degree programme. The project relies on development needs recognised in the organisation by its HR professionals or its management; it may also be based on a current state analysis conducted by a master's student. In either case, certain focus areas are identified and the diversity and inclusion work can start. Since the time frame for a Master's Thesis is one to two years, a full action research cycle can seldom be reached.

The agile development projects where master's students play a key role are related to the following:

- the rising generations,
- leading virtual teams,
- embracing cultural diversity in teams and projects,
- DM from a leadership perspective, and
- ageing and the ability to work.

What can be achieved? Changes in the way of thinking and in skills of perceiving equity and diversity can most likely be seen. The potential methods of inclusion that are appropriate in the organisation as a result of agile pilot projects in specified HR or other areas are expected to lead to rapid improvements. More profound changes in the operative level, let alone changes in the organisational culture—for example, a proactive strategic approach—require a longer time. This is where one of the benefits comes from: the master's students, who study alongside their work, can keep on working and promoting DM after they graduate. In the next sections we examine four Master's Theses that provide examples on how the master's students work as diversity and inclusion promoters in practice.

Case One: How to Promote Ability to Work?

One perspective on equity in working life is to explore how the working community and especially the management level ensure equal opportunities for ageing community members and support their ability to work to enable their full contribution and participation. This question is highly topical in Finland as the working communities in the future are even more diverse in relation to age due to the rising retirement age. Huppunen-Vänskä and Tietäväinen (2015a, 2015b) conducted their Master's Theses on this issue and suggested applying both a systemic follow-up on work ability and a model of an early-stage intervention immediately when a need arises. This kind of process has been applied to some extent in Finnish working communities, but Huppunen-Vänskä and Tietäväinen suggest it be systematically applied in the healthcare and welfare sectors.

The data analysed by Huppunen-Vänskä and Tietäväinen was collected by the National Institute for Health and Welfare conducting regional research of health and welfare covering the whole country, yet the researchers analysed only the data from the North Karelia region. The ability to work was seen as personal, situational and interpretive. It was discussed from the dimensions of physical and mental workload, discrimination, roles in the community, way of life and health. Huppunen-Vänskä and Tietäväinen (2015a) emphasised an interplay between the work, employee, working community and the superior being in the scope affecting the ability to work—when the community feels well and is properly managed, each member also feels well. Furthermore, when the community feels well, productivity rises. However, a well working and trustful relationship with the superior and skilful management were seen as the most important factors to support the employee's ability to work.

For the superiors, Huppunen-Vänskä and Tietäväinen (2015a, 2015b) suggested applying a model of a systemic early intervention even if the reasons for decreasing ability to work would come outside of the work and working community. The intervention model should be applied whenever a need arises, not depending on where the reasons come. With the early intervention model the researchers began a process, which includes, first, a mapping discussion between the superior and employee defining the problem or challenges; second, jointly agreed concrete steps to solve the problems; third, a follow-up for the proceedings; and, fourth, feedback and evaluation within a certain time limit. All the steps are documented and visible for both the employee and superior. When needed, the superior works in close cooperation with the occupational healthcare services that offer both preventive and caring services relating to ability to work. Besides the early intervention process, a superior's support and flexibility in organising tasks and working hours were seen as efficient tools to support the ability to work.

Case Two: How Does Leadership Support Equity?

Equity can also be discussed from the perspective of inclusion and inclusive management spractices. Leppänen (2015) explores this phenomenon in the context of Liperi, a North-Karelian municipality nursing and care service. Leppänen identified challenges a manager meets in the management process and searched for suggestions and concrete tools on how to improve management practices. Leppänen formed a development group involving superiors from nursing and welfare services. During the action research, this group created a joint development action plan to increase communality, transparency and continuity of the management practices.

Leppänen (2015) explores the inclusive practices from the perspective of communality. She claims, following Manka et al. (2007), that communality significantly promotes well-being and productivity. Communality reveals itself on both explicit and implicit levels, and a working community calls for an acknowledged organisational culture that aims for visible inclusive practices. Inclusiveness is influenced by the superiors, but it also calls for an active commitment and participation of the whole community. Understanding and acceptance of difference and trust are at the core of communality, which is based on appreciation and equal encountering of the other (Leppänen, 2015, pp. 9–10; see also Gibson, 2003).

Leppänen conducted an extensive research project involving the community members. First, she designed a survey mapping the current state of the community and then enriched the data, with the team of superiors organising three workshops exploring the issue. The workshops were organised to identify points of development and to iterate suggestions of applying concrete tools for the superiors on how to improve their management practices. Leppänen came up with five main areas where the superiors needed to work actively: creation of joint values and goals, development of cooperative practices, development of communality practices, promotion of motivation and commitment, and giving more responsibility to the employees. All the results were documented into the organisational development plan, providing guidelines on increasing communality, thus contributing to the promotion of equity.

Case Three: How to Increase the Commitment of the Rising Generations at Work?

The issue of involving the younger generations—also called the rising generations (e.g., Rahkonen, 2014), referring to Generations Y and Z—is a challenge, especially in the public sector, where wages are generally fairly low, and lifelong careers are not the most desirable outlook for the new recruits. However, the need for skilled and motivated workers is there, increasingly so as the large generations reach their retirement age.

How to manage and lead the rising generations so that they would like to stay instead of 'job hopping'? How to inspire them in contributing to the continuous change taking place in work organisations? What motives them? If it's not the money they make—Generation Y may be the first generation not reaching the income level of their parents (Rahkonen, 2014)—what is it? To what extent can team leaders and other superiors influence their commitment?

This topic area was tackled by Räty (2016) in her Master's Thesis in business administration. A team manager herself in one of the insurance divisions of Kela, the Social Insurance Institution in Finland, Räty explains, 'The choice of the subject was influenced by the awareness of the structural changes like digitalisation and the demand for long careers that will take place in society and working life during the next few years'.

At first, Räty gathered data using group interviews among the employees representing the Generation Y group. Rahkonen's article (2014) was used as discussion material. Second, Räty analysed her data and discussed her findings in the context of DM, age management and motivation theories. Meaningful work, competence development opportunities, good community and team spirit as well as salary issues, where the highly educated young employees felt that they were not paid accordingly, were documented as the main expectations of the young employees of Kela's division. 'The effect of these elements on their work commitment was evident', Räty (2016) claims.

The implementation part of Räty's action research materialised as a virtual handbook to be used by team leaders and supervisors at Kela. Its draft was commented on and the final version was introduced to the targeted user group. The handbook includes text on the special features attached to and the values held by employees representing Generation Y, their career expectations and their wishes for feeling included, that is, feeling equal among more senior colleagues in their work community. Inclusion would mean equal access to training, opportunities to bring new ideas to the table, and fair feedback and overall treatment from their superiors. This should ideally take place from the early stage on at Kela. Räty discovered the managers and leaders of Kela possessing several means to influence the commitment of the rising generations and to respond to their expectations.

Case Four: Who Gets to Know and What? Sharing of Tacit Knowledge in a Service Organisation

The need for Tikkanen's (2014) Master's Thesis arose from the characteristics of the commissioner organisation, the Home and Institutional Health Care and Social Service of the City of Hyvinkää, in southern Finland. The objective of the Master's Thesis was formulated as a change expected to take place in the target organisation with regard to the recognition and use of tacit knowledge.

> More specifically, it attempted to make the personnel, superiors, as well as top management aware of the significance of tacit knowledge; to enable them to recognise the (non)existence of tacit knowledge; as well as encouraging them to share and forward tacit knowledge.
>
> (Tikkanen, 2014)

From an equity perspective, the question inevitably rises: Who has access to worthwhile and necessary knowledge? The power of knowing is a strong tool. Not knowing puts one in a weaker position compared to peers. It was important for the organisation to put more emphasis on sharing tacit knowledge if it was to achieve its ambitious strategic goals and succeed in the ongoing change process.

Tikkanen's approach to her development task was participatory action research. Secondary data was collected from literature and internal data systems, while primary data was gathered with e-questionnaires, team interviews, as well as meetings (observation, participation). Theories of tacit knowledge, recognition and tacit knowledge management, as well as theories of knowledge management were used.

After analyzing the existing level of tacit knowledge management in the organisation, discussions on its usefulness and value—pros and cons—were started. Tacit knowledge was also added to the agenda of individual development discussions carried out in the organisation.

'A follow-up conducted with a questionnaire showed that the employees' experience of the existence and sharing of tacit knowledge had changed to a more positive [model] during the process', states Tikkanen (2014). This would suggest a more equal access to tacit knowledge in the organisation. The improved model for development discussions by Tikkanen served as an inspiration for updating the common development discussion model for the entire city organisation, thus leveraging Tikkanen's outcome. Her work launched a learning process in the target organisation that can favourably contribute to higher work satisfaction, better performance and improved customer satisfaction—all qualities that a service-oriented city organisation values highly. From an individual as well as team perspective, sharing tacit knowledge supports equity. In terms of DM, all three levels—individual, team and organisational—can greatly benefit from improved tacit knowledge management.

Discussion

Curriculum Development and Master's Students' Diversity and Inclusion Projects

In curriculum development, we aim at promoting the following courses in master's degree programmes: first, personal development and self-management; second, management and supervising skills; and, finally, strategic leadership and strategy work. The aim is to support and enhance the crucial competences and skills that the master's students would need to be able to understand equity, diversity and inclusion, and to promote equity through DM in their work organisations. Based on the study, we can also confirm that master's students have many challenges in their growth to the bases of diversity and inclusion management: acceptance, tolerance and understanding of the complexity of the world. They need to have solid motivation to learn, conceptual knowledge, as well as a willingness to achieve personal growth. In addition, one's understanding of the complexity of difference and otherness needs to be supported. The instructor has an important role in enhancing the learning process.

Promoting more Master's Theses reflecting equity and diversity, and inclusion management is one of our aims. A DM project where students are promoters of equity in their partner organisations is expected to increase the impact of the research and development work conducted in master's education. Thus, the connective model (Griffiths & Guile, 2003; Tynjälä, 2008, p. 144), also described as integrative pedagogy (Nykänen & Tynjälä, 2012, pp. 22–23; see also Little, 2004), becomes visible in many real activities implemented in master's studies. Consequently, we believe that the right 'target group' in spreading the understanding of DM in working life is the students attending master's degree programmes at Finnish UASs.

We strongly support the approach of authentic experiential learning in close working life cooperation. In experiential authentic pedagogy, the teacher empowers the student's own ability and willingness to learn and supports her learning processes. The teacher can support student autonomy, authenticity and dialogue by putting herself as a whole person into the teaching (Holec, 1981; Kohonen, 2009; Timonen & Kantelinen, 2013).

Master's Students as Diversity and Inclusion Promoters

Students pursuing their master's studies at UASs are at the focal point of diversity and inclusion management. They can bring about change, if we can make them aware of the topic and its importance. By giving them not only know-how but also tools, the students can experiment and apply their diversity and inclusion awareness and skills in authentic learning environments, typically their employer organisations. They can do this individually or in multidisciplinary teams. In the latter case, they are moving from the integrative model towards the pedagogical model of network culture (Nykänen & Tynjälä, 2012, p. 22) in which students are eager to share their expertise and experiences gained in work life and learn from peer students in return.

It is expected that already during their studies the understanding of the equity and DM competence of master's students is evidenced positively and becomes visible. After the experience of having used some of the tools, having discussed the DM issues in their respective organisations and having internalised the key concepts and the significance and potential of DM, we may well expect the students to continue doing this as their careers progress. Multiple impacts on a larger scale may take place, thus fulfilling the expectation of this sector of higher education; master's students and future alumni from Finnish UASs are change agents of renewing the working life (e.g., Juuti & Luoma, 2009).

Whether this can be achieved depends greatly on how empowered the master's students feel. As found out in our study, not everyone is in a position to influence diversity and inclusion policymaking. Leaving the power issue aside, we may ask: Can we encourage the students to take action also in situations where traditional organisational structures may hinder or prevent them from doing so? DM is a complex area where sensibility and diplomacy combined with a determined mode of action are needed. Have the students, many of whom started their studies and careers according to the rules and expectations of modern society, been able to step into the postmodern society where one's identity is under continuous renewal (Juuti & Luoma 2009, p. 181)? What kind of pedagogical approach would best support the action research-type diversity and inclusion interventions we are expecting our master's students to plan and implement in their partner organisations (see Conley & Wright, 2011; European Commission, 2012)?

Our Vision: Competence and Impact

Our vision is that DM competence becomes a part of the competence profile of all master's students at Finnish UASs. Equity, diversity, inclusion and strengthening of vitality give a new meaning to managerial and leadership work. New work and the renewing working life call for a new kind of leadership. The joy of work must not disappear, well-being at work can and must be increased and, at the same time, productivity and efficiency have to stay at a high level in work organisations.

DM is both a strategic and an operative issue supporting equity. Shaping the organisational reality towards proactive equity, diversity and inclusion policies could be a role well fitted for master's students with understanding and appreciation of DM content. From being empowered enough to act as DM promoters in their organisations master's students of UASs could reach the level of employee engagement (Byrne, 2015, pp. 41–43), where they not only transform their own work to something meaningful and purposeful but feel empowered to empower others as well. Diversity and inclusion management could offer them and their colleagues a framework for collaborative shaping of the equity, vitality and well-being of the whole organisation.

There is so much unused or unrecognised human potential that diversity and inclusion management can bring to the surface. When understood, recognised, appreciated, and, finally, utilised for the benefit of an individual, a team and the whole organisation, a favourable development can reach the working life on an even larger scale, as was expected in Case 4 by Tikkanen (2014). This is an area our project team will continue to take a look at in the next few years.

References

Bruner, J. (1986) *Actual minds, possible worlds.* Cambridge: Vintage Books.

Buber, M. (1961) *The writings of Martin Buber.* Selected, edited, and introduced by Herberg, W. Cleveland: World Publishing Company.

Byrne, Z. S. (2015) *Understanding employee engagement. Theory, research, and practice.* New York: Routledge.

Cohen, L., Manion, L. & Morrison, K. (2007) *Research methods in education.* Sixth edition. New York: Routledge.

Conley, H. & Wright, T. (2011) *Gower handbook of discrimination at work.* London: Routledge.

European Commission. (2012) Implementation checklist for diversity management. Support for voluntary initiatives promoting diversity management at the workplace across the EU. European Commission. Available from: www.ec.europa.eu/migrant-integration/librarydoc/implementation-checklist-for-diversity-management.

Gibson, L. (2003) Trust and the development of health care as a social institution. *Social Science and Medicine.* 56 (7), 1453–1468.

Griffiths, T. & Guile, D. (2003) A connective model of learning: the implications for work process knowledge. *European Educational Research Journal.* 2 (1), 56–73.

Hall, S. & du Gay, P. (eds.) (1996) *Questions of cultural identity.* London: SAGE.

Heschung, S. (2014) *Diversity and inclusion mean business.* Goal-oriented diversity and inclusion work at Sodexo Group. FIBS seminar 'Miten myyt, seuraat ja mittaat monimuotoisuustyötä?' 4.9.2015, Helsinki. Corporate Responsibility Network FIBS, Diversity Charter Finland.

Holec, H. (1981) *Autonomy in foreign language learning.* Oxford: Pergamon Press.

Huppunen-Vänskä, M. R. & Tietäväinen, M. (2015a) *How to support aging workers to maintain their ability to work as the retirement age rises.* Master's Thesis. Karelia University of Applied Sciences, Finland [in Finnish].

Huppunen-Vänskä, M. R. & Tietäväinen, M. (2015b) Aging workers' ability to work when the careers prolong. In: Timonen, L., Mäkelä, J. & Raivio, A. M. (eds.) 2015. Diversity: a feature of a good working community. *Jyväskylä University of Applied Sciences* 213, 147–155 [in Finnish].

Juuti, P. & Luoma, M. (2009) *Strateginen johtaminen - miten vastata kompleksisen ja postmodernin ajan haasteisiin?* Keuruu: Otava. [in Finnish].

Kaikkonen, P. (2001) Intercultural learning in foreign language education. In: Kohonen, V., Jaatinen, R., Kaikkonen, P. & Lehtovaara, L. (eds.) *Experiential Learning in foreign language education* (pp. 61–105). Harlow: Pearson Education Limited.

Kakkori, L. & Huttunen, R. (2007) Aristotle and pedagogical ethics. *Paideusis.* 16 (1), 17–28.

Kauppinen, T., Mattila-Holappa, P., Perkiö-Mäkelä, M., Saalo, A., Toikkanen, J., Tuomivaara, S., Uuksulainen, S., Viluksela, M. & Virtanen, S. (eds.) (2013) *Työ ja terveys Suomessa 2012*. Seurantatietoa työoloista ja työhyvinnoinnista. Työterveyslaitos. Tampere [in Finnish].

Kohonen, V. (2009) Autonomy, authenticity and agency in language education: the European language portfolio as a pedagogical resource. In: Kantelinen, R. & Pollari, P. (eds.) *Language education and lifelong learning* (pp. 9–44). Joensuu: University of Eastern Finland. Philosophical Faculty. School of Applied Educational Science and Teacher Education.

Leppänen, P. (2015) *Leadership – workplace community developer*. [Master's Thesis]. Karelia University of Applied Sciences [in Finnish].

Little, D. (2004) Constructing a theory of learner autonomy: some steps along the way. In: Mäkinen, K., Kaikkonen, P. & Kohonen, V. (eds.) Future perspectives in foreign language education. University of Oulu. *Research in Education*. 101, 15–25.

Manka, M.-L., Kaikkonen, M.-L. & Nuutinen, S. (2007) *Hyvinvointia työyhteisöön – Eväitä kehittämistyön avuksi*. Tampereen yliopiston kauppakorkeakoulun tutkimus-ja koulutuskeskus Synergos [in Finnish].

Nieto, S. & Bode, P. (2008) Affirming diversity. *The sociopolitical context of multicultural education*. Boston, MA: Pearson/Ally and Bacon.

Nykänen, S. & Tynjälä, P. (2012) Työelämätaitojen kehittämisen mallit korkeakoulutuksessa. *Aikuiskasvatus* 1, 17–28 [in Finnish].

Rahkonen, J. (2014) Nouseva sukupolvi kaipaa työltä mielekkyyttä ja elämältä onnellisuutta. *Journal of Finnish Universities of Applied Sciences*. 4. Available from: www.arkisto.uasjournal.fi/uasjournal_2014-4/rahkonen.html [in Finnish].

Räty, M. (2016) *Diversity management: developing the management of generation Y*. [Master's Thesis]. Helsinki Metropolia University of Applied Sciences [in Finnish]. Available from: www.urn.fi/URN:NBN:fi:amk-2016060712304.

Robertson, Q. (2013) *The Oxford handbook of diversity and work*. Oxford: Oxford University Press.

Savileppä, A. (2012) *Erilaisuus energiaksi*. Diversa Consulting. [in Finnish].

Sippola, A. (2007) *Essays on human resource management perspectives on diversity management* [Doctoral dissertation]. Acta Wasaensia 180, Business Administration 75. Vaasa: Universitat Wasaensis.

Sippola, A. & Kasurinen, R. (2014) *Miten myyt, seuraat ja mittaat monimuotoisuustyötä? A FIBS seminar 4.9.2015 in Helsinki*. Corporate Responsibility Network FIBS, Diversity Charter Finland [in Finnish].

Taylor, C. (1991) *The ethics of authenticity*. Cambridge: Harvard University Press.

Tikkanen, M. (2014) *How to use tacit knowledge in customer-valued organization culture – management aspect* [Master's Thesis]. Helsinki Metropolia University of Applied Sciences [in Finnish]. Available from: www.urn.fi/URN:NBN:fi:amk-201501021005.

Timonen, L. (2011) Kansainvälisty tai väisty? Tapaustutkimus kansainvälisyysosaamisen ja kulttuurienvälisen oppimisen merkityksenannoista oppijan, opettajan ja korkeakoulutoimijan pedagogisen suhteen rajaamissa kohtaamisen tiloissa. Dissertations in Education, Humanities and Theology. *Publications of the University of Eastern Finland*. 16. [in Finnish].

Timonen, L. & Kantelinen, R. (2013) Moninaisuus opettajankouluttajan ja korkeakouluopettajan työssä – näkökulmia monikulttuuriseen kasvatukseen. *Kasvatus* 3, 258–269 [in Finnish].

Timonen, L. & Piironen, M. (2014) Supporting the development of professional identity through intercultural communication and language courses. In: Paola, P. E. (ed.) Identities in and across cultures series: Linguistic Insights. *Studies in language and communication.* 189 (pp. 269–288). Bern: Peter Lang.

Tynjälä, P. (2008) Perspectives into learning at the workplace. *Educational Research Review.* 3, 130–154.

Welsch, W. (2009) On the acquisition and procession of communalities. In: Schulze-Engler, F. & Helff, S. (eds.) Transcultural English Studies. Theories, Fictions, Realities. *Cross/Cultures* 102. ASNEL. Papers 12, 3–36.

7 Diversity and Inclusion in Institutional Development in Science and Engineering in Switzerland

A Bird's-Eye View

Ursula Gut

Introduction

This chapter explores different perspectives on power and privilege in the context of institutional development and diversity in academia. It addresses the question of how to introduce and enhance the institutional[1] embedding of processes that facilitate innovation in research, fairness and inclusion in parallel, using a mixed compilation of theories and research results from different domains, including sociology, social and organisational psychology as well as system theory. It also explores underlying patterns that tend to self-perpetuate prevailing structures or offer promising approaches to foster open-minded and adaptive organisations.[2]

It also draws on my direct observations and data obtained on the current situation of male and female researchers during my practical experience as an institutional developer and diversity coordinator. The data and reflections should throw light on the interface between diversity and inclusion practice, and selected theoretical approaches as well as help to deal with the current situation as an essential first step towards increased fairness, diversity and inclusion.

Methods

Data collected recently by the Human Resource Department of the Swiss Federal Institute of Forest, Snow and Landscape Research (WSL) was statistically analyzed. The focus was on interactions within the organisation with white female researchers as an example of a minority group working in the domain of natural science research in Switzerland. Further input came from direct observations as a participant in the Swiss Federal Institutes of Technology (ETH) Domain,[3] the outcomes of organisational surveys at WSL and inputs from an interview cycle with the members of the human resources (HR) board of the ETH Domain and the members of the Directorate of WSL. The analysis was intended to contribute to the general understanding of key conditions researchers need to meet in academia, and drew on explanatory theories and research results from the literature.

The theoretical analysis was based on the work of Geoffrey Hodgson (2006), who provides clear definitions of terms such as 'institution' and 'organisation'. Dobbin et al. (2011) provide a set of preconditions to explain and analyze the degree of inclusiveness of an organisation at a given point in time. Lenski's analysis (1984) on power and privilege, as well as the theoretical framework of Luhmann (2012), offers relief from conceptual impasse and helps to enlarge perspectives. The latter in particular is helpful for understanding communication processes. In addition, Davidson (2011) on leveraging differences provides a new focus on the domain of managing and coordinating diversity.

These different theoretical perspectives and studies suggest that a substantial growth in fairness and inclusion depends on multiple factors, such as the prevailing culture of an organisation and existing societal norms as well as the relative proportion of diversity groups in a given organisation. In essence, they offer different approaches to addressing the question as to why a shift towards more inclusive environments is challenging. They also provide conceptual frameworks that challenge prejudice and may generate promising ideas to foster inclusion in practice.

Findings

A glance at the basic essentials of life situations of most researchers, in particular of those younger than 40 years, reveals that their work setting is becoming increasingly demanding. Research is driven by a permanent competition for the best ranking positions within worldwide measurement systems based on quantitative indicators comparable to those in banking. To assure survival and success, academic organisations, especially those at the top of the league, have optimised production by radically increasing flexibility, which requires an increased job mobility of researchers. All organisations of the ETH Domain are tending to raise the number of short-term contracts. At WSL, 55 per cent of the male researchers and 80 per cent of the female researchers worked in non-permanent positions in 2014. In addition, openings regarding permanent positions are reserved for experienced researchers in highly specialised research or technical domains.

At the same time, the performance mandate of the Swiss Federal Council for the ETH Domain for the period 2013–2016 states, among other things: 'It will support women at all levels and in all functional groups. It will ensure a substantial increase in the proportion of women in management positions and on decision-making bodies'. The Swiss Federal mandate unlocks a wide area between gender-oriented policies and the realities in practice.

As an example, in 2014 at WSL, 321 persons worked in research; of these, 198 were male, and 123 were female. Nine men were in the position of head of department, but only one woman was. Similarly, there were 34 male and 5 female group leaders (see Table 7.1). Furthermore, all of the WSL Directorate were white males. Some of the researchers worked in permanent positions. All scientists in a higher hierarchical position than researcher occupied permanent positions. At WSL the probability of obtaining a permanent job in research averaged roughly 10 per cent for the 35–39 age group in 2014. As a result, most hierarchical decision-making power, as well as most prestige, is still in the hands of white males.

According to the ETH Domain's political performance mandate, a multitude of projects, such as the 'Fix the leaky pipeline training program' of the ETH Domain and various other equal opportunity programmes, have been, and still are, carried out. In most research organisations, few of them have led to sustainable embedded processes or have had a measurable impact on the distribution of career or leadership positions according to gender. Only one of the four research organisations, headed by a woman director, does better, which fits in with the findings of Dobbin et al. (2011, p. 386) that suggest that 'firms that lack workforce diversity are no more likely than others to adopt [diversity] programs, but firms with large contingents of women managers are more likely to do so'.

The research organisations in the ETH Domain produce excellent research and are correspondingly ranked high; however, there is no clear functional necessity for more diversity and inclusion. Under these circumstances, what basic understanding of diversity and inclusion best fits the current situation? Which type of embedding best serves the purpose of the organisations' 'key business': namely to produce

Table 7.1 Percent of WSL Scientists in Different Hierarchical Levels

Position	*Male*	*Female*
Short-term temporary staff	3.0	8.1
Trainees	4.6	10.6
PhD students	21.2	21.1
Post Docs	7.6	13.8
Research assistants	4.0	8.1
Researchers	35.4	31.7
Group leaders	17.2	4.1
Senior scientists	1.5	0.8
Program leaders	1.0	0.8
Department leaders	4.6	0.8
Grand total	**100.00**	**100.00**

Source: WSL, Human Resources Department 2014 (pers. comm.).

high-quality research generating innovation? How does this fit with the research organisations' aim to continuously improve their ranking positions with respect to production indicators, such as number of papers published in renowned journals? And what about the goal of the Swiss Federal performance mandate to enhance equal opportunity and fairness?

Diversity coordination in the past has, in practice, been mostly understood as a kind of service involving trouble shooting. Diversity seems to have been perceived as a source of potential problems that might hinder knowledge production. The activities of the Human Resources Department were mainly taken up with handling a growing number of non-permanent contracts, with little capacity to consider diversity issues. The political performance mandate of the ETH Board, however, implies that the WSL Directorate is interested in diversity in the context of real institutional development and sees benefits in including diversity groups, such as women, different age groups or members of different hierarchical levels (Davidson, 2011; Lenski, 1984).

To better understand what type of benefit such a decision-making body may perceive as being motivating, the question 'who gets what and why?' (Lenski, 1984, p. 1), or more formally what represents power, privilege and prestige in academia, will be briefly examined. According to Lenski, privilege and prestige are defined as a function of power, where power is the key variable. Furthermore, power is based on commonly accepted laws and rules of persuasion and incentive. Some groups in academia benefit from the privilege of a permanent position, whereas others do not. They have higher incomes and more decision-making rights and duties within the organisation due to their position. The commonly accepted convention of competitiveness is a major individual, group and organisational driver. In practice, each male or female researcher, including the members of the decision-making body and of other minority groups, is part of the system driven by the worldwide ranking system (h-index) of publication performance. They function as agents of the consensus to strive for additional power, privilege and prestige within the system.

Dobbin et al. (2011, p. 387) suggest that 'for legitimacy-enhancing innovations adoption will be driven primarily by corporate culture, not by need [for more diversity]. More important than a firm's … susceptibility to regulatory scrutiny will be its past pattern of attentiveness to social norms'. To a certain extent, within WSL and the ETH Domain, no effective social norm or pressure exists with explicit constraints issued by male peer groups or decision-making bodies related to equal opportunity regarding minority groups or increased diversity per se. Indeed, the subliminal message is to advertise positions emphasising equal opportunity to allow female career opportunities and to use politically correct wording. Practice shows, however, that the often assumed norm that research in natural sciences is traditionally reserved for men has not yet been completely extinguished in either male or female minds.

Direct observations indicate that most male researchers, especially those who are part of a decision-making body, are either very sensitive to issues related to equal career opportunities for female researchers or members of other minority groups or not interested in them at all. Real or potential requests from members of any minority group tend to immediately provoke conscious or unconscious resistance. Members of decision-making bodies and most male HR managers seem to behave as if they were brought to bay whenever the issue arises on the horizon. Most discussion partners then compete in producing a multitude of arguments. Decision-making bodies seem to consider activities to facilitate the organisational embedding of processes enhancing the inclusion of minority groups as part of an important political, but not pressing, project.

From the observations, experience and interviews, however, it is clear that each member of a decision-making body is in some respect part of a minority group due to their age, position in the hierarchy and so on, and feels occasionally unfairly treated. In 2014, the Directorate of WSL decided to widen the perspective by creating a staff function embracing institutional development as well as diversity. In practice, this involved implementing conceptual outcomes in the development of the institute through staff development activities and open discussion of diversity and inclusion issues. Positive effects are already apparent since discussions have become more open and fruitful. Furthermore, most members of the decision-making body and the research staff sense that they may benefit personally from jointly developed actions.

Taking Action on Survey Outcomes: Inclusive Institutional Development Policy and Strategies, Training Modules, Focus on Career: Work-Life Balance and Facilitating Day Care

The results of a staff survey on possible domains of action regarding different groups of researchers, such as part-time workers, researchers with young children and members of the decision-making body, as well as a list of propositions established in collaboration with the staff council, led to the following steps being selected for 2015 by the Directorate of WSL. Most of the actions are designed to cover at the same time a current organisational challenge (a need) and to improve the working conditions of a particular minority group. As an example, training modules to optimise the annual performance appraisals, including individual development in career opportunity discussions, will be introduced to all members of the decision-making body from the position of group leader onwards. Other examples are the introduction of two bottom-up sounding board processes that will consider possible improvements for long-term researchers older than 58 years and, with respect to a work-life balance, collect best practice on how to facilitate childcare.

At WSL, a process of institutional development means making a joint effort to gradually adapt prevailing and often unconscious norms and rules towards a naturally embedded construction of a more inclusive environment for different minority groups. These groups include those based on age, gender and different positions in the hierarchy. Since literally everybody is part of at least one minority group due to their personal characteristics, a development towards more inclusiveness may also increase their effectiveness to contributing to qualitatively high-end research and help to enhance communication and managerial skills.

From the point of view of the Diversity Coordinator, these developments may serve to promote diverse teams with members from often very different backgrounds and with different ways of thinking. This should foster more acceptance of different values and ways of doing something and enhance people's willingness to openly discuss any perceived fields of tension. The following statement on gender diversity could serve as a basis for all minority groups: 'Gender diversity can provide different perspectives and insights. The combination of these offers a wider range of ideas and, thus, greater creativity, facilitating decision-making processes' (Díaz-García et al., 2013).

Another interesting and recent development is that the Directorate of WSL decided to implement a subgroup as a task force to shorten the decision-making processes for institutional development and diversity, including staff development issues. The task force is composed of the associate general director, two directors representing the research departments, the head of finance and HR as well as the institutional developer and diversity coordinator. Research results from Dobbin et al. (2011) suggest that the most effective actions to foster diverse and inclusive organisations are task forces and mentoring programmes. Therefore, this decision to implement a task force can be considered a first valuable, trendsetting step.

Conclusions

Promoting the development of a more inclusive environment in an organisation means encouraging a more diverse group of employees. This is challenging in the technical world of natural science research in Switzerland as a corresponding boost in performance is not directly evident from the point of view of traditionally white male-dominated decision-making bodies. Consequently they tend, at first, to see no functional necessity to foster diversity and inclusion. Conscious or unconscious adherence to prevailing peer group values and goals at individual, group and organisational levels often serves to perpetuate the present situation. As the report of the European Commission EUR 24905 (2011) suggests, the majority of academic organisations in Europe and Switzerland are currently similar in their settings. However, both theory and research findings indicate that diverse populations can do better than monocultures since different task-oriented points of view foster better quality decision-making and team performance (Díaz-García et al., 2013). Leveraging differences helps to improve the results of the 'key business' (Davidson, 2011).

The research findings of Dobbin et al. (2015) 'suggest that the regulation of specific behaviour may backfire, but that engaging people in helping to achieve organisational goals may succeed by influencing their motives'. Insights drawn from my experience in and reflection on institutional development and diversity at WSL and the ETH Domain lead to the same conclusions.

According to Luhmann (2013), power and communication function as a result of selection processes to reduce complexity in order to benefit organisations.[4] The function of power can thus be described as a generalisation of the relevance of individual decision-making processes. The members of decision-making bodies have power due to their positions in the organisation. Moreover, the receiver of any message is free to select from a range of messages, according to his/her individual selection processes. Thus the members of decision-making bodies are not forced to comply with prevailing norms or prevailing peer group values, especially if they could hinder the development of their organisation towards more innovation and inclusiveness.

The people with the most power, privilege and prestige in an organisation may still choose to help to create structures and processes to enhance the fair treatment of very different individuals. In the end, this will also usually be in their own personal interests.

Acknowledgements

My thanks to the staff and the Directorate of WSL, in particular to Christoph Hegg, for their time and their direct and indirect contributions to the content of this chapter. The comments of the reviewers were greatly appreciated, as was the feedback from Silvia Dingwall on the English.

Notes

1 'Institutions are systems of established and embedded social rules that structure social interactions' (Hodgson, 2006, p. 18).

2 'Organisations are special institutions that involve (a) criteria to establish their boundaries and to distinguish their members from nonmembers, (b) principles of sovereignty concerning who is in charge, and (c) chains of command delineating responsibilities within the organisation' (Hodgson, 2006, p. 18).

3 The ETH Domain consists of ETH Zurich, EPF Lausanne and the four research institutes Eawag, WSL, Empa and PSI.
4 Due to the limited capacity of concentration of the human being, influencing power only can take effect if the result of a selection process of a participant is communicated to another participant who accepts it as a reduction of his mental possibilities or the range of possible actions, without proceeding to a selection process on his/her own.

References

Davidson, M. (2011) *The end of diversity as we know it: why diversity efforts fail and how leveraging differences can succeed.* Oakland: Berrett-Koehler.

Díaz-García, C., González-Moreno, A. & Sáez-Martínez, F. J. (2013) Gender diversity within R&D teams: its impact on radicalness of innovation. *Innovation: Management, Policy & Practice.* 15 (2), 149.

Dobbin, F., Kim, S. & Kalev, A. (2011) You can't always get what you need: organizational determinants of diversity programs. *American Sociological Review.* 76 (3), 386–411.

Dobbin, F., Schrage, D. & Kalev, A. (2015) Rage against the iron cage: the varied effects of bureaucratic personnel reforms on diversity. *American Sociological Review.* 80 (5), 1014–1044.

European Commission, EUR 24905 (2011) *Structural change in research institutions: Enhancing excellence, gender equality and efficiency in research and innovation.* Luxembourg: Publications Office of the European Union.

Hodgson, G. M. (2006) What are institutions? *Journal of Economic Issues.* 40 (1), 1–25.

Lenski, G. E. (1984) *Power and privilege, a theory of social stratification.* Chapel Hill, NC: The University of North Carolina Press.

Luhmann, N. (2012) *Soziale Système: Grundriss einer allgemeinen Theorie.* Berlin: Suhrkamp Verlag.

Luhmann, N. (2013) *Macht im system.* Berlin: Suhrkamp Verlag.

8 Are We There Yet? Advancing Women at Work in Canada and Australia

Similar Goals, Different Policies

Eddy S. Ng and Erica French

Introduction

Differences in opportunities and outcomes in the workplace are inherent in a free and competitive market. However, when differences between individuals and groups are identified as resulting from particular policies, behaviours or attitudes, any resulting inequality may be identified as unfair. Increasingly, unfair disparities in societies and their workplaces are regularly challenged. Many of the unfair disparities are recognised as caused by unfair discrimination (Anker, 1997). The International Labour Organization Convention (ILO) No. 111 (ILO, 1958) defines discrimination as 'any distinction, exclusion or preference made on the basis of race, colour, sex, religion, political opinion, national extraction, or social origin, which has the effect of nullifying or impairing equality of opportunity or treatment in employment or occupation'. Yet, the argument for addressing this ideal of 'equality of opportunity' is complex. Ekmekci (2013) identifies the difficulties as the determination of whether any process should be based on equality of opportunity or equality of outcome. In addition, there is the difficulty of determining what exactly constitutes a process for addressing unfair disparity due to the haziness of what constitutes discrimination and controversy in the meaning as well as policy implications of equality (Tomei, 2003).

This chapter considers the policies and practices on achieving equality for men and women at work in Canada and Australia. Both countries are compared because of their similarities in terms of their political, economic and social values (O'Connor, Orloff & Shaver, 1999). Canada and Australia are also similar in many aspects on efforts to promote equality for women. The Organization for Economic Cooperation and Development (OECD) has monitored the economic and social well-being of people internationally with a 'wealth distribution equality' measured through the Gini coefficient (OECD, 2012). Currently this index indicates that wealth distribution equality is regressing in 17 of 24 OECD countries, but this is not the case in Canada and Australia. Australia's

Gini coefficient score was 0.63 in 1985 and 0.34 in 2008, while Canada's was 0.40 and 0.32, respectively. Both countries implement different policies and regulations to encourage gender equality in wealth distribution, including pay equity.[1]

It is almost 30 years since Canada and Australia first implemented employment equity and equal opportunity policies in 1986. In this chapter we compare and contrast the differences and similarities in the approaches to gender equality policies and practices, including employment equity and equality of opportunity and pay equity. We also assess the goals and outcomes in the attainment of gender equality with a view to understanding the progress and limitations that have both assisted or hampered women's advancement in both jurisdictions. Our analysis suggests that while legislative and policy change is patchy across the workplace, employer responses are prolific, but these may not be well targeted to achieve substantive results in terms of equality of opportunity outcomes and pay equity.

Employment Equity and Equal Employment Opportunity

Employment Equity in Canada

The federal *Employment Equity Act* (EEA) officially came into effect in 1986, following the Report of the Commission on Equality in Employment (Abella, 1984). Under the EEA, no one should be denied employment opportunities, and benefits for reasons unrelated to ability and systemic barriers faced by designated groups are identified and eliminated. Furthermore, the EEA requires that employers take special measures to eliminate employment barriers and to ensure that members of designated groups are proportionately represented and distributed in their workforces.

The EEA applies to all federally regulated industries (banking, communications, transportation) with 100 or more employees, which are the federal civil service, Crown corporations, the Canadian Forces and the Royal Canadian Mounted Police. Employers must file an annual report to the Minister of Labour and submit to a compliance audit by the Canadian Human Rights Commission. In 2015 (the 2016 report has the most recent data available, reporting on 2015), 486 employers with a total workforce of 730,485 employees (representing 4 per cent of the Canadian workforce) filed their annual reports under the Legislated Employment Equity Program (LEEP) (ESDC, 2016). Additionally, employers with 100 or more employees that are not covered under LEEP, but have been awarded a federal government contract for goods and services of $1 million[2] or more (effective 2013), are also required to comply under the Federal Contractors Program (FCP), with essentially the same requirements as LEEP employers. While the focus of the EEA and LEEP is on the four designated groups, we focus our examination on women in the workplace.

Although the Canadian Charter of Rights and Freedoms (part of the *Constitution Act* of 1982) protects the rights and freedom of Canadians, and the *Canadian Human Rights Act* (CHRA) prohibits discrimination on the basis of race, sex, sexual orientation and marital status, among others, these legislations are reactive in nature (i.e., complaints based) as they do not correct for imbalances in the workforce (Ng, Haq & Tremblay, 2014). The LEEP requires employers to take positive action to eliminate barriers and to ensure that women and other designated group members are proportionately represented and distributed across different occupation groups and levels in the workforce. Section 2 of the EEA specifically states that

> employment equity means more than treating persons in the same way but also requires special measures and the accommodation of differences.
>
> (*Employment Equity Act*, 1995, c. 44, s. 2)

Consequently, employers are compelled to conduct a workforce analysis comprising a workforce survey and a review of existing human resource policies and practices. In this regard, employers are required to consult with employee representatives (e.g., unions), introduce positive measures to accommodate the four designated groups, implement an employment equity plan to close any gaps in representation, inform employees on the purpose of employment equity and maintain employment equity records. It is noted that employment equity is not about filling quotas, and no employer is required to hire any employee who is not qualified. Therefore, employment equity is considered to be a form of positive action rather than reverse discrimination (Busby, 2006).

Legislation requires that the EEA be reviewed every five years. The last review was conducted in 1995, where the original EEA of 1986 was strengthened and broadened. Requirements for compliance for federal contractors were made the same as LEEP employers with the exception of annual reporting. Employers who fail to comply with their employment equity reporting obligations may be subject to a monetary penalty (up to $50,000) levied by the Labour Program. Cases of non-compliance are referred to the Canadian Human Rights Commission (Haq & Ng, 2010).

The EEA of 1995 was undergoing a parliamentary review in 2006, but the review lapsed (cf. Haq & Ng, 2010). The former Conservative government had quietly modified aspects of LEEP and FCP reporting and compliance requirements. Reporting for public-sector employees, including the Royal Canadian Mounted Police and the Canadian Forces, have not been included in EEA Annual reports since 2011. Additionally, the contract threshold for compliance under the FCP rose from $200,000 to $1 million, and small- to medium-sized employers have been excluded since 2013.

Equal Employment Opportunity in Australia

Australia has experienced three waves of equality of employment action. The first between 1975 and 1999 heralded the Anti-Discrimination and Affirmative Action approach. Anti-discrimination legislation made it unlawful to discriminate in the workplace based on numerous identity differences, such as race, sex, religion, disability and ethnicity (ADCQ, n.d.). Numerous State and Federal Acts were implemented beginning with the *Race Discrimination Act of 1975. The Affirmative Action (Equal Opportunity for Women) Act* of 1986 added to the anti-discrimination approach by promoting the principle that employment for women be based on merit and not sex. The Act covered all private-sector organisations (and educational institutions) with more than 100 employees in the private sector and sought to encourage special measures for a group that had been heavily discriminated against in the past. Reports consisted of numbers of men and women employed and their roles, salary as well as policy information on HR and organisational processes in the form of a tick-the-box survey.

The second wave saw a change in the focus of Affirmative Action to Equal Employment Opportunity. The *Equal Opportunity for Women in the Workplace Act 1999* replaced the previously named *Affirmative Action (Equal Opportunity for Women) Act 1986* following a legislative review. While it still promoted the principle of merit, it encouraged private organisations over 100 in size to implement their own strategic actions based on their research and their analysis of organisational and industry needs, particularly encouraging a business case approach. Progress reports from private-sector organisations to the government's Equal Opportunity for Women in the Workplace Agency remained a requirement for reporting on seven actionable employment matters: recruitment and selection, promotion and transfer, training and development, work organisation, conditions of service, sex-based harassment and pregnancy and breastfeeding. The number of women and men across the organisation and their positions and salary were also a requirement.

The third wave again involved a change from the *Equal Opportunity for Women in the Workplace Act 1999* to the *Workplace Gender Equality Act 2012* following a legislative review. The new legislation aims to improve and promote equality for both women and men in the workplace but in a different way to the previous two acts. This time it is not the strategic policies or the actions taken by employers that are the most important but rather the outcomes. The aim is to achieve broadly equal outcomes for women and men. Under previous Acts, employers reported on their policies and strategies or their actions in seven employment matters. This new Act requires employers (still private-sector organisations with more than 100 employees) to report against a set of six standardised gender equality indicators (GEIs). The latest Gender Equality Scorecard, published on the 16 November 2016 (WGEA, 2016a), offered key results. The third year of data collected by the Workplace Gender Equality Agency (WGEA) (and reported by the Australia Bureau of Statistics (ABS)) covers over 12,000 employers and 4 million employees, which is approximately 40 per cent of Australia's workforce of 11,650,800 (ABS, 2015c).

Policy Differences between Canada and Australia

Although Canada and Australia implemented equality legislation for women in 1986, both countries espoused different philosophies and pursued separate policy trajectories. The Canadian approach is aimed at addressing past discrimination when individuals and institutions fail to provide women with opportunities for economic and social advancement (Blakely & Harvey, 1988). To correct this imbalance, employment equity legislation aims to address the underutilisation of women (i.e., when women are under-represented in the workforce relative to their availability rates in the labour market). In contrast, the Australian approach to equality, while originally about addressing past discrimination, changed focus to the business case but more recently has refocussed on an 'under recognition' of the value of women, particularly in relation to their position in the workplace relative to pay and opportunity, and keeping pace with the changing workplace. It is important to note that the Canadian legislation has only undergone a single revision in 1995 since its inception, while the Australian legislation has undergone three revisions. In this regard, Canada has had to rely on separate pieces of legislation (e.g., the CHRA) and provincial-level legislation (e.g., Pay Equity in Ontario and Parental Leave and Childcare in Quebec, see the following) to achieve the same policy effect (see Ng, Haq & Tremblay, 2014) as Australia. Furthermore, because Canada is a loose federation of provinces, the federal Canadian legislation only covers the federal civil service and federally regulated industries, although this extends to employers who wish to do business with the federal government. In contrast, the Australian legislation has far wider coverage, and includes all private-sector employers. As a result, more than one-third of the Australian workforce is covered compared to less than five percent of the Canadian workforce. Apart from coverage differences, the Canadian legislation appears to have 'more teeth' in its enforcement. The Canadian EEA legislation can impose fines of up to $50,000 as a penalty for non-compliance and refer a complaint to the Canadian

Human Rights Tribunal. A monetary penalty is not provided under the Australian legislation, as the Australian government has sought to publicly shame employers who are found to be non-compliant.

Measure of Progress in Canada

For Canada, we use data from 1987 as a benchmark year, since the EEA was official in 1986, allowing for a full year of reporting following its inception. Data from 1996 was also selected in our assessment, as the EEA was revised in 1995. This provides us with a ten-year interval to measure the progress since the EEA was introduced. We also included data from 2006 (census year) to 2014 (the most recent data available is from 2016 Annual Report (EEA, 2016)) to reflect current trends in the employment outcomes for women. In general, research has documented that firms covered under the LEEP and FCP are much more responsive in implementing employment equity measures than firms that are not covered (Ng & Burke, 2010).

Table 8.1 shows the representation of women relative to their availability rates in the labour market in Canada. From Figure 8.1, the gap in the representation of women has widened in recent years (2006–2015). This is in contrast to the first two decades of the implementation of the EEA (1987–2001), where LEEP has narrowed the gap between women's representation in the labour market relative to their availability rates (Ng et al., 2014). Leck and Saunders (1992) examined early results from the EEA (from the 1989 EEA Annual Report) and found that EEA employers with more formalised, comprehensive and supportive programmes hired more women. Indeed, Agocs (2002) confirmed that the representation of women closed in on their availability rates in the labour market in the early years (1987–1998). However, Jain et al. (2010) examined more recent EEA reporting (between 1997 and 2004) and reported that the effectiveness of the EEA for women declined after 2002. They suggested that weak enforcement (i.e., weak penalties and low likelihood of being sanctioned) was a cause for the decline.

Our chapter extends the analysis undertaken by Jain et al. (2010) post 2006 and confirms the continuing decline for women. A possible explanation for the widening of the gap in recent years may be explained by the net outflow of women in the workforce. There were more women leaving the workforce (termination) than entering the workforce (hiring) between 2008 and 2012 (Figure 8.2, Table 8.2). In recent years, a shift in the economy (e.g., towards the oil and mining industry) in Canada also saw fewer jobs for women (Canadian Labour Congress, n.d.).

Women's participation at higher-level occupational groups appears mixed. Women's representation in senior manager roles has increased and is closing in on their available rates (Figure 8.3, Table 8.3). Women's

Table 8.1 Comparison of Equality Legislation for Women in Canada and Australia

	Canada	*Australia*
Equality Legislation for Women	*Employment Equity Act* (1986); subsequently revised in 1995.	*Workplace Gender Equality Act 2012* (from AA in 1986 and EEO in 1999).
Year First Implemented	1986	1986
Employers Covered	Federally regulated industries (banking, communications, transportation) with 100 or more employees, federal civil service, Crown corporations, RCMP, Canadian Forces.	All employers in the private sector with more than 100 employees.
Workforce Covered	Four percent (2016) of the Canadian workforce.	Forty percent (2016) of the Australian workforce.
Objectives	Setting and meeting numerical targets for women to achieve proportionate representation in the workplace.	Promote and improve gender equality (including equal remuneration).
Measure of Progress	Number, representation, hires, promotions and terminations of women in the workplace.	Gender composition of the workforce; remuneration of women and men; availability and utility of conditions and practices relating to flexible working; sex-based harassment and discrimination.
Compliance Requirement	Employers must file an Annual Report to the Labour Program by 1 June of each year.	Employers must file an annual report by 31 May each year.
Penalties for Non-Compliance	Monetary penalty of up to $50,000 and cases of non-compliance are referred to the Canadian Human Rights Commission.	Named in parliament for non-compliance. Contracts with governments may not be offered.

Figure 8.1 Representation of women in the Canadian labour market.

Table 8.2 Representation of Women Relative to the Labour Market Availabilities (LMAs) in the Workforce for Select Years (in Percentages)

	1987	*LMA*[a]	*1996b*	*LMA*[a]	*2006*	*2007*	*2008*	*2009*	*2010*	*2011*	*2012*	*LMA*[a]
Women	40.9	44.0	44.8	46.4	43.1	42.7	42.6	42.3	41.7	41.2	40.9	47.9

	2013	*2014*	*2015*	*LMA*[a]
Women	41.4	41.6	41.0	48.2

a LMA rates based on census data for 1996 and 2006. Reporting for 1987 was matched with 1986 census data, as census is undertaken once every five years in Canada. The 2013 and 2014 LMAs are based on 2011 NHS and 2012 CSD data.

b Data obtained from Agocs (2002).

Source: EEA: Annual Reports (2007, 2008, 2009, 2010, 2011, 2012, 2013, 2014, 2015, 2016).

representation at middle-level management also exceeded their labour market availabilities; however they are trending downwards from a high of 47.9 per cent in 1996 to 43.6 per cent in 2012. Women in professional occupations are also trending downwards and remain below their availability rates in the labour market. As more women attend post-secondary institutions, it contributes to the availabilities of women (LMA) as professionals and managers (Zeman, Allen & Bussière, 2004)

Figure 8.2 Hiring and termination rates for women in Canada.

(Table 8.4). As a consequence, the pool of female human capital (or pipeline) can no longer serve as an excuse for a lack of women representation in senior roles. Instead, occupational segregation and institutional discrimination, such as gender-role stereotyping (Fortin & Huberman, 2002; Jain et al., 2010; Ng & Wiesner, 2007; Schweitzer et al., 2014), explain the persistent under-representation of women. In an industry analysis, Ng and Sears (2016) reported that women in management are under-represented in IT/technology, manufacturing and transportation and are comparably represented in banking/financial services and government (public sector).

Measure of Progress in Australia

In a study of almost 2,000 private-sector organisations using their progress reports submitted to the Affirmative Action Agency, French (2001) notes the interplay between structures and strategies used by organisations in implementing equal opportunity for women and the limited numbers of women in management and in nontraditional roles. Of note was the finding that more than 64 per cent of all organisations in the year of study (1997) had implemented strategies in the name of equal opportunity for women, but these had no demonstrable link to the improved status of women in those organisations, including the numbers of women in any tier of management, in nontraditional work areas and in employment generally (Table 8.5). Only those organisations that

Table 8.3 Hiring, Promotion and Termination Rates for Women for Select Years (in Percentages)

	1987	*1996*	*2006*	*2007*	*2008*	*2009*	*2010*	*2011*	*2012*	*2013*	*2014*	*2015*
Hiring	42.7	39.8	40.0	37.8	36.4	35.6	35.5	35.3	35.4	35.9	35.0	35.7
Promotion	52.5	56.0	54.0	51.8	50.1	50.1	50.2	46.2	47.2	47.2	47.9	48.2
Termination	40.3	39.3	39.8	37.5	37.3	37.3	37.9	35.9	36.9	37.3	37.0	38.1
	2.4	0.4	0.2	0.3	−0.9	−2.0	−2.4	−0.6	−1.5	−1.4	−2.0	−2.4

Source: EEA: Annual Reports (2007, 2008, 2009, 2010, 2011, 2012, 2013, 2014, 2015, 2016).

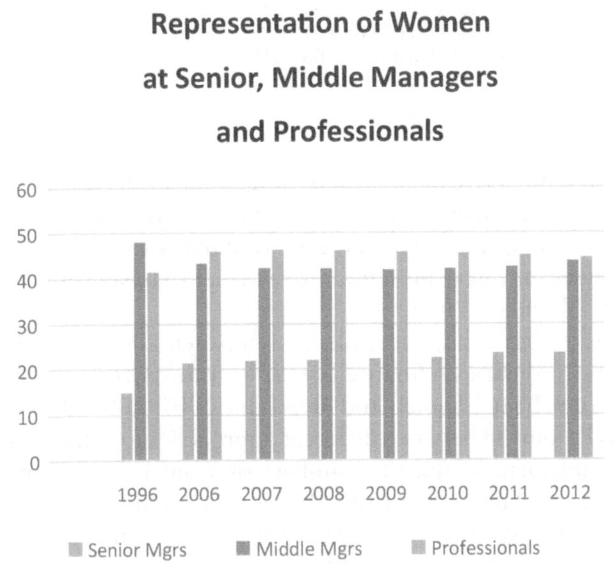

Figure 8.3 Representation of women in professional, middle and senior management positions (data for 2013 and 2014 no longer reported in EEA annual reports).

Table 8.4 Representation of Women in Management and Professional Occupational Groups (in Percentages)

	1987	*1996*	*2006*	*2007*	*2008*	*2009*	*2010*	*2011*	*2012*	*LMA*[a]
Sr Managers	n/a	14.9	22.2	21.9	22.0	22.3	22.5	23.5	23.5	24.2
Middle Mgrs	n/a	47.9	42.4	42.2	42.1	41.8	42.1	42.4	43.6	39.1
Professionals	n/a	41.4	44.5	46.1	46.0	45.7	45.7	45.0	44.4	54.2

a LMA rates based on census data for 2006. Reporting for 1987 was matched with 1986 census data, as census is undertaken once every five years in Canada. The 2013 and 2014 LMAs are based on 2011 NHS and 2012 CSD data.

Source: EEA: Annual Reports (2007, 2008, 2009, 2010, 2011, 2012, 2013).

Table 8.5 Women Employed in Significant Years (in Percentages)

	1973	*1986*	*1999*	*2012*	*2014/2015*
Women Employed	41.3	45.3	53.6	58.7	65.1
Men Employed	82.1	76.3	72.2	71.7	78.3
Pay Gap	—	20.2	15.6	17.6	17.3

Significance of dates

1973 Australia signed Discrimination (Employment and Occupation) Convention 111 of 1958.

1986 *Affirmative Action Equal Opportunity for Women in the Workplace Act 1986.*

1999 Change from AA to EEO.

2012 Change from EEO to *Workplace Gender Equality Act 2013.*

ABS 6291.0.55.001 Labour Force (ABS 2015a).

ABS 6302.0 Average Weekly Earnings (ABS 2015b).

ABS 4123.0 Labour Force Participation (ABS 2015c).

implemented proactive identity-conscious EEO strategies (approximately 32 per cent) had evidence of increased numbers of women across any of the tiers of management. This suggests that many formal EEO structures and strategies may have been figurative rather than substantive in nature (French & Sheridan, 2010).

In three studies using data collected between 2005 and 2012 investigating three industries—finance (n = 200), transport (n = 100) and construction (n = 100)—French and Strachan (2007, 2009, 2015) identified that the relationship between different approaches to equity management policies implemented and the numbers of women in management was not significant. The only statistically significant variable was organisation size, which was the only contributing factor to increased numbers of women in management. None of the strategic activities across any of the seven policy areas was a statistically significant indicator of increased numbers of women in management. Indeed the multitude of strategies, structure and policy options for managing equity and diversity appears to have confounded the determination, implementation and outcomes for EEO and Managing Diversity policies. Relatively few organisations in each industry report the implementation of proactive strategies in the areas of recruitment, promotion and development of women in addressing the inequities between men and women in management or in nontraditional roles. This supports the premise that women are doing it alone. The person-centred or deficit model suggested by Meyerson and Fletcher (2000) recognises that many organisations offer interventions designed to support women to overcome their so-called skill deficits and to adapt their behaviours and skills to the male culture rather than real organisational reform and change.

While policies that could be classed as gender diverse were available to both genders in the areas of work organisation and conditions of service, these policies only appeared to meet the EEO requirements for

Table 8.6 Women in Management in Australia 2004–2016 (in Percentages)

	2004	2006	2008	2010	2012	2014	2016
ASX200 Chairs	1.1	2.0	2.0	2.5	3.0	na	7.1
ASX200 CEOs	2.3	3.0	2.0	3.0	3.5	na	8.7
ASX200 Board Directors	8.6	8.7	8.3	8.4	12.3	na	21.5
ASX Executive KMP	—	—	—	8.0	9.7	na	20.2
ASX200 Exec Managers	10.2	12.0	10.7	na	na	na	28.4
ASX200 Senior Managers						na	29.5
ASX200 Other Managers	44.4	44.2	45.5	44.6	na	na	37.5

Source: EOWA (2008, 2006, 2004) cited in Strachan (2010), EOWA (2010), EOWA (2012) and WGEA (2016c).
ASX200 = Australian Stock Exchange Top 200 Companies.

equality of care opportunities. In reality these policies were argued to allow women opportunities to move in and out of organisations rather than up the corporate ladder. The degree to which organisations rely on these policies to deliver equity is alarming, as substantive equity outcomes are unlikely to result from a single policy type (French & Sheridan, 2010). However, evidence for change comes in a small study of early career women in Australia. Burke, Burgess and Fallon (2006) identified five areas of organisational practice aimed at supporting and developing professional and managerial women with significant results (Table 8.6). Organisations with polices across the board in the five areas—management, resources, administration, training and development and recruiting and external relations—had significantly higher performance across all the areas, with women identifying higher career satisfaction and higher levels of psychological well-being.

Discussion on the Progress of Women in Canada and Australia

Based on the reporting contained in the Annual Reports, Canada appears to collect a broader range of statistics compared to Australia, reflecting the evidence-based approach to approaching employment equity. Given that the reportings are different, we focus our analyses on the trends observed in the respective countries. Women's employment in Canada is on a downward trend, while women's participation has climbed steadily in recent years. Australia revised its legislation three times, thus modernising it (e.g., by adding remuneration and family-friendly policies), and it is broader in employer coverage (all private-sector employers covering a third of the Australian workforce). Canada, on the other hand, revised its legislation only once, and its coverage is limited to federally regulated industries only (covering less than 5 per cent of its workforce). Thus, as more women enter the workforce and want to balance work with family, the Canadian (federal) legislation may be lagging in its ability to support women's labour market participation, compared to Australia. Australia is reporting significant progress in women's advancement into senior management, but this is not the case for Canada. Both Canada and Australia also appear to be making slower progress (increase in initial years but stagnant in recent years) for women's representation in management and professional roles. It is possible that Australia's shift from equality to the business case may be partly responsible for the rise in senior roles for women.

Pay Equity

Pay Equity in Canada

In Canada, pay equity refers to *equal pay for work of equal value*, which goes beyond 'equal pay for equal work' (i.e., a requirement for women and men to be paid essentially the same wages for doing the same work). Pay equity is aimed at addressing gender-based wage discrimination, whereby work that is traditionally performed by women is undervalued (England & Gad, 2002). The federal Pay Equity Program focusses on education and promotion of pay equity to federally regulated employers only. Therefore, women must file a complaint to address a violation of the CHRA, the *Equal Wages Guidelines* and the *Canadian Labour Code,* to seek redress under a complaints-based approach to pay equity (Weiner, 2002). However, separate provincial legislations provide greater enforcement of pay equity on a more proactive basis. For example, Ontario's pay equity legislation (introduced in 1988), widely considered to be one of the most progressive pay equity policies, requires employers to implement pay equity in both the public and private sectors (McDonald & Thornton, 1998; Singh & Peng, 2010). This requires employers to identify female and male job classes, conduct job evaluations based on compensable factors and make equity adjustments.

Although the federal EEA and LEEP are focussed on removing employment barriers for women (and other designated group members), it does examine the distribution of compensation between women and men. From Table 8.7, it is evident that a majority of women continue to make below $50,000, although the proportion is trending down. Although women's share of salary above $60,000 is rising, that proportion is far below men on the same salary level. However, the lack of proactive measures in federal legislation confines the pay inequity largely to data collection and reporting only.

Table 8.7 Percentage distribution of Salary Ranges between Women and Men (Selected Recent Years)

	2001		*2010*		*2013*		*2014*		*2015*	
	F	*M*	*F*	*M*	*F*	*M*	*F*	*M*	*F*	*M*
Above $60,000	14.5	52.6	30.5	48.2	38.7	55.6	41.5	57.7	44.5	59.8
$50,000–$59,999	10.7	16.3	20.9	20.1	21.0	19.4	20.1	18.3	19.9	17.3
Below $50,000	74.8	31.1	48.6	31.7	40.3	25.0	38.4	24.0	35.6	22.9

Source: EEA: Annual Reports (2009, 2011, 2014, 2015, 2016).

Research suggests that the pay gap between men and women is narrowing because women have better access to higher paying jobs due to the EEA (Leck, St. Onge & Lalancette, 1995). Despite improving trends, Table 8.7 indicates the relatively modest gains made by women. This finding corroborates with an earlier study by McDonald and Thornton (1998), who found that, despite pay equity legislation in Ontario, fewer than 15 per cent of women received pay adjustments, and these adjustments amounted to less than 1.5 per cent of the employer's payroll, with women receiving approximately 5 per cent of their base salary.

Several explanations are offered for the slow progress in closing the gender wage gap despite proactive policies and legislation. McDonald and Thornton (1998) found that employers manipulated the application of the law (e.g., by expanding the pool of male comparators to include lower paying jobs) to minimise their payouts. Gunderson (1994) also suggested that limited application of the policies as well as their limited scope were responsible for the gap. Unions, which are party to wage setting in the collective bargaining process, also hinder the application of pay equity principles (Weiner, 2002). The unions' requirement that pay equity be undertaken at the bargaining unit rather than at the organisational level limits job comparison with other male-dominated higher paying jobs. The definition of an establishment in making job comparisons in the 'Airlines Case' illustrates this limitation (see Kainer & McDermott, 2004). England and Gad (2002), in their review of employment and pay equity policies, noted that some women benefit more than the others. This assertion is confirmed in our findings from Table 8.7, where women making over $60,000 increased their share by 146 per cent between 2001 and 2012, while women making below $50,000 decreased by only 42 per cent over the same time period.

Pay Equity in Australia

Australia ratified the ILO *Equal Remuneration Convention 1951 (No. 100)* in 1974 (ILO, 1958; HREOC, 1998), yet pay equity between men and women in Australia has still not been reached. Pay equity is a simple concept—men and women receive equal remuneration for work of equal value—although there is nothing simple about it (Lyons & Smith, 2008). There is complexity in understanding what constitutes equal remuneration and also in the concept of what is 'work of equal value'. The gender pay gap is the difference between women and men's average weekly full-time equivalent earnings, expressed as a percentage of men's earnings (WGEA, 2014). Using Average Weekly Earnings data from the Australian Bureau of Statistics, the Workplace Gender Equality Agency calculated the national gender pay gap to be 16.2 per cent for full-time employees, a difference of $261.10 per week (WGEA, 2016b). This climbs to 23 per cent when part time and casual workers are included. This means that full-time working women must work 14 months to earn the same amount that men earn in 12 months. The Gender Equity Insights 2017: Inside Australia's Gender Pay Gap report (WGEA, 2017) captured information on four million employees and more than 12,000 employers in the 2015 to 2016 reporting period. In positive news, the average full-time gender pay gap has declined since 2015, as have gender pay gaps in 12 of the 19 major industry groupings. Key findings indicate that increasing the representation of women in executive leadership roles is associated with lowering gender pay gaps. Organisations with the lowest share of female executive leaders have an average gender pay gap double the size of those with an equal share of women in senior roles: 20 per cent compared with 10 per cent. Organisation-wide reductions in the gender pay gap were recorded for those companies that improved gender balance at the executive leadership level between 2015 and 2016. Organisations that increased the share of women in executive leadership roles by more than 10 per cent recorded a reduction in the organisational gender pay gap of 3 percentage points over the course of a single year (Cassells, Duncan & Ong, 2017). For a long period, pay differentials in Australia were based on social assumptions and perceptions of what a full-time family breadwinner should be like, and these assumptions and perceptions influenced the decisions made by industrial tribunals under a centralised industrial relations system (Lyons & Smith, 2008). According to Watson (2010), three equal pay cases and the resulting decisions in 1969, 1972 and 1974 ended this, and helped close the gap considerably (see, e.g., Gregory & Duncan, 1981; Borland, 1999). However, Justice Mary Gaudron, the first female High Court Judge in Australia, noted 'We got equal pay once, then we got it again, but we still haven't got it' (Gaudron, 1998).

In Australia, there are differences in the gender pay gap according to the State or Territory of work: those states high in mining and construction have a larger pay gap and those with a lower pay gap, such as the Australian Capital Territory, have a workforce predominately in the public administration and safety sector. Industry differences are also identified in Australia, with the Financial and Insurance Services identified as the highest pay gap at 31.9 per cent, mining in the middle at 22 per cent, Public Administration and Safety at 7.3 per cent and wholesale trade at 7.2 per cent. However, more women are affected by the Health Care and Social Assistance Industry, where the pay gap is 31.7 per cent because 71 per cent of this industry's full-time workforce is female. Increasingly, evidence also shows that the pay gap is not equal across the wage distribution, with a smaller gap for lower paid workers and a larger gap between men and women higher up the pay scale (Watson, 2010).

Since 1986, Australian organisations greater than 100 employees in size have been writing and submitting annual and biennial progress reports on the equal opportunities of men and women within these organisations along with pay rates and employment positions to the variously titled Government Agency (now the Workplace Gender Equality Agency (The Agency)). French and Strachan (2007, 2009), in a study of 300 Australian organisations in the Transport Industry and the Financial and Insurance Industry, noted that only 20 per cent of organisations identified equity issues related to their current remuneration structures. Some organisations identified the use of recommended pay equity systems or consultants to assist in the process of developing equity in remuneration; however, more than half of these organisations were vague in identifying any action for change, suggesting that either staff consultation or the process of enterprise bargaining or market benchmarking would ultimately address any unfair pay differentials. The balance of organisations (80 per cent) either did not address remuneration differences or identified that staff had equal access to additional pay entitlements such as bonuses or paid leave. The Agency (WEGA 2016a) reported in 2016 that the average full-time female employee took home $26,853 less than the average male employee in 2015–2016, with the salary difference rising to $93,884 at the top level of management. Women are also under-represented in leadership roles, holding just 16.3 per cent of CEO and 37.4 per cent of all manager roles. However, the scorecard shows improvement in key GEIs with lower pay gaps, greater movement of women into management roles and increased action from employers to address gender equality.

Pay Equity Differences in Canada and Australia

Despite having pay equity policies, Canada and Australia remain challenged in closing the pay gap for women. Canada's federal pay policy programme lacks positive action and is limited to employers reporting in their annual reports to the Labour Program. Efforts to close the pay gap rest primarily with the provinces. The Province of Ontario, which leads in pay equity legislation, is complaint based. Under the EEA, employers face penalties for non-compliance; however, in the absence of such pressures, statistical reporting alone is limited in closing the pay gap. Employment equity legislation does have a spill over effect on wage levels for women as their representation in management jobs rises. Pay equity reporting (as part of EEA reporting in Canada) benefits women at higher pay levels but less so for women at lower levels. In Australia, the pay gap for women is persistent despite multiple attempts at reducing it through legislation and varies in different industries due to gender-based occupational segregation. In our view, legislation without enforcement mechanisms, as in the case for Australia, or positive action as in the case for Canada, will not likely bring about the closing of the pay gap. Thus, although women's wages are on the rise as they enter management ranks, the gap that exists between women and men will continue to persist.

Conclusion

In more than one international report on equity and equal opportunity, Australia and Canada achieve similar outcomes. They are rated as comparable when judged against similar systems of corporate governance, legislation and policy among others, on many of the factors or elements of equal opportunity, pay equity and women in management as well as equality of wealth distribution overall. In both countries the equal opportunity policy areas have been proactive through legislation, with obligations for employers in reporting and an overall lack of penalty or enforcement. Yet, due to internal policy differences, the implementation has had slightly different coverage and different reporting as well as different outcomes. However, advancing women in terms of opportunity to work in management, nontraditional areas and achieving equal pay in both jurisdictions has been painfully slow, in fact, glacial. Neither jurisdiction is there yet in achieving equity for women! In both jurisdictions the early years saw the greatest improvements (e.g., Ng & Burke, 2010), and in many cases EEO implementation has had little effect due to lack of substantive organisational culture change and globalisation of the labour market (e.g., Ng & Sears, 2014; Strachan, French & Burgess, 2010). Conflicting beliefs as to the cause of the inequality and competing views as to the means of addressing it has contributed to a paralysis of movement in terms of substantive cultural and structural change in organisations (French, 2001; French & Sheridan, 2010).

Notes

1 The Gini Coefficient is grounded in the Lorenz Curve, which is a visual depiction of the gap between the ideal line of wealth distribution and the actual cumulative distribution for a given population. The Gini Coefficient is the ratio of the area represented by the gap in relation to the total area of the triangle formed by the line of perfect equity and the two axes. In an ideal society, where every member was to receive an equal share of the total wealth produced, the Lorenz curve would sit right on top of the perfect line of equity and the Gini Coefficient would be zero.

2 All dollars pertaining to Canadian legislation are in Canadian currency and likewise for Australian currency.

References

Abella, J. R. (1984) *Royal commission report–equality in employment*. Ottawa: Supply and Services Canada.

ABS. (2015a) *Labour force, Australia, detailed – electronic delivery*, Jan 2015. Australian Bureau of Statistics. Report ABS 6291.0.55.001. Available from: www.abs.gov.au/AUSSTATS/abs@.nsf/DetailsPage/6291.0.55.001Jan%20 2015? [Accessed 26th February 2015].

ABS. (2015b) *Average weekly earnings, Australia*, Nov 2012. Australian Bureau of Statistics. Report ABS 6302.0. Available from: www.abs.gov.au/AUSSTATS /abs@.nsf/second+level+view?ReadForm&prodno=6302.0&viewtitle= Average%20Weekly%20Earnings,%20Australia~Nov%202012~Previous ~21/02/2013&&tabname=Past%20Future%20Issues&prodno=6302.0& issue=Nov%202012&num=&view=& [Accessed 26th February 2015].

ABS. (2015c) *Gender indicators, Australia*, Feb 2016. Australian Bureau of Statistics. Report ABS 4125.0. Available from: www.abs.gov.au/ausstats/ abs@.nsf/Lookup/by%20Subject/4125.0~Feb%202016~Main%20Features~ Economic%20Security~6151 [Accessed 26th February 2015].

ADCQ. (n.d.) Report, 2013–2014. *Anti-discrimination commission Queensland*. Available from: www.adcq.qld.gov.au/about-us/annual-reports [Accessed 1st March 2015].

Agocs, C. (2002) Canada's employment equity legislation and policy, 1987–2000: the gap between policy and practice. *International Journal of Manpower*. 23 (3), 256–276.

Anker, R. (1997) Theories of occupational segregation by sex: An overview. *International Labour Review*. 136 (3), 315–339.

Blakely, J. H. & Harvey, E. B. (1988) Socioeconomic change and lack of change: employment equity policies in the Canadian context. *Journal of Business Ethics*. 7 (3), 133–150.

Borland, J. (1999) The equal pay case–thirty years on. *Australian Economic Review*. 32, 265–272.

Burke, R. J., Burgess, Z. & Fallon, B. (2006) Organizational practices supporting women and their satisfaction and well-being. *Women in Management Review*. 21 (5), 416–425.

Busby, N. (2006) Affirmative action in women's employment: lessons from Canada. *Journal of Law and Society*. 33 (1), 42–58.

Canadian Labour Congress. (n.d.) *Women and work*. Available from: www.canadianlabour.ca/human-rights-and-equality/women-and-work.

Cassells, R., Duncan, A. & Ong, R. (2017) Gender equity insights 2017: Inside Australia's gender pay gap. *BCEC|WGEA Gender Equity Series*. 2, March 2017.

Ekmekci, O. (2013) Equality of outcome or equality of opportunity? A simulation of wealth distribution using agent-based modeling. *Research in World Economy*. 4 (2).

Employment Equity Act (EEA). (2007) *Employment Equity Act: Annual Report 2007*. Gatineau, Quebec: Human Resources and Social Development Canada.

Employment Equity Act (EEA). (2008) *Employment Equity Act: Annual Report 2008*. Gatineau, Quebec: Human Resources and Social Development Canada.

Employment Equity Act (EEA). (2009) *Employment Equity Act: Annual Report 2009*. Gatineau, Quebec: Human Resources and Social Development Canada.

Employment Equity Act (EEA). (2010) *Employment Equity Act: Annual Report 2010*. Gatineau, Quebec: Human Resources and Social Development Canada.

Employment Equity Act (EEA). (2011) *Employment Equity Act: Annual Report 2011*. Gatineau, Quebec: Human Resources and Social Development Canada.

Employment Equity Act (EEA). (2012) *Employment Equity Act: Annual Report 2012*. Gatineau, Quebec: Human Resources and Social Development Canada.

Employment Equity Act (EEA). (2013) *Employment Equity Act: Annual Report 2013*. Gatineau, Quebec: Human Resources and Social Development Canada.

Employment Equity Act (EEA). (2014) *Employment Equity Act: Annual Report 2014*. Retrieved from www.canada.ca/en/employment-social-development/services/labour-standards/reports/employment-equity-2014.html [Accessed August 2017].

Employment Equity Act (EEA). (2015) *Employment Equity Act: Annual Report 2015*. Retrieved from www.canada.ca/en/employment-social-development/services/labour-standards/reports/employment-equity-2015.html [Accessed August 2017].

Employment Equity Act (EEA). (2016) *Employment Equity Act: Annual Report 2016*. Retrieved from www.canada.ca/en/employment-social-development/services/labour-standards/reports/employment-equity-2016.html [Accessed August 2017].

England, K. & Gad, G. (2002) Social policy at work? Equality and equity in women's paid employment in Canada. *GeoJournal*. 56 (4), 281–294.

EOWA. (2010) *Australian census of women in leadership*. Equal Opportunity for Women in the Workplace Agency. Available from: www.wgea.gov.au/sites/default/files/2010_census_tag.pdf [Accessed 28th February 2015].

EOWA (2004) (Equal Opportunity for Women in the Workplace Agency). Australian Census of Women in Leadership.

EOWA (2006) (Equal Opportunity for Women in the Workplace Agency). Australian Census of Women in Leadership.

EOWA (2008) (Equal Opportunity for Women in the Workplace Agency). Australian Census of Women in Leadership.

EOWA (2012) (Equal Opportunity for Women in the Workplace Agency) Australian Census of Women in Leadership. Available from: www.wgea.gov.au/sites/default/files/2012_CENSUS%20REPORT.pdf [Accessed 1st March 2015].

ESDC. (2016) *Employment Equity Act: Annual Report 2016*. Employment and Social Development Canada. Available from: www.canada.ca/en/employment-social-development/services/labour-standards/reports/employment-equity-2016.html [Accessed August 2017].

Fortin, N. & Huberman, M. (2002) Occupational gender segregation and women's wages in Canada: an historical perspective. *Canadian Public Policy/Analyse de Politiques*. 28 (S1), 11–39.

French, E. (2001) Approaches to equity management and their relationship to women in management. *British Journal of Management*. 12 (4), 267–286.

French, E. & Strachan G. (2007) Equal opportunity outcomes for women in the finance industry in Australia: evaluating the merit of EEO plans. *Asia Pacific Journal of Human Resources*. 43 (3), 314–332.

French, E. & Strachan, G. (2009) Evaluating equal employment opportunity and its impact on the increased participation of men and women in the transport industry in Australia. *Transport Research Part A: Policy and Practice*. 43A (1), 78–89.

French, E. & Strachan, G. (2015) Women at work! Evaluating equal employment policies and outcomes in construction. *Equality, Diversity and Inclusion: An International Journal*. 34 (3), 1–19.

French, E. & Sheridan, A. (2010) Women in management: limited progress and uncertain prospects. In: Strachan, G., Burgess, J. & French, E. (eds.). *Managing diversity in Australia: theory and practice* (pp. 153–168). AUS McGraw Hill.

Gaudron, Justice M. Cited in Ex 456 Pay Equity Inquiry p97—Final Submissions of NPEC and others, cited in *Report to the Minister: Volume I*, 14 December 1998, p. 5.

Gregory, R. G. & Duncan R. C. (1981) Segmented labor market theories and the Australian experience of equal pay for women. *Journal of Post Keynesian Economics*. 3 (3): 403–428.

Gunderson, M. (1994) Pay and employment equity in the United States and Canada. *International Journal of Manpower*. 15 (7), 26–43.

Haq, R. & Ng, E. S. (2010) Employment equity and workplace diversity in Canada. *International Handbook on Diversity Management at Work: Country Perspectives on Diversity and Equal Treatment*. 51436, 68–82.

Human Rights and Equal Opportunity Commission. (1998) *Equal pay handbook*. Commonwealth of Australia.

ILO. (1958) C111-Discrimination (Employment and Occupation) Convention, 1958 (No. 111). Convention concerning Discrimination in Respect of Employment and Occupation (Entry into force: 15 Jun 1960). International Labour Organization, United Nations, New York.

Jain, H. C., Lawler, J. J., Bai, B. & Lee, E. K. (2010) Effectiveness of Canada's employment equity legislation for women (1997–2004): implications for policy makers. *Relations Industrielles/Industrial Relations*. 65 (2), 304–329.

Kainer, J. & McDermott, P. (2004) Pay equity in the sky: The case of Air Canada and Canadian Airlines. *Canadian Woman Studies*. 23 (3), 78–83.

Leck, J. D. & Saunders, D. M. (1992) Hiring women: the effects of Canada's Employment Equity Act. *Canadian Public Policy/Analyse de Politiques*. 18 (2), 203–220. University of Toronto Press.

Leck, J. D., St. Onge, S. & Lalancette, I. (1995) Wage gap changes among organizations subject to the Employment Equity Act. *Canadian Public Policy*. 21, 387–400.

Lyons, M. & Smith, M. (2008) Gender pay equity, wage fixation and industrial relations reform in Australia. *Employee Relations*. 30 (1), 4.

McDonald, J. A. & Thornton, R. J. (1998) Private-sector experience with pay equity in Ontario. *Canadian Public Policy*, University of Toronto Press. 22 (2), 185–208.

McGrath-Champ, S. & Jefferson, T. (2013) Gender and pay equity in a global knowledge organisation. *The Economic and Labour Relations Review*. 24 (1), 97–123.

Meyerson, D. & Fletcher, J. K. (2000) A modest manifesto for shattering the glass ceiling, *Harvard Business Review*. January–February 2000.

Ng, E. S. & Burke, R. J. (2010) A comparison of the legislated employment equity program, federal contractors program, and Financial Post 500 firms. *Canadian Journal of Administrative Sciences/Revue Canadienne des Sciences de l'Administration*. 27 (3), 224–235.

Ng, E. S. & Sears, G. J. (2014) Toward representative bureaucracy: predicting public service attraction among underrepresented groups in Canada. *Review of Public Personnel Administration*. 35 (4), 367–385.

Ng, E. S. & Sears, G. J. (2016) The glass ceiling in context: the influence of CEO gender, recruitment practices and firm internationalisation on the representation of women in management. *Human Resource Management Journal*. 27 (1). Available from: doi: 10.1111/1748-8583.12135.

Ng, E. S. & Wiesner, W. H. (2007) Are men always picked over women? The effects of employment equity directives on selection decisions. *Journal of Business Ethics*. 76 (2), 177–187.

Ng, E., Haq, R. & Tremblay, D. (2014) A review of two decades of employment equity in Canada: progress and propositions. *International handbook on diversity management at work: second edition. Country perspectives on diversity and equal treatment*. pp. 46–67.

O'Connor, J. S., Orloff, A. S. & Shaver, S. (1999) *States, markets, families: gender, liberalism and social policy in Australia, Canada, Great Britain and the United States*. Cambridge: Cambridge University Press.

OECD. (2012) *Gender equality in education, employment and entrepreneurship: final report to the MCM 2012*. Organization for Economic Co-operation and Development. C/MIN(2012)5. Available from: www.oecd.org/employment/50423364.pdf.

Schweitzer, L., Lyons, S., Kuron, L. K. J. & Ng, E. S. W. (2014) The gender gap in pre-career salary expectations: a test of five explanations. *Career Development International*. 19 (4), 404–425.

Singh, P. & Peng, P. (2010) Canada's bold experiment with pay equity. *Gender in Management: An International Journal*. 25 (7), 570–585.

Strachan, G. (2010) Still working for the man? Women's employment experiences since 1950. *Australian Journal of Social Issues*. 45 (1), 117–130.

Strachan G., French, E. L. & Burgess, J. (2010) *Managing diversity in Australia: theory and practice*. McGraw-Hill.

Tomei, M. (2003) Discrimination and equality at work: A review of the concepts. *International Labour Review*. 142 (4), 401–418.

Watson, I. (2010) Decomposing the gender pay gap in the Australian managerial labour market. *Australian Journal of Labour Economics*. 13 (1), 49–79.

Weiner, N. (2002) Effective redress of pay inequities. *Canadian Public Policy/Analyse de Politiques*. 28, Supplement: Occupational Gender Segregation: Public Policies and Economic Forces (May, 2002), pp. S101–S115.

Workplace Gender Equality Agency. (2014) Game-changing gender data launched. Available from: www.wgea.gov.au/media-releases/game-changing-gender-data-launched [Accessed March 2017].

Workplace Gender Equality Agency. (2016a) *Australia's latest gender equality scorecard released today. Women are still undervalued, but key indicators improving*. [Media release, 16 November 2016]. Available from: www.wgea.gov.au/sites/default/files/2015-16-gender-equality-scorecard-mr.pdf [Accessed March 2017].

Workplace Gender Equality Agency. (2016b) *Equal pay day 4th September 2017* [Media release, 16 November 2016]. Available from: www.wgea.gov.au/news-and-media/media-releases.

Workplace Gender Equality Agency. (2017) *The gender equity insights 2017: inside Australia's gender pay gap report*. Available from: www.wgea.gov.au/sites/default/files/BCEC%20WGEA%20Gender%20Pay%20Equity%20Insights%202017%20Report.pdf [Accessed December 2017].

Zeman, K., Allen, M. & Bussière, P. (2004) *Who pursues postsecondary education, who leaves and why: results from the youth in transition survey*. Ottawa, ON: Culture, Tourism and the Centre for Education Statistics Division, Statistics Canada.

Conclusion

Marilee Reimer

This collection has introduced insights brought by feminist and policy theorists in the following areas:

- how inequality in higher education might be better managed to respond to the priorities of low income and marginalized women whose skills base may be very broad due to their employment history;
- how we might learn from the European Union community development projects where women's capabilities are enhanced through participation in informal education, as well as community-based education and political participation, in order to address industry flight in rural Atlantic Canada; and
- how successful employment equity policy might be developed in academic and science-based contexts (Finland and Switzerland) but requires systems of accountability that go beyond the primarily public-sector equity programmes in Australia and Canada that have been able to develop.

All of these point towards a future research direction quite different than that raised traditionally around career process to community engagement. What we saw in the political context of community-based programmes is the potential for community actors and action such as the Hodgett study found.

Section 1: Political Contexts of Community-Based Development and Work-Based Careers

Hodgett's chapter introduced one of the women's projects in the EU designed to incorporate Belfast's Protestant women into political participation beyond what such a marginalized group as women in the 1990s had ever experienced. We learn from other participants in that era that a Women's Coalition was formed by women who had interacted across the Catholic-Protestant divide in that period to work towards the resolution of conflict at the Peace Table where the Good Friday Agreement was arrived at between the warring factions in Northern Ireland and the Republic of Ireland.

Hodgett shares the stories of women from downtrodden, severely disadvantaged and traumatized communities, women who bear the brunt of the violence in the privacy of their homes and families and the responsibilities of healing other damaged family members. Through community-based educational projects, these women are finding ways to penetrate the sectarian divide to work with other women across community lines. It is perhaps because women are less directly drawn into the gun violence on the streets, and more responsible for repairing damaged lives, that they are more able to find ways to create new forms of community life. Peace negotiator Monica McWilliams explained that the work of the early Northern Irish women's movement in the 1960s and 1970s laid the groundwork for participating in the Peace Agreement: women were very active in grassroots, community-based movements that crossed divides, including religion, which was not previously bridged by any other group at the peace table (McWilliams, 2018). She was a co-founder of the Northern Ireland Women's Coalition that participated in the multiparty peace negotiations that led to the Good Friday/Belfast Agreement in 1998. Just as the Belfast women's group benefitted from the EU Project that allowed them to associate for the first time with a Catholic women's group, the peace agreement would likely have been very different if the Women's Coalition had not brought that broad approach of being able to work cooperatively with other groups across a religious divide (Doucet, 2018). More research is needed into how women do this work and what processes are involved in community education through which women envision opportunities to shape, to bring into existence cooperative life options in Northern Ireland.

Cassin brings a feminist perspective on public administration to shed light on paths not followed by the Atlantic Canada Opportunities Agency (ACOA). After the devastation brought by the collapse of industrial jobs in the region, what alternatives exist? How might it be possible to shape a future in more cooperative, socially embedded forms of enterprise through which to 'make a living'? Women in Atlantic Canada are finding new paths. Cassin's research points to the need for ACOA to look beyond obvious routes to professional qualifications, to find other ways in which people create opportunities for themselves, and to see women as at the centre of this new work.

While the former Northern Ireland politician McWilliams points to the importance of the coalition building of the women's movement in the 1960s and 1970s to further coalition building in that country, the #MeToo Movement has recently carried on a number of talks on Maine Public Radio (PBS, 2018) in which the importance of having supportive allies became a part of the discussion. Mychal Denzel Smith, author and panellist, underlined the importance for the #MeToo Movement of allies speaking up across colour and gender lines (Smith, 2018). Given the importance of allies, women fighting discrimination could only benefit by having progressive allies for social change.

The Reimer research tracks the traditional focus on barriers to entry and to career success for first generation women students and the need for more specifically targeted university support services to rectify these disadvantages. The research conclusion, however, points in a different direction. It tracks four high-performing 'A' average students who rejected the traditional career paths of undergraduate honours into postgraduate training for professional careers. Two of the four actually started traditional paths towards bachelor's and master's in education but then 'dropped out'. It is what they dropped into that is the more interesting focus. All four entered managerial and administrative careers managing complex projects for a non-profit organization, and managing diverse business networks and relationships. There is very little research that even conceptualizes nontraditional career process as processes, and ways in which people shape for themselves how they navigate precarious working worlds.

The Bourgeois study similarly shows that the Newfoundland government's White Paper on education for the knowledge economy almost entirely misses or regards as marginal value the liberal arts focus that so many women from rural communities 'misguidedly' seem to choose. The White Paper actually debates how to try to discourage such choices, and persuade more women to study STEM subjects—science, technology, engineering and mathematics, as the way to achieve gender-pay equity. What the government policy planners miss is again what these women drop into. What these women talk about is memories of the role of literature, of readings shared between parents, aunts and cousins, and how important it was to their lives in isolated rural communities. What draws these women students into studying liberal arts is also what they hope to give back, to inspire other women to think about their lives differently, and in the process to revitalize the heart of their communities. This opens up a vast area of potential new research into exactly how these women, steeped in liberal arts, will actively change their rural worlds.

Lu's study begins with a focus on the seven-fold increase in the number of university graduates in China and the reality that half the women she interviews have no immediate job prospects. What the women themselves talk about, in between discussions of jobs and debts, is their own sense that their futures are open-ended and will not involve a return to patriarchal closure of their former lives. This research leaves open the possibility and the promise that China might avoid some of the pitfalls of the neo-liberal Western model of development, to a more socialist, community-based way forward. These women graduates, already powerfully nontraditional in bucking the patriarchal assumptions and family structures that shaped their past lives, may well hold the key to creating new paths for themselves.

Section 2: Equity Policy and Diversity Goals

Having women represented at the peace table was just one of the goals that activists like Monica McWilliams achieved as she later became an advocate for voting equality and fair employment, and worked for acceptance of the Sex Discrimination Act in the 1970s. We see the importance of women being 'at the table' and the connection of community development work to coalitions towards that end. An example of a Canadian discrimination battle over workplace harassment/assault that has been in the courts is that of the Royal Canadian Mounted Police (RCMP) who have more than a problem with 'organizational culture'. The federal government has appointed Brenda Lucki as the first female head to the 145-year-old organization (CBC Radio, 2018), which has left many curious of her strategy. Commissioner Lucki plans to achieve a transformation of how women officers are treated in the RCMP, first, by holding herself to high standards and, second, by holding people accountable for their behaviour. This strategy addresses a theme that all of the articles on employment equity programmes raise: How do we assess the results of equity policies and to whom are they accountable?

Gut's study of Swiss forestry scientists focusses on women who have achieved professional status, who have the best STEM qualifications and who have achieved jobs in top research laboratories. Logically they should succeed as the men do, but it doesn't work out that way. Opportunities have not materialized. Women find precarity in advanced professions in a period when only contractually limited jobs are available to them. Tenured positions are mostly occupied and an expansion isn't planned. Women find themselves in a competitive process where they are not advancing quickly enough. This research hints at the need to restructure ways of organizing elite scientific research laboratories into more non-hierarchical cooperative networks of research teams. The work of Hodgett and Cassin could be useful as models of alternative ways to organize work at the top. Women may become leaders in reshaping ways of doing things that go beyond hierarchy and competitive individualism.

Employment equity legislation in Canada and Australia is among the most advanced in the world, yet Ng and French's research finds again that outcomes are less egalitarian than expected. Their work shows that the accountability of these programmes appears to have been lax and not entirely enforceable; an organizational culture prevails in which women's participation is not treated as an urgent priority. Those in position to evaluate the contributions of others tend to see the merits of those most like themselves; in these contexts, it is easy to question the merits of employees who were selected as employment equity candidates as undeserving. There is need for research into alternative ways to organize work to be less hierarchical and more cooperative and communalistic in how responsibilities are shared in public administration and in science institutes. Abandoning the deficit model to get women to better compete with men may involve finding a model that values the skills of women's leadership styles and requires a rethink of the competitive process itself.

It is here that the master's programmes in diversity and inclusion management in Finland, in Timonen and Turunen's chapter, may have much to offer. These creative programmes offer students advanced training on implementing diversity promotion in their workplaces as a part of their Master's of Human Resources requirements. Their curriculum transforms the deficit model to an inclusive one on the basis of gender, ethnicity, age and ability, attempting to retain the current workforce and facilitate their career objectives. These educational programmes are re-conceptualizing workplaces as ones where community development is accomplished from a more communalistic starting point.

In conclusion, this wide-ranging research collection asks us to open ourselves to the possibilities that we see developing in diverse workplaces and where women are in leadership roles previously not imagined. These are the workplaces of the future that we can only hope to have a hand in developing as a community; for example, European Union-inspired adult education projects that the graduates go on to develop, as in Finland and Northern Ireland; an expansion of the credit unions, retail cooperatives and social housing at which women often excel as organizers; and the Canadian federal housing programme and other social enterprises, such as the anti-poverty movement/anti-homelessness movement in Southern New Brunswick. This is also a challenge for researchers in the liberal arts and social sciences in this era of inclusion for women and a kaleidoscope of minorities joining public life.

References

CBC Radio. (2018) 'We have to eradicate this behaviour': RCMP commissioner tasked to reform workplace harassment. May 23, 2018. *The Current*, Canadian Broadcasting Corporation. Available from: www.cbc.ca/radio/thecurrent/the-current-for-may-23-2018-1.4674090/we-have-to-eradicate-this-behaviour-rcmp-commissioner-tasked-to-reform-workplace-harassment-1.4674095 [Accessed 1 June 2018].

Doucet, L. (2018) Her story made history—Monica McWilliams. January 24, 2018. *Seriously...*, BBC Radio 4, British Broadcasting Corporation. Available from: www.bbc.co.uk/programmes/p05vzcpz [Accessed 1 June 2018].

McWilliams, M. (2018) 'Equality is an Unfinished Business'—activist and former politician Monica McWilliams. February 27, 2018. *Voices Magazine*, British Council, UK. Available from: www.britishcouncil.org/voices-magazine/women-equality-northern-ireland-monica-mcwilliams-peace-agreement-belfast [Accessed 1 June 2018].

PBS. (2018) Episode 3: Masculinity in Crisis? *#MeToo, Now What?* Public Broadcasting Service. February 16, 2018, PBSHD. Available from: www.pbs.org/program/metoo-now-what/#about [Accessed 1 June 2018].

Index

Note: Page numbers followed by 'n' refers to endnotes.

academic choices 37–8
Academic Mentorship/bursary programme 13
academic subject, gendered 38–9
ACOA *see* Atlantic Canada Opportunities Agency (ACOA)
Administrative Assistant 21, 22
affiliation 73, 79, 90, 95, 98
Affirmative Action (Equal Opportunity for Women) Act 143
Agocs, C. 145
Alkire, S. 72–3
Anti-Discrimination approach 143
The Appalachian Mountains 101
Arts degrees 36
Atlantic Canada 15, 18, 90, 91, 94, 102, 106, 163
Atlantic Canada Opportunities Agency (ACOA) 93–4, 96, 97, 102–3, 163
Australia 107–9, 140, 141, 146; equal employment opportunity in 143–4; pay equity in 154–6; policy differences 148–51
Australian Capital Territory 155

bachelor's degree persistence 15
Belfast women 79, 162, 163
belongingness and communality 121–2
bilingualism 21, 24, 93
Bill C-65 3
'black box' 91, 92
Bourdieu, P. 5, 48, 54–5, 61, 62
Bourgeois, M. 6, 164
budget restraint and efficiency approach 97
building management system 22
Burgess, Z. 151
Burke, R. J. 151
business 92–6, 143; diversity management to 114; residents and 99; and social goals 7; success 42; workforce for small 102, 103; and work forces 93

Campbellton 102, 106
Canada 2, 3, 10, 29–31, 107; Employment Equity Act 145; employment equity in 141–3; hiring and termination rates 148; labour market 145–7; pay equity in 152–3, 155–6; policy differences 145–8
Canada Student Loans programme 24
Canadian Charter of Rights and Freedoms 142
Canadian EEA legislation 144–5
Canadian Human Rights Act (CHRA) 142, 152
Canadian Human Rights Commission 141, 142
Canadian Labour Code 152
Canadian university graduates 11
capabilities and human development 72–5; expansion 77–80; policymakers 75–7
Capability Approach (CA) 72–4, 76, 81
capital and habitus 54–5
Cassin, M. 2, 6, 7, 26, 90, 163, 165
CBDC *see* Community Business Development Corporation (CBDC)
CDHN *see* Community Development and Health Network (CDHN)
CEGEP *see* Collège d'enseignement général et professionnel (CEGEP)

China 2, 47; Communist Party of China membership 61; first generation female university students in 55; higher education in 63; inequalities in 48–52; rural 56, 58
Chinese university students: cultural capital and social capital 60–1; data and method 52–4; gender discrimination 59–60; habitus and capital, Bourdieu's concepts 54–5; incompatible habitus 58–9; inequalities 48–52; overview 47–8; rural and urban education, poverty 56–8; traditional gender role 59–60
choice of university education 14–16
CHRA *see* Canadian Human Rights Act (CHRA)
cognitive diversity 119
Collège d'enseignement général et professionnel (CEGEP) 16, 25
Communist Party of China (CPC) 61
community: college 22, 25, 38, 93, 95, 98, 100; confidence 99–100; development 1, 2, 20, 41, 77–9, 97, 100–2, 165, 166; education 73–5, 79, 83, 84, 163
community-based organizations 76
Community Business Development Corporation (CBDC) 97, 102–3, 106
Community Development and Health Network (CDHN) 78–9
Community Infrastructure (CI) measure 73–9
Conservative Government 30
conservative/traditional communities 95
'convertibility of capitals' 55
co-op-type programmes 16–17
criminality and social challenges 99–100
cultural capital 54–5; and social capital 60–1
cultural hybrids 112
culture: concepts of 112; and identity 69–72
curriculum development 110, 116, 126–7

Davidson, M. 133
debt, student 14
decline of industrial economy 95
democratization 73
'Difference-Educational Intervention' 25
difference, sense of 113
direct observations 136
discrimination 140
disparity, rural and urban education 58
diversity: coordination 135; and inclusion 111, 115, 117, 132–8
diversity coordinator 132, 135, 137
diversity management (DM) 110, 114–15, 120–1, 127; competence 128–9; equity and diversity 117–20; and inclusion management 121–2; issues 128; multiculturalism 111; research context 115–16
domestic violence 68, 69, 84n3
dominant discourses, university career process 17–18

economic: capital 54, 62; change 100; decline 7, 11, 95; dislocation 98
economic development policy: Atlantic Canada Opportunities Agency 93–4; Enterprise Restigouche 94–5; gender relations and 95, 103; and implementation 96–8; institutional practices 91–2; northern New Brunswick 92–3; overview 89–91
Economic Development Project 106
education: equity in 3–4; inequalities in 48–52; Northern Ireland culture and identity 69–72
EEA *see* Employment Equity Act (EEA)
Ekmekci, O. 140
employment: equity 141–3; inequalities in 48–52
Employment Equity Act (EEA) 141–3, 145, 156
England, K. 153
English Canada 10, 15
English education: difficulties 57; studying 38
English-speaking student 18
Enterprise Restigouche (ER) 94–7
equal employment opportunity 143–4
equality: Australian approach 144; Canadian approach 144
Equality, Diversity and Inclusion (EDI) Conference of 2015 1

Equal Opportunity for Women in the Workplace Act 143–4
Equal Remuneration Convention 1951 (No. 100) 154
Equal Wages Guidelines 152
equity: ability to work 123; and diversity 117–20; in education and government 3–4; leadership support 124; rising generations 124–5; tacit knowledge 125–6; in working life 110–11. *See also* work-life equity. *See also* masters students' on equity and DM
eudaimonia 74, 81, 82, 84
European Commission EUR 24905 (2011) 137–8
European Social Model 75, 85n8
European Union (EU) 1–2, 67, 74; conference 76–7; interventions to Northern Ireland 76–7; Structural Funds 77

Fallon, B. 151
family background, disadvantaged 56–7
family formation 95, 98
family-supported families 95
Federal Contractors Program (FCP) 141
FGFUSs *see* first generation female university students (FGFUSs)
financial burden 60
financial responsibility, first generation students 13–14
Finland 107, 114, 116, 123, 125, 162, 166
Finnish higher education 107
Finnish Universities of Applied Sciences (UAS), work-life equity 110; data analysis 116–17; diversity 111; diversity management *see* diversity management (DM); equity 110–11; inclusion 121–2; multiculturalism and transculturalism 111, 112; sense of difference and similarity 113–14; vision 128–9
first generation female student 53–4
first generation female university students (FGFUSs) 48–50, 55, 58, 61, 63
first generation students, career outcomes 9–11, 19–23; choice of university education 14–16; dominant discourses 17–18; financial responsibility 13–14; institutional ethnography 18; intention to university 12–13; New Brunswick 18; professional success 19; public discourse 11; university process 12, 16–17; *vs.* non-first generation students 15
Fletcher, J. K. 150
Flores-Crespo, P. 81
Foster, K. R. 90
Freire, Paulo 5
French, E. 3, 108, 148, 150, 155, 165
French-speaking student 16, 18, 21–3, 25
funded education system 29–30
funding 2, 16, 31, 77, 91, 94, 100, 102

Gad, G. 153
Gaudron, M. 154
gender discrimination 59–60
gendered academic subject 38–9
gender equality indicators (GEIs) 144, 155
gender inequality 49–52
gender relations and economic development policy 90, 95, 103
Generation Y group 124–5
Gini coefficient 140, 141, 157n1
Globe and Mail (Wente) 11
Good Friday/Belfast Agreement 163
government: democratic 71; equity in 3–4; and higher education 41; municipal 100–2; New Brunswick 26; Northern Ireland 81; non-government organization 24; policy measures 76; taxes to 93; White Paper 31, 36, 42, 164
Gravatt, J. 75
Gunderson, M. 153
Gut, U. 2, 165

habitus and capital 54–5
Harris, Mike 11
Hattersley 71
higher education: barriers 56–8; in China 48–9 *see also* Chinese university students; expansion of 47, 50–2; gaining upward mobility 52; state funding of 2
Hodgett, S. 6–7, 162–3, 165

Hodgson, G. 133
Home and Institutional Health Care and Social Service 125–6
honours degrees and upgrading programmes 11
household registration *(Hukou)* institution 50, 51
human capital theory 29, 30
human development and capabilities 72–5; expansion 77–80; policymakers 75–7
Human Development Index 72
human flourishing 75
human resources (HR) 2, 19, 93, 107, 108, 111, 132, 135, 142, 166
Human Resources and Skills Development Canada 100
Huppunen-Vänskä, M. R. 123

Ibrahim, S. 76, 82
identity 113
income gap, inequalities 49–51
incompatible habitus 58–9
industrial jobs 89–90, 93
industrial shifts 89
inequalities and structural barriers 52
inequalities in educational and employment (China): changes in higher education 48–9; income gap and gender 49–52; rural-urban division 50–1
Inglis, F. 69, 71
institutional developer 132, 137
institutional ethnography 17–18, 90; and New Brunswick 18; public policy analysis and 91–2
integrated economic development 92–3
intention, first generation students 12–13
International Labour Organization Convention (ILO) 140
interpretive approach 76

job assignment system 48–9
job losses 7, 26, 90, 98, 102
job market 5, 6, 11, 14, 19, 36, 41, 47, 49, 51, 63; incompatible habitus 58–9; traditional gender role and gender discrimination 59–60
jobs for rural Newfoundland women 32–4

Karelia Universities of Applied Sciences (UAS) 116
Kasurinen, R. 114
Knight, K. 68
knowledge, tacit 125–6
Krawchenko, T. 90, 103

labour force participation 95
labour market 10, 15, 18, 25, 47, 48, 52, 55; in Canada 145–7; tremendous gender bias and discrimination 59
Labour Market Availabilities (LMAs) 147
lack of participation 16
lack of visibility 16
language, cultural bonds of 114
Lanzhou University 48, 52
leadership 99–100
leadership support equity 124
Leathwood, C. 43
Leck, J. D. 145
Legislated Employment Equity Program (LEEP) 141–3, 145
legislation: anti-discrimination 143; Canada and Australia 142–7; diversity 108; equity 144; pay equity 153, 156; for women 67
Lehman, W. 25
Lendvai, N. 83
Lenski, G. E. 133, 135
Leppänen, P. 124
liberal arts education 36–7, 39–41
local development and social enterprise 102–3
Loots, S. 81, 83
Luhmann, N. 133, 138
Lu, Y. 47–64

McDonald, J. A. 153
McManus, C. 70, 71
McWilliams, M. 68–9, 163
'Management Specialist' 20–1
masters students' on equity and DM: ability to work 123; competence 128–9; curriculum development 126–7; diversity management 120–1; equity and diversity 117–20; inclusion 121–2; leadership support 124; rising generations 124–5; tacit knowledge 125–6
Master's Theses 116, 117, 122, 123, 127

mathematics 37–8
Medical Instruments Re-processing Technician 22–3
Member of the Legislative Assembly (MLA) 93, 98
#MeToo Movement 1, 163
Metropolia Universities of Applied Sciences (UAS) 116
Meyerson, D. 150
middle class parents, university career process 12
migration and formal education 34
money 36, 42, 56, 57, 80, 94, 96, 125
Montreal English university 19
Mulroney administration in Canada 29
multiculturalism 111–13
municipal government and community development 100–2

National Educational Longitudinal Study of 2000 10
nationwide development programme for master's-level education 115–16
neo-liberal public policies 29–31; post-secondary education 41; White Paper of 2005 31–2
New Brunswick 1, 2, 7, 9, 10, 14, 15, 17–24, 26, 90, 92–5, 97, 101, 166
Newfoundland and Labrador Government White Paper of 2005 29–31, 36, 41–3
Newfoundland women 31–2; families and communities 34–6; and gendered academic subject 38–9; jobs for 32–4; liberal arts 39–41; prioritizing of happiness 41–2
New Public Administration 97
Ng, E. 3, 4, 108, 148, 165
NI (Northern Ireland) Department of Health 79
NI (Northern Ireland) Programme for Building Sustainable Development 80
non-government organization 19, 24
normative diversity 118
Northern Ireland (NI) 1, 2, 6; Capability Approach 72–4, 76; Community Infrastructure measure 73–9; culture and identity 69–72; European interventions 76–7; overview 67–9; policymakers, challenge for 75–7; position of women 68; schools in 70
Northern Ireland Council for Voluntary Action 78
Northern Ireland Women's Coalition (NIWC) 85n10
northern New Brunswick 2, 7, 90, 100; Atlantic Canada Opportunities Agency 93–4; public economic development policy 90, 92–3
Norway 3
Numerous State and Federal Acts 143
Nussbaum, M. 73, 74, 77, 79, 81

Ontario 4, 11, 144, 153, 156
O'Reilly, Bill 11
Organization for Economic Cooperation and Development (OECD) 140–1
Orientation and Pre-University programmes 25

parental expectations 34
pay equity: in Australia 154–6; in Canada 152–3, 155–16
paying student debt 14
Peace Agreement 163
People's Republic of China (PRC) 47
Pinhorn, L. 34
police and policing 99
policy differences 144–5; in Australia 148–51; in Canada 145–8
politics 98
population decline 98
Porter, Paige 43
post-secondary education 5, 6, 16, 30–5, 37, 39, 41, 43, 51, 61, 90, 93, 95, 98
post-secondary tuition and fees 49
poverty 7, 33, 56–8, 60–1, 63, 73, 75, 78, 79, 81, 99, 166
productivity 97
professional success, first generation students 19
'Program Delivery Officer' 20
Program Manager 24
Project Coordinator 21
projects: to community development 77–9; DM *see* diversity management (DM); EU-sponsored 2; Finnish *see* Finnish Universities of Applied Sciences (UAS), work-life equity; and policies 76–7

Property Administrator's position 22
property tax base 93
Province of Ontario 156
provincial and federal government 93
public discourse 10, 11, 15–16
public policy analysis and institutional ethnography 91–2

Quebec 16, 19, 21, 22, 106, 144
Quebec approach 2; French-speaking 16, 21–3, 25; province of 19
Quebec post-secondary educational system 16
Quiet Revolution 16

Race Discrimination Act of 1975 143
Räty, M. 125
Reagan administration in the USA 29
recruitment 31, 52, 59, 143, 150
regional and cooperative perspectives 101
Regional Commission 101, 106
regulatory diversity 118
Reimer, M. 6, 164
research-based development 122
rising generations, equity 124–5
Rodl, S. 73
Royal Canadian Mounted Police (RCMP) 165
rural schooling, quality of 39
rural-urban division, inequalities 50–1

Saunders, D. M. 145
scholarships 11–14, 24, 30, 31, 56, 60, 104
schooling 10, 13, 19, 21, 38, 39, 51
science, technology, engineering and mathematics (STEM) subjects 5, 164, 165
Sears, G. J. 148
second generation student, career outcomes 19
'sectoral approach' 78
self identity 113
self-seeking employment 49
Sen, A. 5, 71–5, 77–82
sense of difference and similarity 113–14
Sex Discrimination Act 165
Sippola, A. 111, 114, 117–18
situation of crisis 55
Slaughter, S. 30
Smith, D. E. 17, 92
social capital 54; cultural capital and 60–1
social enterprise and local development 102–3
Social Insurance Institution 125
social relations 9, 92
Social Sciences and Humanities Research Council of Canada (SSHRC) 30
society and working community 113
socioeconomic status (SES) 49; demographic characteristics and 53–4; disadvantaged family 56–7; inequalities 51; students from 58
Sociology degree 22
Sodexo case 114–15
Sparrow, David 3
Stanistreet, P. 75
Strachan, G. 150, 155
Strydom, W. 82
Stubbs, P. 83
supporting identity 113
Sweden 3
Swiss Federal Council 133
Swiss Federal Institute of Forest, Snow and Landscape Research (WSL) 132–7
Swiss Federal Institutes of Technology (ETH) Domain 132, 134–5, 139n3
Swiss Forestry Research Institutes 108
Switzerland 107, 108, 132, 137, 138
symbolic capital 54

tacit knowledge 125–6
taxes 2, 93
Taylor, C. 71, 73
team building and systemic interaction 121
Thornton, R. J. 153
Tietäväinen, M. 123
Tikkanen, M. 125–6, 129
Timonen, Liisa 2, 166
tourism 100–2
traditional gender role 58–60
'traditional women's work' 93
transculturalism 112
Transition Survey for 2005 10
Trump, Donald 2
tuition freeze 49
tuition-income ratio 50, 51
tuition prices 49

unemployment 51, 68, 99, 106
United Nation's Development Program (UNDP) 72, 79
university career process: choices 14–16; dominant discourses 17–18; first generation students 12, 16–17; intention 12–13
University of Applied Sciences (UAS) 107, 110, 115, 116
University of Quebec's eight campuses 16
University of Regina 16
University of Waterloo programme 16
unorthodox female cooperation 79
Unterhalter, E. 82

vitality 99–100
voluntary contributions 93

Walker, M. 73–4, 79, 81, 83
Watson, I. 154
Wente, M. 11
West, R. 73, 82–3
White Paper *see* Newfoundland and Labrador Government White Paper of 2005
Williams, D. 29
Williams, M. 68, 69, 163, 165
women: decision-making 36; distribution of salary ranges 153; empowerment of 79–80; hiring and termination rates 148, 149; labour market in Canada 145–7; management in Australia 151; in NI *see* Northern Ireland (NI) education system; pay equity 152–6; perspectives on money 36; prioritizing of happiness 41–2
Women's Coalition Party 79
workers, loss of 99
work-life equity: Finnish UAS *see* Finnish Universities of Applied Sciences (UAS), work-life equity; overview 107–9 *see also* equity
Workplace Gender Equality Act 2012 143–4
Workplace Gender Equality Agency (WGEA) 144, 154, 155

Xi'an Jiaotong University 48, 52